Java Programming
with CORBA

ANDREAS VOGEL

KEITH DUDDY

WILEY COMPUTER PUBLISHING

John Wiley & Sons, Inc.

New York • Chichester • Weinheim • Brisbane • Singapore • Toronto

Publisher: Katherine Schowalter
Editor: Robert M. Elliott
Managing Editor: Erin Singletary
Text Design & Composition: North Market Street Graphics

This text is printed on acid-free paper.

Library of Congress Cataloging-in-Publication Data:
Vogel, Andreas, 1965–
    Java programming with CORBA / Andreas Vogel, Keith Duddy.
      p.   cm.
    "Wiley Computer Publishing."
    Includes index.
    ISBN 0-471-17986-8 (paper/online : alk. paper)
    1. Java (Computer program language)   2. ORB (Computer file)
  I. Duddy, Keith, 1967– . II. Title.
  QA76.73.J38V64   1997
  005.2'762—dc21
                                 96-29919
                                    CIP

Printed in the United States of America
10 9 8 7 6 5 4 3 2 1

In memory of my father Wolfgang Vogel.

Contents

Foreword

The meteoric rise of the World Wide Web (dragging along with it the 25-year-old "overnight success" of the Internet) has managed, as I write this, to mask a pertinent fact: to wit, the Web is full of trash. Given the fantastic rate at which the Web continues to grow, it is truly impossible to estimate the average number of Web pages that have any intrinsic value, but any guess of that percentage above even my own inflated shoe size is likely to be too high.

Nevertheless, there is an amazing amount of value on the Web, from deep-space photographs to dictionaries, from world histories to cinematic masterpieces. Why the paradox? The reasons are simple: posting information (regardless of utility) is inexpensive, and the Web is still primarily static. Even Web pages that boast dynamic content tend to consist of lookup mechanisms onto static databases.

The next leap of the Internet will be the wide connection of the popular, simple Web browser-user interface to personal, corporate, national and international legacies not only of data, but of services as well. These services will mirror—in fact, they will **be**, in many instances—telecommunications services, and also other computerized services, from home electronics management to intercorporate data interchange to international flows of monetary instruments. The urge to standardize on a simple, single-user interface that can be taught to the beginning user—and that can yet be accessible to the power user—is impossible to ignore.

What technological leaps are holding us back from this dream? The primary reason is the poor programming model that underlies most Web services. The server-side Common Gateway Interface, and its logical mirror client-side Common Client Interface, rely on arcane bits of programming lore to be useful. Proprietary replacements exist but, unfortunately, lose the open, portable, interoperable nature of the rest of the Web structure.

Meanwhile, great strides have been made in the related distributed-object computing realm. Systems based on Object Management Architecture (OMA) and in particular CORBA, developed by the members of the Object Management Group, address enterprise integration issues, cross-platform portability and interoperability—but, interestingly enough, not user interfaces.

These two technologies, plus the exciting new programming language and virtual machine design named Java, provide a powerful potential solution to the elusive problem of simple interfaces to complex, distributed enterprise systems. This book presents the most comprehensive yet readable approach to understanding these three important technologies individually and in concert. Java-based CORBA extensions to Web browsers and servers—literally, the general communications devices of the future—are already in use at major banks, manufacturing companies, telecommunications utilities and health-care facilities. This important book brings us a vision of a heterogeneous, but integrated, future system based on these technologies.

Richard Mark Soley, Ph.D.
Object Management Group, Inc.
Somewhere over the Atlantic Ocean

Acknowledgments

First of all, we want to thank those people who made it possible for us to write this book. These are our editor at John Wiley and Sons, Robert Elliott, and his assistant Brian Calandra; OMG's Lydia Bennett and Richard Soley; V. Juggy Jagannathan of West Virginia University; and our employer, the Distributed Systems Technology Centre (DSTC) in Brisbane, Australia. DSTC's CEO David Barbagallo, Research Director Melfyn Lloyd, and Architecture Unit Leader Kerry Raymond have been very supportive and made arrangements that allowed us to get the book written.

We owe our colleague David Jackson a great debt as he edited and proofread the whole book and very much improved its readability in terms of organization and English expression. Thanks a lot, David!

Our colleagues at the DSTC helped us resolve technical questions. Thanks for sharing your expertise. The CORBA experts are Kerry Raymond, Douglas Kosovic, Michi Henning, and Mark Fitzpatrick. The Java experts are Ted Phelps and Tim Mansfield, the authors of the Java programming environment Kalimantan. Thanks also to Michael Neville and Derek Thompson, the implementers of DSTC's CORBA Trading Service product.

Gerald Vogt, a student from the University of Stuttgart, spent the second half of 1996 at the DSTC working on his Master's thesis. He worked on the Universal CORBA Client and contributed substantially to Chapter 10.

Particular thanks are also due to the three ORB vendors, Visigenic Software, Iona Technologies, and Sun Microsystems, whose Java ORB products we used throughout the book. The companies provided early access releases of their Java ORBs and their staffs have been very supportive. In particular, we would like to thank Alain Demour, Jonathan Weedon, and Neguine Navab of Visigenic, Ellen Siegel, Jeff Nisewanger, and Geoff Lewis of Sun, and David Glance and Mark Dunleavy of Iona.

Special thanks goes to Dean Halford, representing the Department of Mathematics of Massey University, Palmerston North, New Zealand, who provided Andreas with the necessary computing facilities during a difficult time.

We would also like to thank the many and diverse participants of the Java ORB course from which the book evolved. The participants' feedback gave us the confidence to go ahead with the book project and all their questions improved the content of the book.

Finally, we would like to thank DSTC's Anonymous Coffee Society, which managed to install an espresso machine on Level 7.

How to Read this Book

This book introduces Java ORBs to an audience familiar with the basic concepts of object-oriented programming and distributed systems. The book has chapters of different categories: introductory and background information, tutorials, and chapters containing reference information. The chapters and appendices of the book fall into three categories as follows:

♦ *Introduction and background.* Chapter 1 gives motivation for the use of Java ORBs. It also compares Java ORBs with alternatives such as CGI integration and Java RMI. Chapter 2 is an introduction to CORBA. Chapter 3 is an introduction to Java. Chapter 4 gives a more detailed overview of Java ORBs.

♦ *Tutorial chapters.* Chapter 5 provides first examples demonstrating the basic use of Java ORBs. Chapter 8 introduces two fundamental CORBA Services, the Naming and the Trading Service, and demonstrates their use. Chapter 9 shows how to build applications with Java ORBs using a room booking example. Advanced features are explained in Chapter 10. They include the Any type and TypeCodes, the Dynamic Invocation Interface, the Tie mechanism, and applet server. Appendix A provides a more comprehensive CORBA tutorial than Chapter 2.

♦ *Reference.* A complete overview of the mappings from OMG IDL to Java as they are currently implemented by the three leading Java ORB vendors is given in Chapter 6. Chapter 7 documents the Java implementation of the pseudo-IDL interfaces ORB, BOA, and Object. Chapter 8 is also somewhat of a reference chapter as it documents the interfaces of

CORBA Naming and Trading Services. Appendix B provides a number of tables extending issues from Chapters 6 and 7. Appendix C lists the source code (OMG IDL and Java) of all examples introduced throughout the book.

Besides the default approach of reading the book front to back we suggest the following paths through the book.

◆ *Novice approach*. Beginners should read the book from Chapter 1 to Chapter 5 and then continue with Chapters 8, 9, and 10. We also recommend the reading of Appendix A to provide a more thorough understanding of CORBA.

◆ *Advanced approach*. An advanced programmer will have experience with Java and CORBA. They can start reading with Chapter 4, but if they have already had some exposure to Java ORBs they can go straight to Chapter 8 and continue from there to Chapter 10.

◆ *Expert approach*. We expect that the expert will use the book as a reference only. They may also look up particular details of ORB implementations from Chapters 6 and 7 and familiarize themselves with the CORBA Services using Chapter 8, and advanced features using Chapter 10 as needed.

We recommend the book for self-teaching as well as base material for training and university courses. In any case, users are recommended to work thoroughly through the examples provided. The source code can be obtained from the John Wiley & Sons web site at htttp://www.wiley.com/compbooks/.

About the Authors

Dr. Andreas Vogel has been a Senior Research Scientist with the Distributed Systems Technology Centre (DSTC) in Brisbane, Australia, since 1994. Among other projects, Andreas leads CORBAnet, OMG's Internet-accessible ORB-interoperability showcase. Prior to this appointment he worked as a Research Scientist for the University of Montreal, Canada. He has worked on various topics in the area of distributed computing including Formal Description Techniques, Distributed Middleware (DCE and CORBA), Distributed Multimedia, and Quality of Service. His research results have been published in over 30 publications in international conferences, workshops, and journals. Andreas holds a Ph.D. in Computer Science from the Humboldt-University at Berlin, Germany.

Andreas was recently married to long-time partner Dorit Hillmann and is the father of Meta Hillmann. They have lived in Berlin, Montreal, and Brisbane and are looking forward to enjoying life in San Francisco.

Keith Duddy is a Research Scientist with the Distributed Systems Technology Centre (DSTC). His special area of interest is CORBA and he is one of the authors of the CORBA Trader Service specification which has recently been adopted by the OMG. He studied computer science at the University of Queensland. He has worked in the Australian and European computer industries as a UNIX operating systems and network programmer, and at the University of Queensland in the specification of real-time systems.

He enjoys taking and printing black-and-white photographs, red wine, trash TV, and cultural criticism. He will accept any opportunities to travel to places where he can practice his bad German (or any other language for that matter), but lives quite happily in inner Brisbane, a country town of about 1.2 million residents. He lives in a flat with long-term flat-mate Kathleen (bigk) Williamson, a few hundred meters from his partner of eight years, and fellow research scientist, Tim Mansfield.

Java Programming
with CORBA

C H A P T E R

Benefits of Java Programming with CORBA

This book brings together two of the major object models used in distributed computing: *Common Object Request Broker Architecture* (*CORBA*) and Java. They each introduce a different approach to distributed computing. CORBA provides an infrastructure which enables invocations of operations on objects located anywhere on a network as if they were local to the application using them. Java introduces platform-independent, low-level code, which, when integrated with World Wide Web protocols and browsers, results in what are known as *applets*. In this approach, instead of invoking a method on a remote object, the code for the class providing the method is transferred across the network, run locally, and then the method is invoked on a local object instance.

These two approaches converge when a mapping is defined from CORBA's interface definition language, *Object Management Group Interface Definition Language* (*OMG IDL*), to Java. When combined with a run-time system which supports this language mapping, the result is a *Java Object Request Broker* (*Java ORB*). For the remainder of this chapter we discuss this combination of the two paradigms in the form of Java ORBs. We explain the advantages of Java for CORBA users and the advantages of

CORBA for Java users. The relevance of Java ORBs to the Web and configuration management is also discussed. We also compare Java Remote Method Invocation (RMI) interface mechanisms with Java ORBs.

1 *What Does Java Offer CORBA Programmers*

The main reason for using a Java language mapping of OMG IDL is to exploit the combination of features unique to the Java language:

◆ Portability across platforms
◆ Internet programming
◆ Object-oriented language

1.1 Portability of Applications Across Platforms

Java programs are highly portable due to the standardized byte-code representation generated by Java compilers. Wide industry support means that compilers and run-time systems for virtually any hardware platform and operating system are available. This is a significant advantage over other programming languages, in particular for client applications, since a single source code or compiled byte-code set will be usable on any platform without porting. Consequently, development and maintenance costs can be significantly reduced.

1.2 Internet Programming

The Java language binding allows implementation of CORBA clients as applets. This enables access to CORBA objects, and potentially to legacy applications wrapped into objects, using popular Web browsers. In fact, Java-enabled Web browsers are becoming the universal graphical user interface (GUI). In an enterprise the same technology can be used in intranets because the same TCP/IP protocols are used.

Although having applets that are only clients to CORBA objects is useful, applets can also implement CORBA objects. This approach is somewhat limited because the Java security model does not give applets access to resources on the machine where they execute. This means, for example, that those objects cannot be made persistent. However, applets can at least provide call-back interfaces so that they can respond to requests from other objects.

1.3   Friendly Object-Oriented
Programming Language

Java ORBs provide the same functionality as any other ORB. The main language bindings offered by currently available ORB products are C++, C, and Smalltalk. In our experience, Java provides a cleaner approach to object-oriented programming than C++, with fewer memory management responsibilities, no pointers, a less confusing syntax, and simpler method resolution rules. Additionally, Java provides features not available in C or C++ such as automatic garbage collection, exception handling, and integrated thread support. These features are generally desirable and are particularly useful for distributed systems programming, as we shall see throughout this book.

2   *What Does CORBA Offer*
Java Programmers?

The Java programming language does not directly support the development of distributed applications or systems. The only way to implement distributed applications that is directly supported in Java is to use the network library classes in the package `java.net`. Those classes provide an Application Programming Interface (API) for the handling of URLs and an API to UDP/IP and TCP/IP sockets.

The URL API provides high-level access to Web resources. For example, it provides a mechanism to fetch the document specified in a URL using the protocol specifier in the URL. Hence the API provides the same approach to distributed computing as a Web browser, that is, either fetching documents from a remote server or using the Common Gateway Interface (CGI) to invoke a program at a HTTP server that creates an HTML document on the fly. Below we outline the limitations and drawbacks of the CGI.

UDP/IP and TCP/IP sockets are relatively low-level abstractions providing access to transport protocols. The socket API does not provide distribution transparency or connection management.

The Java language binding for OMG IDL provides an application programmer with CORBA's high-level distributed object paradigm:

- ♦ Interfaces defined independently of implementations
- ♦ Access to objects implemented in other programming languages
- ♦ Access to objects regardless of their location (location transparency)
- ♦ Automatic code generation to deal with remote invocations
- ♦ Access to standard CORBA services and facilities

These advantages are discussed in detail in Sections 2.1–2.6.

2.1 OMG IDL Defined Interfaces

OMG IDL provides a means of separating interfaces from implementations for distributed object applications. This separation is particularly useful for software engineering processes. Systems designs based on object-oriented design methodologies and tools, such as Object Modelling Technique (OMT) or Booch, can be expressed in OMG IDL. Once components are specified in IDL, different teams or individuals can independently implement different components.

The separation of interface from implementation is also useful for managing software component evolution. In particular, it allows access to multiple implementations conforming to the same interface specification. Additionally, interfaces can be extended by inheritance, where derived interfaces are substitutable for base interfaces.

2.2 Programming Language Independence

CORBA supports multiple language mappings for OMG IDL so that different components of a system or application can be implemented in different programming languages. However, all interactions between components happen through interfaces which are specified independently of the programming language they are implemented in.

Previously, distributed applications were implemented in a particular programming language because of the availability of remote invocation libraries for that language. With CORBA the most appropriate programming language can be chosen for each component object, based on the need for legacy integration, the prior experience of a development team, or the suitability of the language for implementing the object's semantics.

2.3 Location Transparency and Server Activation

Socket- or URL-based distributed applications need to address a server by specifying a host name and a port number. In contrast, CORBA provides location transparency, which means that an object is identified independently of its physical location and can potentially change its location without breaking the application. The ORB provides the necessary mechanisms for this transparency.

In addition, CORBA provides mechanisms to start up services on demand. This can be controlled by various server activation policies.

2.4   Automatic Stub and Skeleton Code Generation

Distributed systems require a number of lower level and repetitious programming efforts, for example,

- ♦ Opening, controlling, and closing network connections
- ♦ Marshaling and unmarshaling of data (conversion of structured data into a programming language and architecture-independent format and back again)
- ♦ Setting up servers to listen for incoming requests on socket ports and forward them to object implementations

IDL compilers and ORB run-time systems free application programmers from these tasks. IDL compilers create representations of IDL-defined constructs such as constants, data types, and interfaces in a particular language binding, for example, C++ or Java. They also create the code to marshal and unmarshal the user-defined data types. Libraries are provided to support predefined CORBA types.

The generated code for the client side, that is, the code invoking an operation on an object, is known as stub code. The server-side generated code, which invokes the method on the implementation of that operation, is called skeleton code. The skeleton code in conjunction with the ORB provides a transparent run-time mechanism for handling incoming invocations and managing associated network connections.

2.5   Reuse of CORBA Services and Facilities

The ORB provides a means for the distribution-transparent invocation of methods on potentially remote objects. Typically, nontrivial distributed applications require additional functionality. Within the OMG these requirements have been analyzed and have led to the specification of corresponding fundamental services. These fundamental services are published with the brand CORBAservices. Examples are

- ♦ *Naming Service*—a white pages service for distributed objects
- ♦ *Trading Service*—a yellow pages service for distributed objects
- ♦ *Event Service*—an asynchronous, subscription-based messaging service
- ♦ *Transaction Service*—transaction processing for distributed objects

There are specifications of higher level application-oriented services which are known as CORBAfacilities. More details of CORBAservices and CORBAfacilities can be found in Chapter 2.

2.6 Vendor Independence Through ORB Interoperability

The current version of CORBA—CORBA2.0—specifies the means by which objects implemented using different ORB implementations can interoperate. These include object addressing through interoperable object references (IORs) and a hierarchy of protocols—the General Inter-ORB Protocol (GIOP) and the TCP/IP-specific Internet Inter-ORB Protocol (IIOP).

This interoperability allows a certain independence from ORB vendor products. Any application developed using a CORBA2.0 compliant ORB can integrate components developed using another interoperable ORB.

3 *The Web, Java, and CORBA*

The progression Web functionality from simple document fetching to more and more complex and interactive applications has followed these steps:

- ◆ Fetching HTML or other formatted documents from fixed locations
- ◆ Fetching documents from back-end systems, such as databases, using the CGI
- ◆ Building interactive systems using HTML forms and CGI
- ◆ Using Java script to increase GUI capabilities
- ◆ Using Java applets to provide client-side functionality

The Web now supports interactive applications. However, there is one thing lacking in the approaches listed above: GUI capabilities combined with remote invocations.

3.1 Overcoming Problems in Current Web Applications

The functionality provided by HTML to create GUIs is not sufficient for commercial applications when judged side by side with applications written for Windows, the Macintosh OS, or Motif. Java provides a package known as `java.awt` that matches the functionality of these systems.

The interactivity of HTML-based interfaces is provided through the CGI. This enables the execution of programs on the server side. Unfortunately, the CGI has a number of limitations and drawbacks:

- ◆ *Stateless clients.* A typical CGI-based application works in a two-phase cycle as illustrated in Figure 1-1. A client has some state which can be changed by data entered into a form, or as a result of state changes in

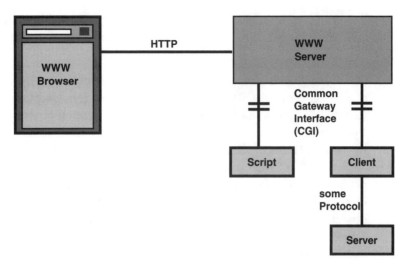

FIGURE 1-1. CGI-based distributed applications.

the server. The client in this case is a sequence of HTML pages where each page is created as the result of a CGI call. Hence all client state information has to be passed to a program behind the CGI. The only way to do this is by encoding it into the URL.

♦ *Non-type-safe interaction.* Writing a client as a sequence of HTML pages and URLs is an extremely tedious task and has great potential for errors. Data transferred from client to server must be encoded in the URL string which must be parsed each time a new CGI call is received.

♦ *Performance bottlenecks.* There are a number of performance bottlenecks in the CGI-based approach. Usually there is some scripting language program that glues the application-specific program and the CGI together. As a result of an invocation a complete HTML page is returned to the client side (including all the hidden state and GUI information). These HTML documents contain a lot of repeated text and formatting data that remains unchanged since the last client action. The amount of unchanged HTML often outweighs the amount of actual data produced by the application program by an order of magnitude.

HTTP, the most popular protocol of the Web protocol suite, is not very efficient. The major performance bottleneck occurs because multiple connections can be created by loading a single URL, and the connection management creates a significant performance overhead. Furthermore, the CGI will start a new operating system process each time an application processes a user input, and any server-side state must be read from persistent storage or communicated from another process.

Java ORBs overcome the statelessness problem by having continuously executing client and server programs which maintain their own state variables. Clients contain their own graphical elements, supported by the Java Abstract Window Toolkit (AWT) package, which avoids the downloading of HTML tags to format the display each time an action takes place.

CORBA's IDL provides typed interface specifications, overcoming the problem of untyped interaction. The performance problems are overcome by the ORB infrastructure allowing the invocation of operations on remote objects, which communicate only the data they need for each interaction. The ORB maintains a network connection between client and server, keeping a reasonable trade-off between lowering connection establishment overhead and freeing idle network resources.

The CORBA approach to Web-based distributed applications is gaining more and more support within the computer industry. For example, Netscape ONE contains support for Java ORBs based on Visigenic's Visibroker for Java.

3.2   Thin Clients and Configuration Management

As HTML-based clients are a sequence of stateless HTML pages downloaded every time from a server, they are considered to be *null clients*. At the other extreme is the case of an applet that executes in the browser without any outside communications or access to local data and contains all the application logic. In between there are a variety of options.

A *thin client* provides a complete GUI and keeps some state information. However, all the application logic and data is kept at the server. Thin clients overcome the limitations of null clients because they contain state and some application logic. They are relatively small in size and can be downloaded quickly over the network. Since they do not contain application logic they are less interesting for hacker attacks.

Thin clients can also overcome a major problem caused by software updates and their distribution. A typical distributed system could have a relatively small number of servers while the client front-ends would number in the hundreds or thousands. When updating the software a new version of the client has to be shipped and installed on each of the client machines. That is a tedious, time-consuming, and high-cost task.

An applet client has the potential to overcome this problem. The shipping and installation process is automatically done by a Web browser.

Caching mechanisms of today are rather simple. However, it would be possible to implement a caching mechanism based on version numbers of applets. That would make the whole configuration process more effective since a client applet is only downloaded when the cached version is older than the one on the server.

4 *Java ORBs Versus Remote Method Invocation*

An alternative approach enabling the invocation of methods on remote Java objects is provided by a mechanism called *Remote Method Invocation* (RMI). The idea is to create objects whose methods can be invoked from another Java virtual machine. This approach provides remote procedure call (RPC) mechanisms for Java objects.

Examples of RMI mechanisms are HORB and JavaSoft's RMI. In both cases, stub and skeleton classes are directly generated from a Java class identified as remote. The stub class deals with binding to the remote object and client-side data marshaling. The skeleton class handles incoming invocations. (See Figure 1-2.)

RMI mechanisms allow the optimization of protocols for communication between Java classes. This optimization, however, comes at the cost of being limited to a single-language environment. In particular, server applications often bring in a certain legacy that makes them hard to wrap in Java.

The main advantage of the CORBA approach over RMI is that it supports multiple programming languages. Although Java is a more friendly language to use than COBOL, C, or C++ and is a good candidate to replace those languages in commercial software development, there will always be legacy applications implemented in other languages. Java applications can access these legacy applications if they are wrapped in a CORBA object, using the most appropriate language binding.

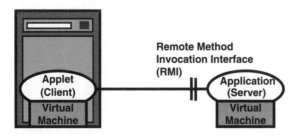

FIGURE 1-2.   Remote method invocation.

CORBA gives additional support for distributed applications by providing CORBAservices. CORBA2.0 interoperability allows application writers to choose ORB products from various vendors and to integrate applications written using different ORBs. See Chapter 2 for details.

RMI is an interesting approach for small and medium-sized applications completely implemented in Java. However, applications that require the integration of legacy components or the use of a particular programming language for some components need a CORBA solution. CORBA IDL's separation of interface definitions from implementations and mappings to many programming languages, in combination with CORBAservices, provide better support for large-scale applications.

2

CORBA Overview

This chapter gives an overview of the Object Management Architecture (OMA) and its object communication mechanism, CORBA. These standards are published by the Object Management Group (OMG), a nonprofit computer industry consortium that aims to establish a framework for distributed object-oriented application integration.

The material covered here is enough to introduce the concepts that you will need to begin writing CORBA applications in Java, but we advise you to consult Appendix A for more details. The Appendix is a complete reference guide to the structure of the OMG, the OMA Guide, and the CORBA2.0 specifications. It provides a full explanation of the OMG standards relevant to CORBA application programmers and a summary of the specifications used only by ORB developers.

The topics covered in this introduction to CORBA include

♦ The OMG technology adoption process
♦ The OMA
♦ The CORBA specifications including

> ♦ An explanation of clients, servers, and object request brokers
> ♦ Operation invocation on objects
> ♦ Interface Definition Language (IDL)
> ♦ The interfaces to components of CORBA
> ♦ Interoperability between ORBs

1 OMG Technology Adoption Process

The OMG does not write any standards or develop any software. It simply administers the process whereby members submit specifications for technology components to its technical committees (Figure 2-1). These committees report to a senior technical board, the Architecture Board (AB). There are two technical committees—the Platform Technical Committee (PTC) and the Domain Technical Committee (DTC)—that oversee several task forces and special interest groups (SIGs).

1.1 Platform Technical Committee

The task forces that report to the PTC are concerned with specifying the infrastructure technologies for the ORB and Object Services and Common Facilities. The PTC task forces and SIGs are

> ♦ ORB/Object Services Task Force (OSTF)
> ♦ Common Facilities Task Force (CFTF)
> ♦ Object Analysis and Design Task Force (OADTF)
> ♦ Internet Special Interest Group (ISIG)
> ♦ Japan Special Interest Group (JSIG)
> ♦ Real Time Special Interest Group (RTSIG)

1.2 Domain Technical Committee

The task forces that report to the DTC are responsible for specifying object technologies that directly support application development in various vertical markets. The task forces and SIGs that specify services for vertical domains are

> ♦ CORBAmed Task Force (Healthcare)
> ♦ Telecommunications Task Force (CORBAtel)
> ♦ Manufacturing Domain Task Force (CORBAmanufacturing)
> ♦ Financial Domain Task Force (CORBA financials)
> ♦ Interactive Multimedia and Electronic Commerce Domain Task Force

♦ Business Objects Task Force (BODTF)
♦ Transportation Special Interest Group (TSIG)

There are also a number of SIGs that are relevant to the OMG as a whole, and they report directly to the Architecture Board:

♦ End User Special Interest Group (EUSIG)
♦ Security Special Interest Group
♦ Metrics Special Interest Group

Descriptions of all the groups can be found in Appendix A.

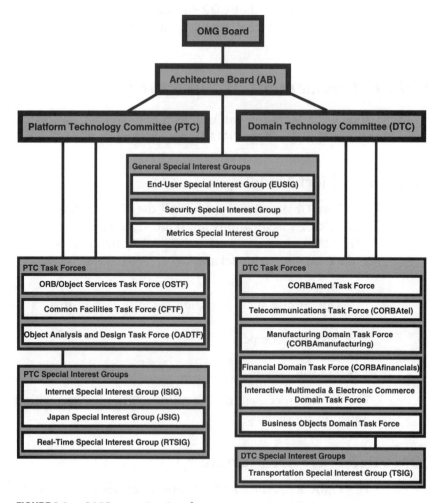

FIGURE 2-1. OMG organizational structure.

Task forces issue *Requests for Proposals* (*RFPs*) for specifications of technologies that fulfill a particular role within the OMA. The specifications take the form of interface definitions, in OMG IDL, with descriptions of their semantics written in English. The submitters are required to implement the technology that they submit specifications for. If their proposal is accepted by the OMG membership then they must make the technology commercially available within 12 months.

The steps in the technology adoption process are given in Appendix A. This process is designed to standardize only the interfaces to technology, and so to allow diverse implementations. It focuses on cooperation and compromise; most final submissions are a merger of specifications from several companies. The requirement for commercial availability is an attempt to ensure that CORBA does not stagnate and that new specifications are based on real, usable implementations.

2 Object Management Architecture

The Object Management Architecture Guide has two components: the Core Object Model and the OMA Reference Architecture.

2.1 The Core Object Model

The Core Object Model defines all the object-oriented concepts on which the CORBA specifications are built. It defines an object model from first principles and a framework for extending that model. The concepts defined in the Core Object Model are

♦ Objects
♦ Operations, including their signatures, parameters, and return values
♦ Non–object types
♦ Interfaces
♦ Substitutability

The CORBA specification is a refinement of the core object model. See the Appendix for details.

2.2 OMA Reference Architecture

The OMA Reference Architecture describes a framework for distributed application integration (Figure 2-2).

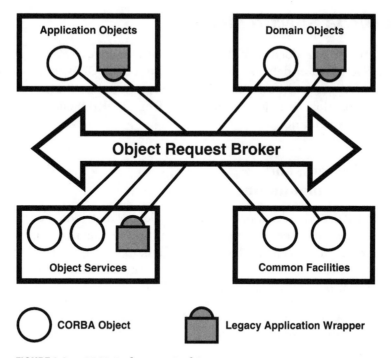

FIGURE 2-2. OMA Reference Architecture.

The architecture contains

◆ *The ORB*. A message bus for communicating requests to invoke opera-
tions on objects, regardless of any object's location or implementation.
The ORB is based on the principles defined in the Core Object Model.
It is specified by CORBA, which is a refinement of the Core Object
Model.

◆ *Object Services*. These are specifications of objects that provide fundamental, lower-level assistance to application developers. They include
services such as Naming (Chapter 8), Event Notification, Transaction
Management, and Trading (Chapter 8).

◆ *Common Facilities*. A set of higher-level object specifications providing
commonly required services to applications such as printing, and com-
pound documents.

◆ *Domain Interfaces*. Specifications that target particular vertical markets
such as healthcare, manufacturing, telecommunications, and so on.

The specifications adopted in each of the groupings above are listed in the
Appendix. The organization of the OMG, which is fully explained in the
Appendix, closely resembles the structure of the OMA.

3 *The CORBA Specification*

The OMG document *Common Object Request Broker Architecture and Specification* defines the functionality of the ORB component of the OMA reference architecture. This is the message bus that conveys requests for invocation of objects' operations from CORBA clients to CORBA object implementations.

3.1 Clients, Servers, and Object Implementations

CORBA provides a peer-to-peer model for distributed computing. In traditional client/server applications you find clients that implement a GUI and some business logic. These clients talk to servers that maintain data stores. In CORBA the terms client and server are used to describe the role played by a component in a distributed application:

- *Client*—the role of making a request of some other component in the distributed application. A *pure client* is a program that does not play the server role.
- *Server*—the role of providing an implementation of a component that a client uses. Servers often also act as clients to other components.

In CORBA the components that provide functionality are CORBA objects, each of which implements the functionality described by an *interface definition*. CORBA clearly separates the interface of an object from its implementation. Clients of CORBA objects rely only on the interface, so implementations can be used interchangeably.

CORBA servers are the programs that provide the implementation of one or more CORBA objects. Aside from implementing the functionality of objects as described by their interface definitions, servers also interact with ORBs to notify them of the availability of the objects they implement. In turn, ORBs are aware of the servers that are available and can start inactive servers running when their objects are required. This is known as *activation* or *launching* of servers.

Figure 2-3 shows a high-level view of a CORBA client interacting with a object in a CORBA server.

3.2 Transparencies

The ORB provides *location transparency* to objects. That is, an object is represented by an *object reference* on which a client can invoke operations as if

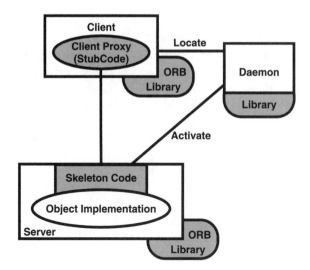

FIGURE 2-3.   CORBA client and server.

they were methods on a local object. Object references may refer to objects that are in the same program, in a different process on the same machine, or located on a remote machine. Each kind of object is used in exactly the same way.

The other transparency that assists in the integration of distributed applications is *programming language transparency*. Because CORBA objects are typed by interface definitions and referenced by object references, the implementation behind the interface can be in one of several programming languages.

These transparencies are achieved by the use of OMG's *Interface Definition Language (IDL)*. OMG IDL makes concrete the notions of interfaces, operation signatures, substitutability (through inheritance) and non object types (data types), which are defined in the OMA Core Object Model. It contains no programming constructs, and the types it defines are used by object implementations and their clients through a mapping to a programming language. These mappings are automatically implemented by IDL compilers, which generate code in a programming language for the types specified in the IDL and facilitate communication between clients and servers wherever they may be located.

3.3   ORB Structure

The ORB is drawn as a single entity in the OMA Reference Architecture diagram (Figure 2-2). However, it is implemented in several parts:

◆ *IDL compiler generated code:*
  ◆ Stub code—linked into a CORBA client.
  ◆ Skeleton code—linked into a CORBA object implementation.
◆ *An ORB agent or daemon process.* Locates and launches servers and facilitates client communication with servers.
◆ *Library code.* Used by all of the components listed above.

Figure 2-4 shows the ORB as a number of components and interfaces:

◆ *IDL stubs.* The code generated for a specific IDL interface to allow *static invocation* of operations of that interface via *proxy objects.*
◆ *Dynamic Invocation Interface (DII).* A way to make operation invocations without IDL stubs.
◆ *ORB Interface.* An interface offering miscellaneous services from the ORB to clients and servers.
◆ *IDL Skeleton.* The code generated for a specific IDL interface that invokes object implementations of that type.
◆ *Dynamic Skeleton Interface (DSI).* A generic interface that allows interpretation of incoming requests to a server for IDL types that were not known at compile time.

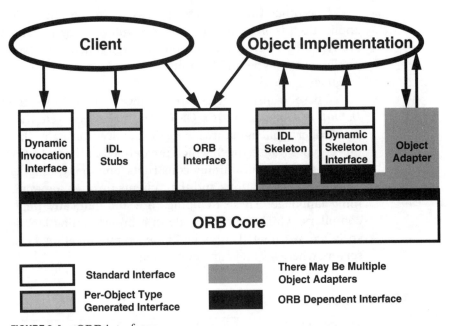

FIGURE 2-4. ORB interfaces.

♦ *Object Adapter.* Because the ORB Core is free to be implemented in a variety of ways, adapter interfaces are defined that provide standard interfaces to servers. There is currently only one standard Object Adapter defined in CORBA2.0, the *Basic Object Adapter* (*BOA*). This is the component of the ORB that is capable of activating servers whose objects are required by invocations. After a server is ready it must inform the BOA that its objects can receive incoming invocation requests.

Figure 2-4 is as close as the CORBA standard comes to specifying the structure of an ORB because CORBA aims to allow a wide variety of implementations. However, the most common implementation style (used by all the Java ORBs we consider in this book) places all the stub, skeleton, DII, and ORB interface components into the client or server executable code, and uses a background process on the server's machine to perform some of the ORB's tasks. Figure 2-5 shows how the components are grouped in terms of executable code.

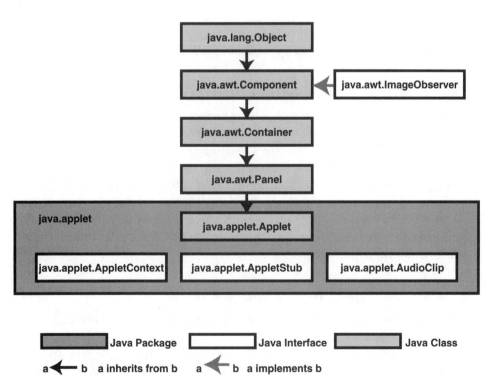

FIGURE 2-5. ORB implementation.

3.4   Invoking Operations on Objects

A CORBA object is a run-time instance of an interface definition specified in IDL. Objects are accessed through object references, which are opaque data used by programmers in the same way as references to local objects in object-oriented programming languages. Object references contain enough information to allow the ORB to locate the machine on which the object implementation resides, the server which implements the object, and the specific object in that server to which the reference refers. The ORB can also activate servers that are not currently running when their objects are required.

3.4.1   Static Invocation Interface

When IDL definitions are compiled by an ORB's IDL compiler, code is generated that allows an operation to be invoked on an object reference as if it were a method on a local object. This code is known as *stub code*. In object-oriented languages the stub code usually implements *proxy objects* which have method implementations that forward the arguments they receive to (possibly remote) object implementations. This is called static invocation because the interface is known at compile time and the code to deliver invocation requests is generated specifically for a particular interface type.

3.4.2   Dynamic Invocation Interface

If the IDL that represents an object's interface is not known when a client is compiled, the interface type can be discovered at run time. This is done by using an operation defined in the Object interface, which is supported by all CORBA objects. An object's operations and their parameter types can then be discovered by querying the Interface Repository (IR). The CORBA specification defines an interface called Request, which allows an operation invocation on an object to be built from this dynamically discovered interface information and then invoked. This part of CORBA is called the Dynamic Invocation Interface (DII).

3.4.3   Operation Invocation Semantics

The invocation semantics of CORBA object operations are known as *at-most-once*. The code making the invocation will block while waiting for the operation to complete, and it will receive back either a result of the type specified in IDL or an exception. A nonexception result means that the object implementation executed exactly once. An exception can be queried to determine whether the invocation request reached the target object or not.

If the IDL signature of an operation contains the oneway keyword, the invocation will return without synchronizing with the termination of the operation's execution. This can occur because oneway operations have no return values or return parameters and cannot raise exceptions. This is known as *best-effort* invocation semantics.

One other type of execution semantics is possible, but only by using the DII. This is called *deferred-synchronous*. When using the DII to invoke an operation, it can send the invocation request and return immediately. Then, after performing some other processing, the client can check the results of the invocation. The DII also implements synchronous and oneway invocations.

3.5 Interface Definition Language

This language is the key to object communication because it provides a definition of the functionality of all objects participating in a distributed application. This definition is then mapped into programming constructs in the programming language chosen by the application developer. The IDL is used to generate programming language code that performs the tedious, error prone, and repetitive tasks of establishing network connections, translating data structures into byte streams (marshaling), locating object implementations, and invoking the right code to perform an operation.

IDL is designed to specify the functionality of objects. Each object has a type that corresponds to an IDL interface. These are known as *object types*. Nonobject types are also required so that structured data types can be specified for use as parameters and result types for operations.

Below we are going to look at the following aspects of IDL:

♦ Data types
♦ Attributes and operations
♦ Inheritance
♦ Name scopes

3.5.1 Data Types

IDL contains the following basic types:

Type Keyword	Description
(unsigned) short	signed [unsigned] 16-bit 2s complement integer
(unsigned) long	signed [unsigned] 32-bit 2s complement integer

float	16-bit IEEE floating point number
double	32-bit IEEE floating point number
char	ISO Latin-1 character
boolean	boolean type taking values TRUE and FALSE
string	variable length string of characters whose length is available at run time
octet	8-bit uninterpreted type
enum	enumerated type with named integer values
any	can represent a value from any possible IDL type, basic or constructed, object or nonobject

IDL also offers constructed types. Here is a short description of each, with some example syntax:

♦ *Structure*—a record type with named members.

```
struct struct_type_name {
    type1 member_name1;
    type2 member_name2;
};
```

♦ *Discriminated union*—a type taking one of several typed values dependent on a discriminator of a scalar type such as numeric and enumerated types.

```
union union_type_name switch(discriminator_type) {
    case value1 : type1 member_name1;
    case value2 : type2 member_name2;
    default : type 3 member_name3;
};
```

♦ *Array*—an indexed list of fixed length.

```
typedef array_type_name1 member_type1(10);
typedef array_type_name2 member_type2(10)(60);
```

♦ *Sequence*—an indexed list of variable length which can have an upper bound.

```
typedef bounded_seq_type_name sequence <member_type1, 30>;
typedef unbounded_seq_type_name sequence <member_type2>;
```

♦ *Exception*—a structure that can be returned from an operation as an alternative termination, usually used to indicate an error condition.

```
exception exception_name {
    type1 member_name1;
    type2 member_name2;
};
```

The CORBA specification defines a number of standard exception types, known as *System Exceptions,* that can be raised by any operation or attribute.

3.5.2   *Attributes and Operations*

Attributes and operations are the actions declared in IDL that can be requested of a CORBA object. An attribute is a short way of declaring a pair of operations that act on a value of one type: one to retrieve a value from the object and one to convey a value to the object. The keyword readonly restricts attributes to allow retrieval only. Here are some examples:

```
attribute string message;
readonly attribute boolean unread_message;
```

An attribute is always implemented as one or two operations and does not necessarily refer to a state variable inside the object.

Operations have a name, a return type, a list of parameters, a *raises clause,* and a *context clause.* Let's have a look at some example IDL before explaining the parts of an operation declaration:

```
interface TheaterBooking {
    enum seating_section {stalls, galleryA, galleryB, balcony};
    struct date {
        short day;
        short month;
    };
    exception no_seats {
        sequence <seating_section> seats_still_available_in;
    };
    exception no_performance {};
    typedef short reservation_code;
    reservation_code make_booking(
        in date performance,
        in seating_section position,
        out float price)
    raises (no_performance, no_seats)
    context (ROW_PREF);
};
```

A raises clause is a list of the possible user exceptions that an operation can raise if an error condition arises. In the example above the make_booking operation can raise a no_performance exception if the theater is closed on the date given, or a no_seats exception if no seats are available in that section. The latter provides some useful information about what other seating sections to try.

A context clause is a list of string names for which there is a string value in the environment of the object's client. The context clause instructs the ORB to convey those string-to-string mappings to the server with each invocation of the operation. In the example the ROW_PREF string is used as an extra input to the booking process if it is defined in the context from which the client makes the booking. We do not encourage the use of contexts because the information they provide is not guaranteed to be in the client's context. The information is always a string, and therefore is not type-safe for most kinds of data that it represents.

Operations may have zero or more parameters, and each parameter must be tagged with a keyword to indicate in which direction arguments will be passed at run time.

- ♦ in—the argument is passed from client to server.
- ♦ out—the argument is returned from server to client.
- ♦ inout—a value is passed from client to server, possibly modified, and then returned.

Each operation must also have a return type or use the keyword void to indicate that no return value is expected.

The operation make_booking has three parameters, two of which are provided by the client to specify the performance date and seating preference. The third is returned by the server as a result of the operation and informs the patron how much the ticket will cost.

3.5.3 Inheritance

Inheritance is used as a way of extending the functionality of an existing interface. It is also the way in which object substitutability is determined in CORBA. When a derived interface inherits from a base interface it can act in place of the base interface type. That is, the derived interface is a subtype of each of the interfaces it derives from. Let's extend our TheaterBooking interface to provide an example of how this works:

```
interface TheaterService : TheaterBooking {
    readonly attribute date next_performance;
    short number_free(
        in date performance,
        in seating_section position)
    raises (no_performance);
};
```

Our new TheaterService interface adds an attribute and an operation to the functionality declared in TheaterBooking to provide information as well as bookings. When using objects of these types we now have the option of substituting a TheaterService object wherever a TheaterBooking object is required. This is because a TheaterService object is a TheaterBooking object. This is *polymorphism,* and it relies on the inheritance relationship between the two interfaces to determine substitutability.

Interfaces can inherit from any number of other interfaces, with the following restriction: any attribute or operation name that becomes a part of the derived interface must be declared in only one of its base interfaces. OMG IDL does not allow any overriding or overloading of operation signatures.

3.5.4 *Name Scopes*

In order to allow interface and type names to be simple and descriptive, IDL provides the *module* construct to group declarations together and prevent their names from clashing with other unrelated declarations. Modules can be nested within other modules so that declarations can be placed into subgroups. Here is an example of how we might simplify the naming of the interfaces defined above:

```
module Theater {
        interface Booking {
                // contains types and make_booking operation
        };
        interface Service : Booking {
                // contains information access
        };
};
```

The names of the interfaces above are written as a concatenation of the module name and the interface name separated by a double colon, for example, Theater::Booking. Naming within a module is context relative, so the declaration of Service does not need the scoped name of Booking since they are in the same module. Unambiguous naming can be achieved by prepending a double colon to a fully scoped name to indicate that the context is the global scope, for example, ::Theater::Service.

3.6   The CORBA Module

The interfaces to the ORB components are all specified in IDL or *pseudo-IDL* in a module named CORBA. Pseudo-IDL describes types and interfaces that will not be implemented as true CORBA data and object types; that is, they cannot be passed as parameters to operations on CORBA objects because they are implemented specifically for the environment in which they are used and cannot be marshaled for transmission and use in another environment. Pseudo-IDL indicates that the IDL syntax is being used to specify interfaces to the ORB in a programming language neutral way.

The CORBA module contains the base interface to all CORBA objects, called Object, which specifies object reference management operations. It contains the ORB interface, which is used to perform miscellaneous housekeeping functions and to get a reference to a BOA object. The BOA is used to notify the ORB when CORBA objects become available for invocation.

The CORBA module contains many type definitions used throughout the ORB. It also defines the DII, the DSI, and the IR (see Appendix A).

We will look at the important parts of these interfaces in overview here, and you are referred to the CORBA Reference Appendix for their detailed descriptions.

Below we discuss the following standard interfaces:

♦ Object
♦ ORB
♦ BOA
♦ Interface Repository

3.6.1 *Object*

In this section we introduce an important subset of the operations defined in the Object interface:

♦ duplicate()
♦ release()
♦ is_nil()
♦ get_interface()

Important operations that all CORBA objects support are those for the copying and destruction of object references. The duplicate() operation is the only way to create a safe copy of an object reference:

```
Object duplicate();
```

Copying an object reference using programming language routines will result in object reference counts being incorrect, and most probably in an object reference becoming invalid before you expect it to.

The only safe way to destroy an object reference is with the release() operation:

```
void release();
```

If you use a programming language's memory management routine to delete an object reference, the object's reference count will be artificially high and resources will not be deallocated when they are no longer needed. To avoid the pitfalls of programming with object references, read Section 3.5.2 in Appendix A (Object reference management), which provides a thorough explanation of the issues.

The other operation specified in the Object interface that is crucial to avoiding programming errors is called is_nil():

```
boolean is_nil();
```

Any object reference returned from an operation or attribute can be *nil*, that is, it refers to no object. If such an object reference is returned, making invocations on it will result in exceptions or worse!

When an object reference is passed as type Object, the receiver of that reference may wish to find out about the object's more specific type (see Section 3.6.4). The following operation allows this information to be discovered using the IR.

```
InterfaceDef get_interface();
```

InterfaceDef is an interface specified in the IR for querying the definition of an object's IDL.

3.6.2   ORB

There are three operations defined in the ORB interface that are needed by most CORBA programmers:

- ♦ BOA_init()
- ♦ object_to_string()
- ♦ string_to_object()

The first is a bootstrap operation to obtain a reference to a **BOA** pseudo-object:

```
BOA BOA_init(inout arg_list argv,
             in OAid oa_identifier);
```

The parameters are designed to allow the **BOA** to extract any command line arguments provided to the CORBA program and to select the correct object adapter by name. Many ORB implementations use variations of this operation, and some require no initialization of the **BOA** at all.

The other two basic operations provided by the ORB interface are to assist programmers in making object references persistent:

```
string object_to_string(in Object obj);
Object string_to_object(in string str);
```

Since the Object interface is the base interface of all CORBA objects, producing a string representation of any object reference is easily achieved by passing it to the object_to_string() operation. However, when passing a stringified object reference to the string_to_object() operation, the result will be a reference of type Object, not of the type that was passed to the converse operation. The way in which you get an object reference to a more specific type from a reference to Object is by using a method called *narrow()*, provided by the generated stub code. See Chapter 6 for details.

3.6.3   BOA

The BOA interface is not needed by CORBA client-only programs, but it is vital for object implementers. The operations of interest are

- ♦ impl_is_ready()—notifies the ORB that objects in this server are ready to be invoked.
- ♦ deactive_impl()—notifies the ORB that this server can no longer take invocation requests for its objects.
- ♦ obj_is_ready()—notifies the ORB that an object is ready to receive invocations.
- ♦ deactive_obj()—notifies the ORB that an object is no longer accepting invocations.

Their signatures are general enough that they can be used in non-object-oriented languages, but we don't reproduce them here because they are mapped in a nonstandard way by most ORB vendors. The BOA specification says that the decision to use impl_is_ready() or obj_is_ready() depends on the *activation policy* of the server (see Appendix). However, in practice it depends on the implementation choice of the ORB vendor. See Chapter 7 for details on Java ORBs.

3.6.4   Interface Repository

The IR is a service specified in the CORBA module that provides IDL interfaces to query the IDL interfaces of objects implemented using the ORB. That is, it allows you to invoke operations on CORBA objects to query the type, operations, and interfaces of all objects implemented in a particular domain.

The IR allows an object reference to be invoked using the DII, even when there is no stub code for its interface type built into a program. Each object supports an operation get_interface(), which returns an object reference

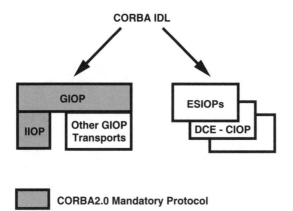

FIGURE 2-6. ORB interoperability protocols.

to an object in the IR. The IR object can describe the interface type of the unknown object reference, and this description can be used to build requests using the DII. These requests can then be used to invoke the object's operations.

3.7 CORBA Interoperability

The second major version of the CORBA standard—CORBA2.0—includes a specification for ORB interoperability called the *General Inter-ORB Protocol (GIOP)*. This is a description of the way in which IDL types are laid out in a message format for invocation requests (Figure 2-6).

The GIOP message format is used as the basis for the specification of the Internet Inter-ORB Protocol (IIOP), which uses TCP/IP as its transport protocol. The IIOP is a mandatory protocol for CORBA2.0 compliance.

An optional additional protocol called DCE Common Inter-ORB Protocol (DCE-CIOP) is also specified, which uses the DCE-RPC mechanism.

CORBA2.0 also provides a specification for *Interoperable Object References (IORs)*, which allow an object reference from any compliant ORB to be used by a client using any other ORB.

C H A P T E R

3

Java Overview

Java is an object-oriented programming language using similar principles to other object-oriented languages. This chapter discusses these principles as they apply to Java; correspondences to CORBA concepts are also noted. This is not a detailed Java tutorial. There are plenty of well-written books on Java and we refer to some of them in the Further Reading Section. The topics we cover are

- ◆ Interfaces, classes and objects
- ◆ Inheritance
- ◆ Methods and exceptions
- ◆ Packages and name scoping
- ◆ Objects at run time
- ◆ Java applets

We close the chapter with a simple Hello-World example. Although it is rather simple, it shows the principles of building Java applications and applets. In Chapter 5 we will distribute this example using various Java ORBs.

1 Interface, Class, and Object

Java's three major object-oriented constructs are

- *Interface.* The Java design concept. An interface only defines types, fields (data variables), and methods (actions); interfaces do not contain programming statements.
- *Class.* The construct that implements the actions that objects perform. A class can either implement methods declared in an interface or it can declare and implement methods of its own.
- *Object.* An instance of a class; a run-time entity. It encapsulates a state that is defined by the values of the fields of the object. The state of the object can be altered by directly modifying the value of public variables or by invoking methods on the object.

Figure 3-1 illustrates the relationship between Java interfaces, classes, and objects. Interfaces define the signature. A class implements the methods defined in the class or in an interface which it *implements.* Objects are run-time instances of a class executed on a virtual machine. Objects contain state.

The Java interface closely resembles CORBA IDL's interface. Java interfaces must be implemented by Java classes, while IDL interfaces can be implemented by constructs from various programming languages, including Java classes.

2 Inheritance

Java distinguishes between the inheritance of interfaces and the inheritance of implementations. Java allows multiple inheritance for interfaces, but only single inheritance for classes.

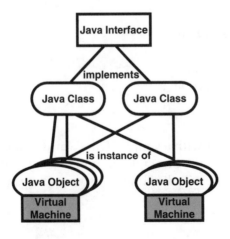

FIGURE 3-1. Relationship between interface, class, and object.

2.1 Classes

The inheritance relationship is declared with the keyword extends. For example, a class Derived inheriting from class Base is declared as

```
class Derived extends Base { ... }
```

The motivation to restrict the inheritance of classes is to avoid inconsistencies in the derived class. A typical example of such an inconsistency occurs in the case of diamond inheritance as illustrated in the Figure 3-2. If both classes Left and Right implement a method m(), then it is unclear if the method m() of the class Derived is Left.m() or Right.m(). If m() is also implemented in the Base class then the situation is even more complex. The restriction to single inheritance prevents such problems.

2.2 Interfaces

As interfaces declare only signatures and not implementations, multiple inheritance is not so problematic. Naming conflicts when using multiple inheritance are handled by a set of clearly defined rules. Let's assume a diamond inheritance case as above, and the interfaces Left and Right both declare a method m(). Then the following cases can occur:

♦ The two signatures differ in number, order or type of arguments. Therefore the two methods are distinguishable. The methods need to be separately implemented in a class that implements the interface Derived.

♦ The two signatures have the same number and order of arguments and corresponding arguments are of the same type, but the methods have different result types. Therefore the two methods are not distinguishable when invoked. The interface Derived cannot be implemented.

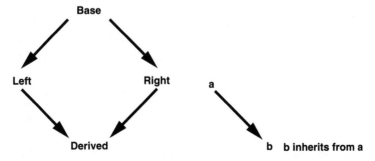

FIGURE 3-2. Diamond inheritance.

- ♦ The two signatures have the same number and order of arguments and corresponding arguments are of the same type. The methods have the same result type. There are two subcases:
  - ♦ The methods raise the same set of exceptions. The methods are identical and there is only one implementation of the two declarations.
  - ♦ The methods raise different sets of exceptions. There is one implementation of the method declaration that can only raise exceptions from the common subset, even if this is the empty set. A common implementation for both method declarations which throws exceptions only defined in one signature is not allowed.

2.3 Implementation of Interfaces

The relationship between interfaces and classes is declared with the keyword `implements`. A class can implement one or more interfaces. The implementation relationship has no influence on the inheritance relationship. For example, a class can extend a base class and implement two interfaces:

```
class Derived
     extends Base
     implements Interface1, Interface2 {
     // ....
}
```

OMG IDL defines multiple inheritance of IDL interfaces. IDL allows no operation over loading and so has an even simpler determination of the signature of derived interfaces. IDL interfaces correspond well to Java interfaces, and inheritance relationships can be mapped to Java naturally.

3 *Methods and Exceptions*

An object has methods that can be declared in an interface and are implemented by a class. Method declarations have parameters with a name and a type. The parameter passing semantics are *call-by-value*. This means that at run time an argument has a value when the method is invoked, which is passed to the implementation of the method. Once the method returns from the invocation the parameter still has the original value. Results of a method can be passed to the invoking object in two ways:

- ♦ As a value of the type specified in the method declaration in the interface or class

♦ As values in fields (members) of an exception in the signature of the method

Exceptions are object instances of classes derived from the predefined class `java.lang.Exception`. Before an exception can be included in the signature of a method a corresponding exception class, and in particular its constructor, must be defined. For example, we can define

```
class mException extends Exception {
     // public member
     public int value;
     //constructor
     mException( int i ) {
          value = i;
     }
}
```

A method signature can contain multiple exceptions that are declared with the keyword `throws`.

```
int m( boolean flag ) throws mException {
     if( flag )
          throw new mException( 1 );
     else
          return 1;
}
```

For example, the method `m()` above can return a value as a result using `return` or as a variable in an exception object.

OMG IDL defines operations that are an equivalent concept to Java methods. Operations can raise exceptions, which is equivalent to methods throwing exceptions. In CORBA there is a predefined type, CORBA::Exception, which is inherited by all CORBA exceptions in the same way that Java exceptions have `java.lang.Exception` as a base class.

4 *Packages*

Packages are Java's name-scoping mechanism. Name scopes achieve the following results:

♦ They group related classes and interfaces together.
♦ They allow the same names to be used inside different scopes and to be distinguished by qualifying them using the scope name.

Packages are declared by using the `package` keyword. There is a convention that the name of a package reflects the name of the directory in which the

Java source code file is located. Package scopes can be nested within other scopes, and subpackages are usually kept in subdirectories. Names are constructed by using dot notation. Here is a package example:

```
// OuterPackage/myClass.java:
package OuterPackage;

public class myClass {
}

// OuterPackage/InnerPackage/myClass.java:

package OuterPackage.InnerPackage;

public class myClass {
     public OuterPackage.myClass my_object1;
     public myClass my_object2;
}
// OuterPackage/InnerPackage/myOtherClass.java:
package OuterPackage.InnerPackage;

public class myOtherClass {
     public myClass my_other_object1;
     public OuterPackage.InnerPackage.myClass my_other_object2;
}
```

In the example above the types of `my_object1` and `my_object2` are different (the latter is a recursive declaration), and the types of `my_other_object1` and `my_other_object2` are the same. Java packages also provide access control to the interfaces and classes defined in the package by use of the `public` keyword.

Modules are OMG IDL's name-scoping construct. They provide grouping and qualified naming, but no usage restrictions. Qualified names in IDL are separated with a double colon—::—and names defined from the global scope can be preceded by a double colon.

5 Objects at Run Time

Objects are run-time instances of classes. An object is always associated with a Java Virtual Machine. The virtual machine allocates the memory for an object to keep its state and executes the Java byte-code that represents the object's semantics.

A virtual machine can execute one or more objects. The machine can be implemented in hardware or run as an operating system process. Java does not handle invocations of methods across virtual machine boundaries.

This has to be done through network or interprocess communication APIs. Java's RMI API and Java ORBs provide high-level facilities to realize these invocations.

Within a Java virtual machine, an object can be represented simply by a piece of memory keeping its state and the byte code of the class representing its functionality. The program execution follows the method invocations and returns in a sequential, or single-threaded, manner. (See Figure 3-3.)

Alternatively, Java enables objects to have their own thread of execution. This is provided by the core package of the language, `java.lang`, in the class `Thread`. This package also provides a predefined interface, `Runnable`, to objects whose behaviors are associated with a thread. The interface defines a single method:

```
public void run();
```

Classes can implement this method to define their particular run-time behavior, for example, the scheduling of the thread with respect to other threads, the synchronization between threads, or the interruption of other threads.

CORBA does not prescribe how to configure the run-time behavior of objects implementing IDL interfaces. Because sequential object implementations can easily lead to deadlocks in distributed systems, it is recom-

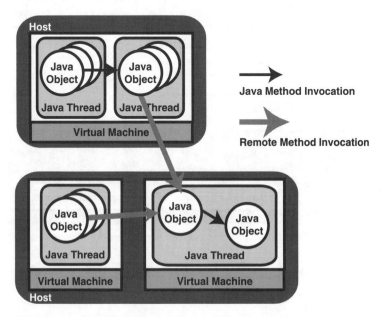

FIGURE 3-3. Java threading and remote invocation.

mended that objects be implemented in separate threads. Java built-in thread support facilitates this.

6 Java Applets

Applets are objects instantiated from the class java.applet.Applet. This class and other interfaces in the package java.applet allow applets to be executed in Web browsers and similar tools. Applets are anchored in documents that are usually marked up in HTML. Figure 3-4 illustrates the interfaces and classes of the package and their relationships to other interfaces and classes.

Any user-written applet extends the class java.applet.Applet. Due to the inheritance structure of the Applet class, an applet contains the basis for a GUI through the inherited class java.awt.Panel.

The interface AppletContext provides information about the applet's environment, for example, the document anchoring the applet. The interface AppletStub provides a communication mechanism between an applet

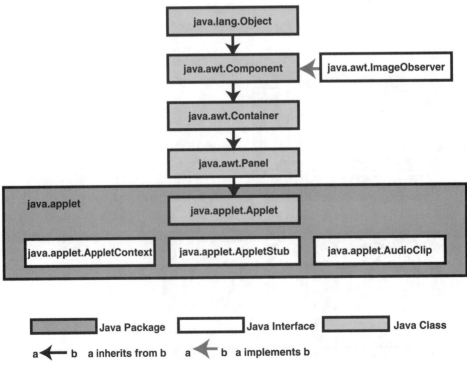

FIGURE 3-4. Package java.applet.

and the browser in which it is executing. The stub, an object conforming to this interface, is attached to the applet using the applet's `setStub()` method. The interface `AudioClip` is a simple abstraction for playing an audio clip.

Applets are executed by the Java virtual machine in the Web browser or similar tool. These virtual machines enforce a number of security restrictions that the stand-alone Java Virtual Machine does not.

First, applets are not allowed to access local resources, such as the file system, on the machine where the browser executes. They also cannot execute native code, for example, C or C++ executables, on that machine, although Java provides an interface to do so. The motivation for these restrictions is to prevent applets acting as viruses, for example, by executing commands to remove or alter local files. On the other hand, these restrictions disable a number of useful features, even some that would increase security. For example, it is not possible for an applet to access a smart card reader on a host machine to authenticate a user.

The second major restriction regards networking. Applets are only allowed to open socket connections to the host from which they were downloaded [the check is based on IP numbers]. This restriction does not ensure any particular privacy—on the Internet an arbitrary host from where an applet is downloaded is not more trustworthy than any other host on the Internet, and on an intranet all hosts may be equally trustworthy. However, the enforcement of this restriction has a major impact on distributed applications involving applets, in particular for CORBA-based applications. CORBA provides the concept of location transparency, that is, one can invoke an operation on an object regardless of its location. In Chapter 4 we explain approaches to achieving location transparency despite this restriction.

7 *Hello World Example*

In this section we introduce a simple Java example, a Hello World program. We show the optional definition of a Java interface and its implementation in a Java class. We then explain how to build both a Java application and an applet. In both cases an object of the implementation class is created and a method is invoked on the object. We return to the same example in Chapter 5 where we distribute the components using various Java ORBs.

The Hello World example contains an object of a class `GoodDay` which provides a method `hello()`. This method returns a string containing the message "Hello World from *location*," where *location* is the name of a geographical location, for example, Brisbane.

7.1   Interface Specification

A Java interface defines the signature of an object, that is, its types, fields, and methods. Hence it allows various substitutable implementations. For our example we define the interface GoodDay, which has one method, hello().

```
interface GoodDay {

    // method
    public String hello();
}
```

7.2   Implementation

An interface is implemented by a class. For our example we have implemented the class GoodDayImpl. The keyword implements defines the relationship between the interface and its implementing class.

```
class GoodDayImpl implements GoodDay {

    private String locality;

    // constructor
    GoodDayImpl( String m_locality ) {
        locality = new String( m_locality );
    }

    // method
    public String hello() {
        return "Hello World, from " + locality;
    }
}
```

Java does not prescribe the use of interfaces. Classes can both define a signature and implement methods. If a programmer chooses not to define an interface, the class declaration above would change to

```
class GoodDayImpl {...}
```

The remainder of the class would be the same.

7.3   Application

The application that makes use of the class GoodDayImpl is also implemented as a class that we call SimpleHelloWorldApplication. We only implement the main() method of this class.

```
import java.io.*;
```

```
public class SimpleHelloWorldApplication {

    public static void main(String args[]) {

        // create object of class GoodDayImpl
      GoodDayImpl good_day = new GoodDayImpl( "Brisbane" );

        // invoke method hello() and print result
        System.out.println( good_day.hello() );
    }
}
```

Within the implementation of the method `main()` we create an object `good_day` of the class `GoodDayImpl`. We invoke the method `hello()` on this object and print the result to standard output.

To run our application we have to compile the Java code

```
.../Java> javac SimpleHelloWorldApplication.java
```

We then start the Java run-time system with the application class. When we execute the application it prints the expected message

```
.../Java> java SimpleHelloWorldApplication
Hello World, from Brisbane.
```

7.4   Applet

An applet differs from an application in that it is only executable in the environment of a Web browser or similar tool. An applet needs to be anchored in an HTML document to be loaded by a browser. For our example we have written the following HTML file:

```
<html>
<header>
<! -- SimpleHelloWorldApplet.html -->
<title>
Simple Hello World Example
</title>
<BODY BGCOLOR=15085A TEXT=FFD700 LINK==FFFFFF VLINK=FFFFFF ALINK=FFFFFF>
<center>
<pre>

</pre>

<h1>
Simple Hello World Example
</h1>
</center>
<pre>
```

```
</pre>
<center>
<applet code=SimpleHelloWorldApplet.class width=400 height=80>
</applet>
</center>

</body>
</html>
```

The HTML tag `<applet>` anchors the file containing our applet class, `SimpleHelloWorldApplet.class`.

An applet always extends the Java Applet class, `java.applet.Applet`. When implementing our applet we override the method `init()` of the Applet class. This method initializes the applet. Applets require a GUI, so we initialize such an interface within the `init()` method. We create two graphical elements, a button object `hello_world_button` of the class `java.awt.Button` and a text field object `text_field` of the class `java.awt.TextField`. The button object is used to cause the invocation of the `hello()` method. The results of the invocation are displayed in the text field. The two objects are displayed on the applet's panel using a simple layout manager, `java.awt.GridLayout`.

```java
import java.awt.*;

public class SimpleHelloWorldApplet extends java.applet.Applet {

    private GoodDayImpl good_day;
    private Button hello_world_button;
    private TextField text_field;

public void init() {

    hello_world_button = new Button("Invoke local method");
    hello_world_button.setFont(new Font("Helvetica",
        Font.BOLD, 20));
    text_field = new TextField();
    text_field.setEditable(false);
    text_field.setFont(new Font("Helvetica", Font.BOLD, 14));

    setLayout( new GridLayout(2,1));
    add( hello_world_button );
    add( text_field );

    // create object of class GoodDay
  good_day = new GoodDay( "Brisbane" );

}
```

To catch and process events we override the method `action()` of the class `java.awt.Component`, which we indirectly inherit via the Java Applet class.

FIGURE 3-5. Applet in initial state.

We compare the target of an event that occurred with our button `hello_world_button`. If the button has been clicked and thus has caused the event, we then invoke the `hello()` method on the object `good_day`. We display the result of the invocation in the text field object using its method `setText()`.

```
public boolean action(Event ev, java.lang.Object arg) {

    // catch and process events
    if(ev.target == hello_world_button ) {

        // invoke the operation and display result
        text_field.setText( good_day.hello() );

        return true;
    }
    return false;
  }
}
```

When the applet is loaded into a Web browser it appears as shown in Figure 3-5. Figure 3-6 shows the applet after the button has been clicked, the `hello()` method has been invoked, and its result displayed.

FIGURE 3-6. Applet after method invocation.

4

Overview of Java ORBs

A Java ORB is an ORB that supports a Java language mapping for OMG IDL. This language mapping, or language binding, allows clients and objects to be implemented in Java. However, not all the Java ORBs currently available support the complete CORBA functionality. Some only allow implementation of clients as Java applications or applets. Typically, Java ORBs are implemented in Java itself.

This chapter introduces the architecture of Java ORB implementations. First we explain some necessary terminology. We then discuss the requirements for Java applications and applets to communicate with CORBA objects. Specifically, we cover the following topics:

- Java applications as clients and servers
- Java applets as clients and servers
- Clients and servers implemented using other programming languages
- An overview of currently available Java ORBs

1   *Terminology*

In this chapter and throughout the rest of the book we will use a number of
terms that have specific technical meanings. Because both CORBA and Java
are object-oriented and have similar object models at the interface level,
some terms will apply to both. However, most of the time we will use different language to refer to concepts in each domain. Here is the way in which
we differentiate:

- *Object.* The term object refers to some program component that has a
  well-defined interface. We usually refer specifically to *CORBA objects,*
  whose interfaces are represented in OMG IDL, and *Java objects,* whose
  interfaces are represented by Java public variables and method declarations. CORBA objects have two parts:
    - The part that allows the object's operations to be invoked from
      any location and using any programming language. The way this
      is implemented will become clear through the rest of this chapter.
    - The part that implements the operations in the interface. This is
      referred to as an *object implementation.* In the ORBs that we are
      interested in, the object implementation will be a Java class.
- *Operation.* An action that can be invoked on a CORBA object, as
  defined in IDL.
- *Method.* An action that can be invoked on a Java object, as defined in
  that object's public class declaration. Java objects can implement
  CORBA interfaces. Methods on these objects correspond to operations
  in the CORBA interface.
- *Client.* A role played by a program when it invokes a CORBA object
  operation.
- *Server.* A role played by a program when it makes an object implementation available to a client. Many programs that are servers are also
  clients to other servers. We use the term *CORBA server* to refer to a program that performs specified interactions with an ORB to make the
  existence of its CORBA object implementations known.

2   *Clients and Servers as Java Applications*

Figure 4-1 illustrates the simplest scenario involving Java ORBs: a client interacting with a server. Client and server are both implemented in Java. Figure
4-1 is an abstract representation of the client-server model in Java ORBs. We
see five components in the figure. Two of these are Java Virtual Machines that

FIGURE 4-1. Client-server model with Java ORBs: abstract view.

allow the execution of the client and server programs. The other three are the client and server programs and the ORB. The client communicates with the ORB in order to convey a request for an operation invocation to the server, which then sends results via the ORB back to the client. The interfaces these components use are defined by the CORBA standard and by the application-specific IDL definitions that the object at the server supports.

Figure 4-2 shows a more concrete view of how the ORB performs the task of conveying an invocation from client to server. The lightly shaded objects in the diagram are all provided by the ORB (compare with Figure 2-4). The following subsections describe the functionality of each of these components.

2.1 Stub and Skeleton Code

The IDL compiler generates a number of Java classes known as *stub classes* for the client and *skeleton classes* for the server. The role of the stub class is

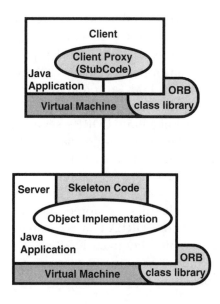

FIGURE 4-2. Client-server model with Java ORBs: concrete view.

to provide proxy objects that clients can invoke methods on. The proxy object method implementations invoke operations on the object implementation, which may be located remotely. If the object implementation is at a remote location the proxy object marshals and transmits the invocation request. That is, it takes the operation name and the types and values of its arguments from language-dependent data structures and places them into a linear representation suitable for transmitting across a network. The code to marshal programmer-defined data types is an essential part of the stub code. The resulting marshaled form of the request is sent to the object implementation using the particular ORB's infrastructure. This infrastructure involves a network transport mechanism and additional mechanisms to locate the implementation object, and perhaps to activate the CORBA server program that provides the implementation.

The skeleton code provides the glue between an object implementation, a CORBA server, and the ORB, in particular the BOA. The CORBA specification leaves many of the interfaces between the ORB Core, BOA, and server program partially or totally unspecified. For this reason different ORBs have different mechanisms for use by the BOA to activate servers and for use by servers to inform the BOA that their objects are ready to receive invocation requests.

The skeleton class implements the mechanisms by which invocation requests coming into a server can be directed to the right method of the right implementation object. The implementation of those methods is the responsibility of the application programmer.

2.2   ORB and BOA Libraries

The BOA has a proprietary interface to the ORB that is not standardized in CORBA. This generally means that the BOA functionality is implemented as part of the same code as the ORB, partially in libraries, partially in stub and skeleton code, and partially in a run-time daemon (background task or process). The marshaling routines in both stub and skeleton code exchange invocation requests and results via a network connection that is set up using ORB library code that must be linked into CORBA servers and clients. This code also communicates with the ORB run-time daemon that knows which servers implement which objects and can locate and/or activate servers when requests are made to them.

The information about how objects and servers are associated with idle or running Java byte code files is stored in the *Implementation Repository*. This is a component of CORBA that is assumed to exist, but its interface is not specified and is different in each ORB.

Figure 4-3 illustrates the interactions between server programs, the objects they support, and the ORB run-time daemon.

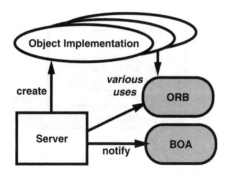

FIGURE 4-3. Java ORB server-side.

As Figure 4-3 shows, a CORBA server usually supports a number of CORBA objects. The server's `main` routine is used to create CORBA object instances and to notify the BOA of their availability to CORBA clients by using the operations `object_is_ready()` and `impl_is_ready()`, which are supported by library methods on a BOA pseudo-object. Remember that a pseudo-object is an implementation of a CORBA pseudo-IDL interface specification in an ORB-dependent manner (usually as library code).

3 Clients as Java Applets

A Java applet can also be a CORBA client, as shown in Figure 4-4. For CORBA there is no difference between a Java application and an applet invoking CORBA objects. However, the Web's security model for applets introduces limitations.

3.1 Security Issues

To prevent damage by untrusted applets, and in particular to ensure privacy, applets are only allowed to open network connections to the host from which they have been downloaded (the identification is based on IP numbers). This model is in conflict with that of CORBA which allows clients to invoke operations on objects regardless of their physical location.

There is some criticism of this model. First of all, when browsing the Internet, a given host is not necessarily trustworthy. Furthermore, a program residing on this host can forward information received from the applet to any other host that it can open a connection to, thus indirectly allowing the applet to open arbitrary network connections.

On the other hand, an applet in an intranet can trust any host in the intranet because of the private nature of the network. The security policy

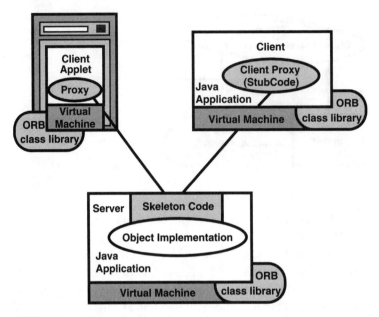

FIGURE 4-4. Clients Java applets.

constrains applications by only allowing applets connections to their source host.

Another problem is created by firewalls. Firewalls restrict the communication between an intranet and the Internet. Firewalls can be configured in various ways, for example, only constraining incoming data to avoid hacker attacks or also constraining outgoing traffic to ensure data integrity within the intranet. Typically firewalls allow e-mail and Web-related traffic to pass. Protocols used for intra-ORB communication (usually UDP/IP or TCP/IP based) and IIOP (TCP/IP based) cannot be used across firewalls. Various Java ORBs have different approaches to solve these two problems.

3.2 HTTP Tunneling

Visibroker and Joe provide an approach called *HTTP tunneling*, which is illustrated in Figure 4-5.

HTTP tunneling does the following:

♦ It puts IIOP calls into an HTTP envelope to enable them to go through firewalls.
♦ It sends all requests to a daemon residing on the host from which the applet was downloaded. This reestablishes CORBA location trans-

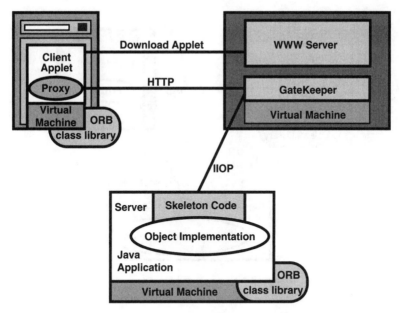

FIGURE 4-5. IIOP tunneling through HTTP.

parency as the daemon forwards the request to the host nominated in the object reference.

Visibroker and Joe implement the HTTP tunneling differently.

Visibroker provides such a special purpose HTTP daemon which is implemented in the class `pomoco.iiop.GateKeeper`. This daemon is also incorporated in Netscape ONE HTTP servers.

Joe is distributed with a module for the Apache HTTP server that allows requests to be sent to other servers by wrapping IIOP in HTTP.

3.3 Wonderwall

OrbixWeb provides an approach to these two problems called Wonderwall. With respect to providing location transparency, Wonderwall is similar to the HTTP tunneling approach. It provides a daemon that receives IIOP requests from clients, forwarding them to the real object and returning the responses in the same way, as shown in Figure 4-6.

The firewall problem is approached by Wonderwall in a different way from HTTP tunneling. Instead of using existing firewalls, Wonderwall is a firewall of its own. Wonderwall is to be installed on the interface between the secure private network and the Internet, that is, the firewall host.

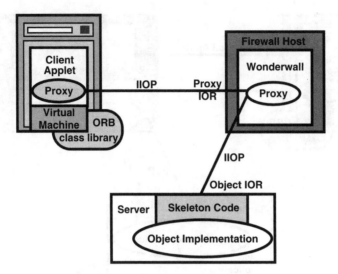

FIGURE 4-6. Wonderwall.

The Wonderwall approach has a number of drawbacks. Wonderwall does not provide an ad hoc solution because it needs installation of new firewall software, which is a complex political and administrative task. Even more problematic is the fact that Wonderwall breaks object identity. To invoke a server across the firewall with Wonderwall, an object reference needs to be modified so that it contains address information of a proxy object at the Wonderwall. This leads to a pair of IORs per object, the original one to be used without Wonderwall and the IOR of the proxy to be used with Wonderwall. When object references are passed around, for example, when obtained from a Naming or Trading Service, they might break, depending on their type (original or modified) and where they are used (inside or outside the firewall).

It is expected that location transparency and firewall access problems will eventually be solved in a more general manner by a subsequent Java/WWW security model. A proper security model for applets will allow firewalls to be configured to let IIOP traffic pass.

4 *Servers as Java Applets*

A server can also be implemented as an applet provided that the particular ORB provides a server-side mapping. Again we face a restriction of CORBA functionality imposed by the applet security model. According to this security model, applets are not allowed to access resources on the host machine.

Hence applet object implementations cannot be persistent nor can they make any data persistent.

The security model for access by applets to local resources is also questionable. The inaccessibility of local resources does shield against applets trying to damage local resources, for example, by removing or altering local files. However, in secure environments such as intranets, there may be no need for such restrictions. Even in the Internet environment there are uses for access to local resources. For example, an applet may need to access a local smart card reader to authenticate a user.

As Java matures we expect a more sophisticated security model for applets to emerge. One could imagine a model that is driven by policies suitable to particular domains, such as intranets. These policies could define the rules for internal and external applets separately.

Nevertheless, the current applet security model allows for interesting features, in particular a call-back mechanism for applets. This means that an applet acting as a server creates one or more CORBA objects. It then passes out references to those objects, for example, as an operation argument. Other clients can then invoke operations on those object references which results in methods of objects within the applet being executed. (See Figure 4-7.)

Applets acting as servers need to handle two event loops: one to handle incoming CORBA requests and the other to deal with applet events such as those caused at the GUI. Java threads handle this issue elegantly. The mechanism is explained in Chapter 9.

5 *Clients and Servers Implemented with Non-Java ORBs*

Since CORBA provides multiple programming language mappings for OMG IDL, clients and servers can be implemented in a wide variety of languages. There are many motivations to use other languages, for example, to integrate legacy code or to exploit specific skills of a software engineering team.

Other programming languages are made available by ORB vendors in these ways:

◆ *Within the same ORB or ORB family.* This requires an IDL compiler that generates the stub and skeleton code in the required programming language. The implementation of the ORB and BOA pseudo-objects must be accessible via an API wrapper in this programming language or they must be reimplemented in this language. The ORB run-time system, including daemons and configuration files, can be

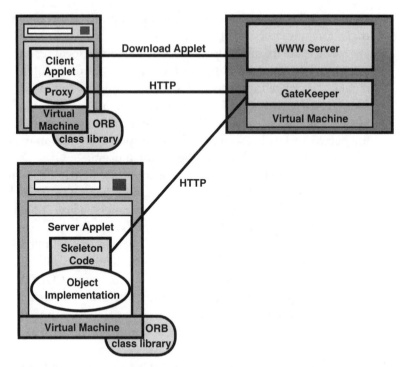

FIGURE 4-7. Applet CORBA server.

shared. The objects implemented in different languages can use an ORB's proprietary protocol. This is the case with Orbix and OrbixWeb, or Joe and NEO. Otherwise IIOP can be used for all CORBA interactions, as in Visibroker.

♦ *With different ORBs using CORBA 2.0 interoperability.* Implementations in different languages using the development and run-time environments of different ORBs can communicate using IORs and IIOP. This is often referred to as communication across ORB domain boundaries.

In Figure 4-8 any of the clients can access any of the servers. The IIOP channel between the Java ORB and the other ORB is symbolic of a bridging of ORB domains. However, when actual communication occurs between a client and a server in different ORB domains, the client's stub code simply uses the information in an IOR to communicate with the foreign ORB daemon on the correct host in order to establish a direct connection to the skeleton code of the remote server. Once this connection is established, the ORB daemon plays no further part in the interaction.

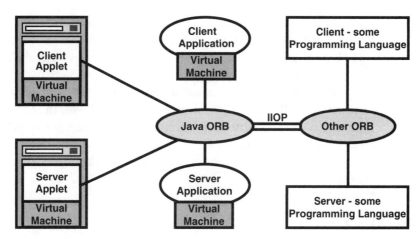

FIGURE 4-8. Interoperation with clients and servers in other ORB domains.

6   *Java ORB Products*

There are several Java ORB products on the market. In this section we give an overview of those products and their particular features. We consider all Java ORBs known to us, but we will concentrate on three Java ORBs:

- Visigenic's Visibroker for Java
- Iona's OrbixWeb
- Sun's Joe

Java ORBs can be seen in action at CORBAnet (http://www.corba.net). CORBAnet is a permanent, Internet-based showcase demonstrating ORB interoperability. This is a joint project by the OMG, the majority of ORB vendors, and the Distributed Systems Technology Centre (DSTC), the Australian research institute where we work. The showcase demonstrates not only IIOP-based interoperability between a large number of ORB products but also shows the Java ORBs Visibroker for Java, OrbixWeb, and Joe in action.

6.1   **Visibroker for Java**

Visibroker for Java is Visigenic's Java ORB. It has been available as a product since April 1996. It supports a full language mapping and complete Java implementations of mandatory CORBA features such as pseudo-interfaces, CORBA::Object, ORB and BOA, and the IR. The CORBA Naming and Event Services are also available as Java implementations.

Visibroker for Java is a complementary product to Visibroker for C++. Both use IIOP as a native transport mechanism. Visibroker supplies an HTTP tunneling mechanism called Gatekeeper to overcome the applet security restrictions.

Visibroker for Java is incorporated into the Netscape ONE browser and server. CORBA class libraries are packaged with the browser and reduce shipped code to a minimum. Visibroker's Gatekeeper is incorporated into the Netscape ONE server.

More information and updates can be obtained from Visigenic's Web home page: htttp://www.visigenic.com.

6.2 OrbixWeb

OrbixWeb is Iona's Java ORB. It was released as a product in July 1996, providing a full client side mapping. OrbixWeb2.0, available as beta since September 1996, provides a full server-side mapping. Iona's approach to enable CORBA's location transparency and firewall tunneling is known as *Wonderwall*.

OrbixWeb provides protocol support for both the native Orbix protocol and IIOP. OrbixWeb is part of the Orbix product family, providing language bindings for C++ and Smalltalk.

More information and updates can be obtained from Iona's Web home page: http://www.iona.ie.

6.3 Joe

Joe is Sun's Java ORB which has been available since July 1996. Joe provides a client-side mapping and a partial server-side mapping allowing the implementation of call-back functionality into applets.

Joe supports a number of protocols: the proprietary Door and NEO protocols, as well as IIOP. Joe is close to Sun's NEO product family, an ORB that provides language bindings for C, Objective C, and C++.

Joe implements firewall tunneling and CORBA location transparency by providing a patch to the Apache HTTP server. Joe's class library is expected to be incorporated in future releases of the Java run-time environment.

More information and updates on Joe can be obtained from http://www.sun.con/sunsoft/neo/joe.

6.4 Other Java ORBs

Most companies providing leading ORB products have announced, or plan to provide, a Java language mapping, either by developing their own Java

ORB or by licensing an existing product. For example, Hewlett-Packard currently has its Java ORB in alpha testing. A product release can be expected for mid-1997. IBM has licensed Sun's Joe technology.

There are also a number of research prototypes dealing with language mappings for Java. Examples are JYLU and Jade. JYLU (http:/www-db.stanford.edu/~hassan/Java/Jylu) from Stanford University is a Java language binding for Xerox PARC's ILU (ftp://beta.xerix.com/pub/ilu/ilu.html). Jade was developed by APM. It has an IIOP communication engine that provides a means to connect CORBA-based servers with the Web.

6.5   Standardizing the Java Language Mapping

As explained in the Appendix, OMG provides two approaches to adopting specifications: Request for Comment (RFC) and Request for Proposals (RFP). The RFC process is the fast-track approach. A consensus-based specification is submitted which is adopted if there are no major technical comments. The RFP process asks for specifications that go through a two-step review process and a vote.

There is an interesting situation regarding products implementing a Java language mapping and OMG's standardization process. Originally the intention among the companies that first implemented a Java language mapping was to use the RFC process to standardize the Java language binding. However, there were a number of differences in each company's language binding which could not be resolved informally (see Chapter 6 for details). This situation eventually led to the issuing of an RFP for the Java language binding in August 1996. The standardized Java language mapping can be expected in mid-1997.

5

Building a First Java ORB Application

In this chapter we will use two simple Hello World examples (see Figure 5-1) to introduce the principles of building distributed applications with Java ORBs. Those examples expand the Hello World example introduced in Chapter 3. We will implement a client which is a Java application, a client that is a Java applet, and a server supporting an object implementation. Figure 5-1 illustrates the components of our examples.

We will present the examples with code for the three Java ORBs we consider in this book, Visibroker for Java, OrbixWeb, and Joe. All code is presented in compact form in the Appendix and is also available in electronic form from htttp://www.wiley.com/compbooks/.

The chapter starts with a summary of the development process for CORBA applications in Java. We give detailed explanations for the development of a simple example application and then extend this to include more features. In Chapter 9 we will return to application development with a substantial example.

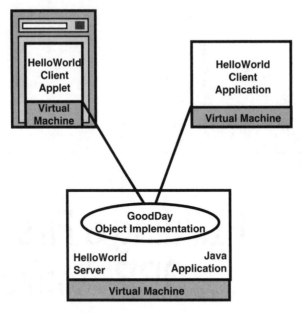

FIGURE 5-1. Hello World application.

1 Summary of the CORBA Development Process

The examples presented in this chapter will follow roughly the same steps:

♦ Write some IDL that describes the interfaces to the object or objects that we will use or implement.

♦ Compile the IDL using the IDL compiler provided by the particular ORB. This produces the stub and skeleton code that implements location transparency. That is, it will convert an object reference into a network connection to a remote server and then marshal the arguments we provide to an operation on the object reference, convey them to the correct method in the object denoted by our object reference, execute the method, and return the results.

♦ Identify the interfaces and classes generated by the IDL compiler that we need to use or specialize in order to invoke or implement operations.

♦ Write code to initialize the ORB and inform it of any CORBA objects that we have created.

♦ Compile all the generated code and our application code with the Java compiler.

♦ Run the distributed application.

Figure 5-2 shows the use of IDL and the IDL compiler when building the application.

When you execute the IDL compiler for the Java ORB you have installed, it will generate two sets of Java code files: stub code to create proxy objects that a client can use for making invocations on object references of the interface types defined in the IDL file, and skeleton code for access to objects that support those interfaces. The diagram shows the former code set being used in an applet client as well as a Java application client.

2   *Environment Set-up*

Before we can start with the examples we have to set up a working environment. We implemented the examples on a Sun/Solaris platform. For set-ups in different environments the reader is referred to the installation manuals for the particular products and platforms.

We use Sun MicroSystem's Java Development Kit (JDK), assuming that the path is set appropriately and the following are installed:

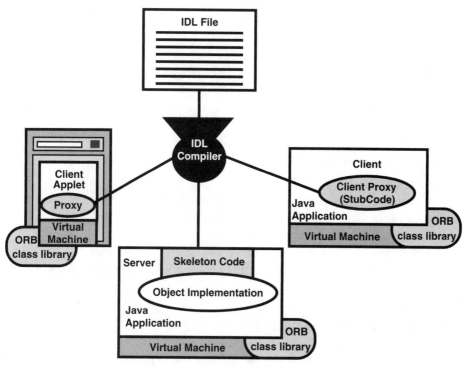

FIGURE 5-2.   Building the Hello World application.

♦ The Java compiler, *javac*
♦ The Java run-time system, *java*

To execute applets we used Sun MicroSystem's Appletviewer as well as Netscape3.0.

2.1 Visibroker for Java

The steps to set up the environment for Visibroker are:

♦ Install the Visibroker IDL compiler *idl2java*.
♦ Set the path appropriately to access the IDL compiler.
♦ Install Visibroker for Java packages.
♦ Set the class path to access the Visibroker classes.
♦ Run Visibroker's directory agent: `prompt> osagent &`
♦ Run a GateKeeper to let applets talk to CORBA objects via HTTP tunneling: `prompt> java pomoco.iiop.GateKeeper`

2.2 OrbixWeb

The steps to set up the environment for OrbixWeb are:

♦ Install the OrbixWeb IDL compiler *idl*.
♦ Set the path appropriately to access the IDL compiler.
♦ Install OrbixWeb Java packages.
♦ Set the class path to access the OrbixWeb classes.
♦ Run the Orbix daemon: `prompt> orbixd &`

2.3 Joe

The steps to set up the environment for Joe are:

♦ Install the Joe package.
♦ Set your path appropriately to access the Joe IDL compiler *idltojava*.
♦ Set your class path to access the Joe classes.
♦ Run the NEO daemon: `prompt> orbd &`
♦ Recompile the Apache HTTP server daemon to include the Joe tunnel module and restart your httpd. See the Joe documentation for details.

3 Interface Specification

Our first example provides the same functionality as the one introduced in Chapter 3. However, a client invokes an operation `hello()` on the interface of a potentially remote object of type GoodDay. The result of the invocation is a message which is printed by the client.

For any CORBA application we must write an IDL specification that defines data types and interfaces, including attributes and operations. For our example, we defined an IDL file called *SimpleHelloWorld.idl*, which resembles the Java interface of the Hello World example from Chapter 3.

```
// SimpleHelloWorld.idl

module SimpleHelloWorld {
  interface GoodDay {
    string hello();
  };
};
```

The file contains the specification of a module SimpleHelloWorld. It is good specification style to

♦ Use modules to create a separate name space for an application or its major components
♦ Have one file per module
♦ Name the file after the module

Within the module we define one interface: GoodDay. The interface is in no inheritance relationship. It provides one operation: hello(). This operation does not have any parameters and returns a result of type string.

As we will see in the implementation, the object returns a string describing its locality as part of the result of the operation hello(). The operation returns a message saying: "Hello World, from *location*."

4   *Compiling the IDL*

The next step in the application development is to compile the IDL to generate the stub and skeleton code. There are differences in the code generated by each of the three compilers, so we will look at the generated code for each separately.

4.1   **Visibroker**

Visibroker for Java's compiler is *idl2java*. The compile command is

```
SimpleHelloWorld/Visibroker> idl2java SimpleHelloWorld.idl
```

The IDL compiler creates a new directory that contains a Java package. Directory and package are named after the IDL module. The Java package contains Java interfaces and classes implementing stub, skeleton, and other code to support your distributed application.

The following files are generated by the IDL compiler:

```
GoodDay.java              GoodDay_var.java         _st_GoodDay.java
GoodDayOperations.java    _sk_GoodDay.java         _tie_GoodDay.java
```

The IDL interface GoodDay is mapped to a Java interface of the same name in the file GoodDay.java. The class _st_GoodDay contains the stub code that forms a client-side proxy for the object implementation. The class _sk_GoodDay contains the skeleton code used on the server side. The class GoodDay_var provides miscellaneous methods. In Chapter 6 we explain the complete mapping from OMG IDL to Java and also the meaning of the generated Java classes and interfaces.

The interface GoodDayOperations and the class _tie_GoodDay are used for the *Tie* mechanism on the server side which is explained in Chapter 10.

4.2   OrbixWeb

OrbixWeb's IDL compiler is called *idl*. To enable IIOP the flag interOp has to be set. The compile command is

```
SimpleHelloWorld/OrbixWeb> idl -m interOp -jP SimpleHelloWorld
SimpleHelloWorld.idl
```

The IDL compiler creates a directory, as specified by the -jP option (the default is java_output). In this directory it creates the following files and sub-directories:

```
SimpleHelloWorld:
GoodDay/      GoodDay.java

SimpleHelloWorld/GoodDay:
Holder.java  Ref.java
```

The module SimpleHelloWorld is mapped to a Java package of the same name and the corresponding directory is created. The IDL interface GoodDay is mapped to a Java interface GoodDay.Ref. The stub code, or client-side proxy, is implemented by the Java class GoodDay. The class GoodDay.Holder deals with in-out and out parameters as explained in Chapter 6.

4.3   Joe

The Joe compiler *idltojava* requires arguments to specify whether you need client stubs, server skeletons, or both:

```
SimpleHelloWorld/Joe> idltojava -fclient -fserver SimpleHelloWorld.idl
```

The compiler creates a package directory called `SimpleHelloWorld` and places the following files in that directory:

GoodDayHolder.java	GoodDayRef.java	GoodDaySkeleton.java
GoodDayOperations.java	GoodDayServant.java	GoodDayStub.java

The IDL interface **GoodDay** is mapped to the Java interface `GoodDayRef`. It is defined in the `SimpleHelloWorld` package, which represents the IDL module of the same name. The class `GoodDayHolder` handles the passing of out and in-out parameters.

The interface `GoodDayOperations` defines the signature of the IDL interface in Java. It is implemented on the client-side by the stub class and on the server-side by the skeleton class.

The skeleton is implemented by the class `GoodDaySkeleton`. It has methods to allow the association of the skeleton with an implementation object, which must be of the class that implements the interface `GoodDayServant`. This is known as the Tie mechanism, which Joe always uses to provide CORBA functionality to implementation objects.

5   A Client as a Java Application

When implementing a client as a Java application, we don't have to worry about the restrictions that exist for applets, and so we can explain CORBA programming in its usual form.

A client implementation follows these steps:

- ♦ Initialize the CORBA environment, that is, initialize the ORB.
- ♦ Obtain an object reference for the object on which it wants to invoke operations.
- ♦ Invoke operations and process the results.

5.1   Generated Java Interfaces

Let's have a look at the Java interfaces that correspond to the interface defined in IDL. All these interfaces extend a base class for CORBA Object and define a Java method `hello()` which returns a Java string and can throw a CORBA System Exception.

5.1.1   Visibroker

Visibroker defines `SimpleHelloWorld.GoodDay` as

```
package SimpleHelloWorld;
public interface GoodDay extends CORBA.Object
{
        public String hello() throws CORBA.SystemException;
};
```

5.1.2 OrbixWeb

OrbixWeb defines `GoodDay.Ref` as

```
package SimpleHelloWorld.GoodDay;

public interface Ref extends IE.Iona.Orbix2.CORBA.Object.Ref {
    public String hello()
        throws IE.Iona.Orbix2.CORBA.SystemException;
}
```

5.1.3 Joe

Joe defines `hello` in `GoodDayOperations` and then extends it, along with `corba.ObjectRef`, in `GoodDayRef`:

```
package SimpleHelloWorld;
public interface GoodDayOperations {
    String hello()
        throws sunw.corba.SystemException;
}

public interface GoodDayRef
    extends sunw.corba.ObjectRef,
            SimpleHelloWorld.GoodDayOperations {
}
```

5.2   Initializing the ORB

We define a Java class `SimpleHelloWorldClient` and define the `main()` method for this class. Initializing an ORB means obtaining a reference to an ORB pseudo-object. The ORB is called a pseudo-object because its methods will be provided by a library in communication with the run-time system, and its pseudo-object reference cannot be passed as a parameter to CORBA interface operations. Excluding that restriction, however, a reference to an ORB looks like any other object reference. The corresponding code looks slightly different for the three Java ORBs.

5.2.1 Visibroker

In Visibroker a static method is used to obtain a reference to an ORB pseudo-object.

```
import java.io.*;

public class SimpleHelloWorldClient {

    public static void main(String args[]) {

        try {
            // initialize the ORB.
            CORBA.ORB orb = CORBA.ORB.init();
```

A call is made to the static `init()` method on the `CORBA.ORB` class.

5.2.2 OrbixWeb

The pseudo-IDL interface **CORBA::ORB** is mapped to a Java class `_CORBA.Orbix`. However, operations on the pseudo-object are implemented as static methods of the class `_CORBA.Orbix`. The ORB can be considered to be implicitly initialized.

5.2.3 Joe

The `Joe` class supports all the operations of the **CORBA::ORB** interface, as well as a number of proprietary naming service methods. A pseudo-object reference to only the ORB part of its functionality can be obtained by calling the method `getOrb()`.

```
public static void main(String args[])
    {
        Joe joe = null;
        try{
            joe = new Joe("");
```

There are many constructors for the `Joe` class, most of them provide different ways of initializing the naming service or specifying the kind of ORB that you want a reference to.

5.3 Obtaining an Object Reference

References to objects can be obtained by various means, as explained in Chapter 8. Here we use a rather unsophisticated method. Object references are opaque data structures. However, an object reference can be made persistent by converting it into a string (as we show when explaining the server). This is known as *stringifying* an object reference. The resulting string is called a *stringified object reference*. Stringified object references are reconvertible into "live" object references. This is done using the two corresponding operations object_to_string() and string_to_object() defined on the **CORBA::ORB** interface. Stringified interoperable object references can be converted into working object references by any CORBA2.0-compliant ORB.

5.3.1 *Visibroker*

```
// Visibroker
        // get object reference from command-line argument
        CORBA.Object obj = orb.string_to_object( args[0] );
```

5.3.2 *OrbixWeb*

```
// OrbixWeb
        // get object reference from command-line argument
        IE.Iona.Orbix2.CORBA.Object.Ref obj =
        _CORBA.Orbix.string_to_object ( args[0] );
```

5.3.3 *Joe*

```
// Joe
        // get object reference from command-line argument
        sunw.corba.ObjectRef obj =
        joe.stringToObject( args[0] );
```

For this example client we assume that a stringified object reference is provided as the first argument to the client program. It is then provided as the argument to the method string_to_object(), which is invoked on the ORB pseudo-object. The method returns an object reference of type CORBA::Object, the base type of all CORBA objects. To make use of the object it needs to be narrowed to the appropriate type. Narrowing is equivalent to *down-casting* in some object-oriented programming languages. The narrow operation is type safe because it can raise a CORBA::SystemException if the object reference passed to it is not of a correct type. If it returns successfully then we know that the reference is valid and of the correct type.

5.3.4 *Visibroker*

Visibroker generates the narrow method in the class SimpleHelloWorld. GoodDay_var.

```
// Visibroker
        // and narrow it to SimpleHelloWorld.GoodDay
        try {
            SimpleHelloWorld.GoodDay good_day =
                SimpleHelloWorld.GoodDay_var.narrow( obj );
```

5.3.5   OrbixWeb

OrbixWeb generates the narrow method `_narrow()` in the class `Simple HelloWorld.GoodDay`. The Java interface that corresponds to the IDL interface is `SimpleHelloWorld.GoodDay.Ref`. Leading underscores are generally used to prevent name conflicts with user-defined type names because IDL syntax does not allow leading underscores.

```
// OrbixWeb
        // and narrow it to SimpleHelloWorld.GoodDay
        try {
           SimpleHelloWorld.GoodDay.Ref good_day =
               SimpleHelloWorld.GoodDay._narrow (obj);
```

5.3.6   Joe

Joe generates the static `narrow()` method in the class `SimpleHelloWorld.GoodDayStub`, and it returns an object of type `SimpleHelloWorld.GoodDayRef`.

```
// Joe
        // and narrow it to SimpleHelloWorld.GoodDay
        try {
           SimpleHelloWorld.GoodDayRef good_day =
               SimpleHelloWorld.GoodDayStub.narrow(obj);
```

5.4   Invoking the Operation

Once the ORB is initialized and an object reference is obtained, CORBA programming looks very much like standard object-oriented programming. One invokes methods on objects and it looks exactly the same for remote and local objects.

```
// Visibroker, OrbixWeb, Joe
        // invoke the operation and print the result
        System.out.println( good_day.hello() );
```

Our simple client invokes the method `hello()` on the object `good_day` and the result is printed to standard output.

The last thing to consider is handling exceptions that might occur. Since there are no user exceptions raised by the hello() operation, we only have to catch and process CORBA system exceptions which can be raised during the initialization of the ORB, the narrow, and the hello() operation.

```
// Visibroker, OrbixWeb, Joe
        // catch CORBA system exceptions
        catch(SystemException ex) {
```

```
                    System.err.println(ex);
            }
        }
    }
```

Note that the `SystemException` class is defined in different packages by different ORBs. The differences have been masked by importing the appropriate packages.

5.5 Compiling and Executing the Client

To make the client program executable by a Java virtual machine it needs to be compiled. This is done by calling the Java compiler:

```
SimpleHelloWorld/...> javac SimpleHelloWorldClient.java
```

We execute the client by calling the Java run-time system with two arguments, the name of the client class and a stringified object reference. When we consider the server implementation we will see how to generate this string.

```
SimpleHelloWorld/...> java SimpleHelloWorldClient IOR:0000000000000021
49444c3a53696d706c6548656c6c6f576f726c642f476f6f644461793a312e300000000
0000000010000000000000004c000100000000000e3133302e3130322e3137362e3900fc
7d0000003000504d43000000010000001a53696d706c6548656c6c6f576f726c643a3a4
76f6f644461790000000000000002febddb22
```

The client then prints the expected message:

```
Hello World, from Brisbane
```

6 *A Client as an Applet*

When writing a client as an applet we have to follow the same steps as for the application client. We also have to make the following additions and alterations:

♦ Anchor the applet in an HTML page to make it addressable and loadable.
♦ Provide a GUI to enable interaction through a Web browser.
♦ Extend the Java Applet class and override some of its methods.
♦ Use a different ORB initialization.

6.1   Anchoring the Applet into HTML

To make an applet accessible over the Web it needs to be anchored into an HTML page. When a browser downloads such a document, the Java byte code representing the anchored applet will also be received and executed by the browser.

Here is an example HTML file:

```
<html>
<header>
<! -- SimpleHelloWorldApplet.html -->
<title>
Simple Hello World Example
</title>
<center>
<pre>

</pre>
<h1>
Simple Hello World Example
</h1>
</center>
<pre>

</pre>
<center>
<applet code=SimpleHelloWorldApplet.class
        width=400 height=80>
</applet>
</center>

</body>
</html>
```

For our simple applet we have an HTML file `SimpleHelloWorldApplet.html` that contains only a header and a reference to our applet `SimpleHelloWorldApplet.class`.

6.2   Initializing the Applet

We define our applet as a class `SimpleHelloWorldApplet` which extends the Java applet class `java.applet.Applet`. Within the class we declare a number of private variables:

- ◆ `good_day`—to hold the object reference of the remote object.
- ◆ `hello_world_button`—a button to enable users to invoke the method.
- ◆ `text_field`—a text field to display the result of the method.

Then we override the method `init()` inherited from the applet class. First, we initialize the GUI components, that is, we create a Button and a TextField object and set some properties of these objects. Then we define the layout of the user interface using the Java layout manager `GridLayout` and add the two GUI components to the layout. The class header is different for each of the three ORBs.

6.2.1   *Visibroker*

```
// SimpleHelloWorldApplet.java
import java.awt.*;

public class SimpleHelloWorldApplet extends java.applet.Applet {

    // Visibroker
    private SimpleHelloWorld.GoodDay good_day;
```

6.2.2   *OrbixWeb*

```
// SimpleHelloWorldApplet.java
import java.awt.*;

public class SimpleHelloWorldApplet extends java.applet.Applet {
    private SimpleHelloWorld.GoodDay.Ref good_day;
```

6.2.3   *Joe*

```
// SimpleHelloWorldApplet.java
import java.awt.*;
import sunw.joe.*;
import sunw.corba.*;
public class SimpleHelloWorldApplet extends JoeApplet {
    private SimpleHelloWorld.GoodDayRef good_day;
```

The remainder of the implementation is the same for the three ORBs.

```
private Button hello_world_button;
private TextField text_field;

public void init() {

    hello_world_button = new Button("Invoke remote method");
    hello_world_button.setFont(new Font("Helvetica", Font.BOLD, 20));
    text_field = new TextField();
    text_field.setEditable(false);
    text_field.setFont(new Font("Helvetica", Font.BOLD, 14));

    setLayout( new GridLayout(2,1));
    add( hello_world_button );
    add( text_field );
```

6.3   Locating Objects

In the next step we locate an object implementation. In the application client we did this using a stringified object reference. This time we use proprietary object location mechanisms provided by each of the three ORBs. We provide details in Chapter 8.

6.3.1   *Visibroker*

To initialize the Visibroker ORB we again call the method `init()`, this time with one argument, the applet object itself (using the Java keyword `this` to do so). This initialization causes a change in the underlying protocol mechanism. Instead of pure IIOP, HTTP tunneling is used. Apart from the different initialization, tunneling is hidden from the application programmer.

To obtain a reference to the remote object we use Visibroker's Smart Agent. The agent provides a proprietary naming service. The interface to this service is a method called `bind()`, which is generated for each IDL interface type and is located in the _var class, for example, `SimpleHelloWorld.` `GoodDay_var`. The `bind()` operation returns a reference to an object of the specified interface type, if available. If there are multiple objects of that interface type available, a random choice is made.

```
// Visibroker

        try {
            // initialize the ORB (using this applet)
            CORBA.ORB orb = CORBA.ORB.init( this );

            // bind to "SimpleHelloWorld.GoodDay"
            good_day = SimpleHelloWorld.GoodDay_var.bind();
        }
```

6.3.2   *OrbixWeb*

Orbix provides a similar bind mechanism that is based on the Orbix daemon and its implementation repository. The method is similarly called `_bind()`. However, it is defined in a different class, namely `SimpleHelloWorld.` `GoodDay`, and returns an object of type `SimpleHelloWorld.GoodDay.Ref`.

```
// OrbixWeb

        try {
            // bind to "SimpleHelloWorld.GoodDay.Ref"
            good_day = SimpleHelloWorld.GoodDay._bind();
        }
```

6.3.3 Joe

In Joe the applet is initialized automatically, as the `JoeApplet` class implements all of the Joe interface (including its ORB functionality). An explicit reference to the ORB pseudo-object can be obtained by calling `getORB()`. Joe uses the NEO naming service and has a method called `find()`, defined in the `JoeApplet` class. This method returns a **CORBA::Object** reference, which must then be narrowed. The server, or some other object, must have registered an object reference of the type we want in the NEO naming service beforehand. This is done using the method `bind()`, which makes an association between a string and an object reference.

```
// Joe
    try{
        ObjectRef obj;

        obj = find("MyGoodDay");
        good_day = SimpleHelloWorld;GoodDayStub.narrow(obj);
    }
```

6.3.4 Catching Exceptions

Applet initialization is finished with the catching and processing of exceptions. The code is the same for the three Java ORBs.

```
// Visibroker, OrbixWeb, Joe
        // catch CORBA system exceptions
        catch(SystemException ex) {
            System.err.println(ex);
        }
    }
```

6.4 Catching and Processing Applet Events

To handle applet events we override the method `action()`, inherited through the class `java.applet.Applet` (originally defined in `java.awt.Component`). This method handles GUI events and it is invoked when an event occurs in the GUI element corresponding to the Component class, in our case the applet. This code is the same for each of the ORBs.

```
// Visibroker, OrbixWeb, Joe
    public boolean action(Event ev, java.lang.Object arg) {

        // catch and process events
        if(ev.target == hello_world_button ) {

            // invoke the operation
            try {
```

```
                text_field.setText( good_day.hello() );
            }

            // catch CORBA system exceptions
            catch(CORBA.SystemException ex) {
                System.err.println(ex);
            }

            return true;
        }

        return false;
    }
}
```

We check if the target of the event was our button `hello_world_button`. If not, we return `false` to indicate that no event was processed. Otherwise we invoke the method `hello()` on the object `good_day`. We display the result of the invocation in the text field. Again we watch for possible CORBA system exceptions and print them if they occur.

6.5   Compiling and Executing the Applet

To make the applet executable it needs to be compiled. This is done by calling the Java compiler:

```
SimpleHelloWorld/...> javac SimpleHelloWorldApplet.java
```

To execute the applet we have to point a Java-enabled Web browser to the URL of the HTML document that anchors our applet. Figure 5-3 shows the initial state of the applet's execution in the browser.

Once the button has been clicked, the result of the operation invocation is displayed in the text field as shown in Figure 5-4.

FIGURE 5-3.   Hello World applet—initial state.

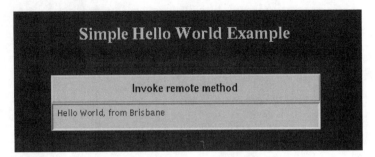

FIGURE 5-4. Hello World applet—invoked method.

7   Object Implementation

Now we turn to the implementation of the object whose interface has been specified in IDL. In this section we only consider Visibroker, since it was the only Java ORB to provide a full server-side language mapping at the time of writing. Iona and Sun have announced server-side mappings for OrbixWeb and Joe, respectively.

Object implementation classes must be associated with the skeleton class generated by the IDL compiler. This can be done by *inheritance* or by *delegation*.

A Java implementation class can extend the skeleton class generated by the IDL compiler. The skeleton class is an implementation of the Java interface which corresponds to the IDL interface. The object implementation is an extension of this class. This is known as associating the skeleton with its implementation by inheritance.

The other way is known as the Tie method, or associating the skeleton with its implementation by delegation. That is, there are separate skeleton and implementation objects, and the skeleton is given a reference to the implementation object. This is explained in detail in Chapter 10.

In our example we have an implementation class `GoodDayImpl` which extends the skeleton class (`SimpleHelloWorld._sk_GoodDay`). As in the implementation of the equally named class shown in Chapter 3, we declare a private variable `locality` which will hold a string identifying the location of the service. Here we mean the geographical location, as shown in the client examples above.

We also have to implement the constructor of the class. The constructor has one parameter which it assigns to the private variable `locality`.

```
// SimpleGoodDayImpl.java

import CORBA.*;
```

```
// Visibroker
class SimpleGoodDayImpl extends SimpleHelloWorld._sk_GoodDay {
    // variable declaration
    private String locality;

    // constructor
    SimpleGoodDayImpl( String m_locality ) {

        // calling the constructor of the super class
        super( "SimpleGoodDayImplV1.0" );

        // initialize locality
        locality = new String( m_locality );
    }

    // method
    public String hello() throws CORBA.SystemException {

        return "Hello World, from " + locality;
    }
}
```

We implement the method `hello()`, which returns a string composed of the message "Hello World, from" and the value of the variable `locality`.

Again we have to compile the Java source into byte code:

```
Visibroker> javac SimpleGoodDayImpl.java
```

8 A Server

Now we have to implement a server class. This class initializes the environment, creates the implementation object, makes it available to clients, and listens for events.

The server class for our example is called `SimpleHelloWorldServer`. We only implement the `main()` method in this class. We check for the right number of arguments, one of which indicates the locality of the server.

A server is responsible for the following tasks:

◆ Initializing the ORB and the BOA
◆ Creating the object
◆ Notifying the BOA of the existence of the object

Although the CORBA2.0 specification defines the interfaces of the pseudo-objects ORB and BOA, the various ORB vendors have implemented these pseudo-interfaces differently.

Visibroker provides a straightforward mapping of the pseudo-interfaces of ORB and BOA. We initialize the ORB in the same way we did on the client-side by calling ORB.init(), which returns a reference to the ORB pseudo-object. With this reference we invoke the method BOA_init(), which initializes the BOA and returns a reference to it. The BOA, like the ORB, is a pseudo-object. The BOA is concerned with the activation and registration of object implementations and servers.

To create an implementation object good_day_impl we call Java's new operator and supply one parameter for the constructor which we copy from the command-line argument.

```
import CORBA.*;

public class SimpleHelloWorldServer {

    public static void main(String[] args) {

        if( args.length != 1 ) {
            System.out.println(
                "Usage: java SimpleHelloWorldServer <location>");
            System.exit( 1 );
        }

        try {
            //init ORB
            CORBA.ORB orb = CORBA.ORB.init();

            //init Basic Object Adapter
            CORBA.BOA boa = orb.BOA_init();

            // create a SimpleGoodDay object
            SimpleGoodDayImpl simple_good_day_impl =
                new SimpleGoodDayImpl( args[0] );

            // export the object reference
            boa.obj_is_ready( simple_good_day_impl );

            // print stringified object reference
            System.out.println( orb.object_to_string( simple_good_day_impl

            // wait for requests
            boa.impl_is_ready();
        }
        catch(CORBA.SystemException e) {
            System.err.println(e);
        }
    }
}
```

Once we have created the implementation object we notify the BOA that this object is available by calling the method obj_is_ready(). We also print out the stringified version of the object reference, which we obtain by calling `object_to_string()` on the ORB. This is the object reference we used in the Java-application client to establish a connection with a server.

We notify the BOA, by calling `impl_is_ready()`, that the server is ready and that it can receive requests from clients. Finally, we catch and handle any CORBA system exceptions.

8.1 Compiling and Starting the Server

We have to compile the Java source into byte code:

```
Visibroker/SimpleHelloWorld> javac SimpleHelloWorldServer.java
```

We now start the server:

```
Visibroker/SimpleHelloWorld> java SimpleHelloWorldServer Brisbane
```

This prints out a stringified IOR:

```
IOR:000000000000002149444c3a53696d706c6548656c6c6f576f726c642f476f6f644
461793a312e300000000000000001000000000000004c000100000000000e3133302e31
30322e3137362e3900fc7d00000003000504d43000000010000001a53696d706c6548656
c6c6f576f726c643a3a476f6f6f64446179000000000000002febddb22
```

9 Extending the Hello World Example

In this section we will modify the simple Hello World example from above to introduce another feature. In this example the server will not only return a message but will also provide the current time at the server's location.

We will look at some new aspects of application development, and we will also revisit some of the issues discussed in the earlier version of this example application. Specifically we deal with

♦ Further aspects of the specification of interfaces
♦ Parameter mapping and the semantics of parameter passing
♦ Development of a client
♦ Applet implementations
♦ Implementation of an object

9.1 Interface Specification

We again specify an interface GoodDay with an operation hello(). However, this time the module is called HelloWorld to avoid name clashes with the previous example. Also the signature of the operation is different. The operation's result is still a string. This time it returns the locality description of the server and has parameters. Those parameters are tagged as out, meaning that their values will be supplied by the invoked object. They are both of type short and their intended meaning is that they hold the current time at the server's location: hour holds the hour and minute holds the minute.

```
module HelloWorld {
  interface GoodDay {
    string hello(
        out short hour,
        out short minute );
  };
};
```

9.2   Parameter Mapping

An out parameter in an IDL operation has pass-by-result semantics. This means that a value for this parameter will be supplied by the invoked object. The value will be available to the client after the invocation is completed.

The parameters in Java operations have pass-by-value semantics, meaning that a value is passed from the caller to the invoked object. There is a mismatch in the semantics of parameter passing between IDL and Java with respect to IDL's out and in-out parameters. The solution is provided by *container objects*. Instead of passing an argument itself, an object is used as an argument to the Java method. The object contains a variable value of the type of the IDL parameter. (See Figure 5-5.) Container classes for predefined data types are provided by a class library. The IDL compiler generates container classes for user-defined types.

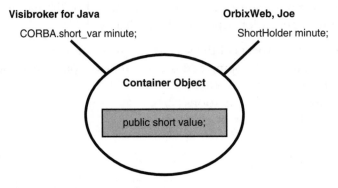

FIGURE 5-5.   Container objects.

Although the three Java ORBs follow the same approach, there are some differences in the notation. Visibroker calls the containers *_var* objects. In our examples we use Visibroker's predefined container class `CORBA.short_var`. OrbixWeb and Joe call the container objects *Holder* objects, in our example we use the pre-defined class `ShortHolder`.

Detailed explanations of parameter mappings are given in Chapter 6.

9.3 A Client

The main difference here, compared to the previous example is that we create two objects, `minute` and `hour`, of the class `CORBA.short_var`(`ShortHolder`) for the out parameters of the `hello()` operation.

```
import java.io.*;

public class HelloWorldClient {

    public static void main(String args[]) {
```

9.3.1 Visibroker

```
// Visibroker
        // create _var objects for out parameters
            CORBA.short_var minute = new CORBA.short_var();
            CORBA.short_var hour = new CORBA.short_var();
```

9.3.2 OrbixWeb and Joe

```
// OrbixWeb, Joe
        // create Holder objects for out parameters
            ShortHolder minute = new ShortHolder();
            ShortHolder hour = new ShortHolder();
```

9.3.3 Invoking the Operation

After we initialize the ORB and obtain a narrowed object reference as above, we invoke the operation. We construct a string `locality` from the result of the operation. After the successful return of the invocation, the variables named `value` in the two container objects will carry values set by the invoked object. Again, this code looks the same for each of the ORBs.

```
            // invoke the operation
            String locality = new String(
                good_day.hello( hour, minute ) );
```

```
                    // print results to stdout
                    System.out.println("Hello World!");
                    if( minute.value < 10 )
                        System.out.println("The local time in " + locality +
                                " is " + hour.value + ":0" + minute.value + "." );
                    else
                        System.out.println("The local time in " + locality +
                                " is " + hour.value + ":" + minute.value + "." );
```

When we print out the results we obtain the time at the remote side via the variable value of the container objects hour.value and minute.value. We compile the client as before and when we execute the client we get the following result:

```
HelloWorld/...> java HelloWorldClient IOR:000000000000001b49444c3a4865
6c6c6f576f726c642f476f6f644461793a312e300000000000010000000000000004c000
100000000000e3133302e3130322e3137362e39008384000000300050534d430000000000
00001448656c6c6f576f726c643a3a476f6f644461790000000000c476f6f6444617949496
d706c00
```

```
Hello World!
The local time in Brisbane is 16:42.
```

9.4 An Applet

The applet implementation does not add much new. We have the same structure as in the simple example and we make additions and modifications as in the client above. We add two private variable declarations to the class and create the corresponding objects within the method init().

9.4.1 Visibroker

```
public class HelloWorldApplet extends java.applet.Applet {

// Visibroker
    private CORBA.short_var minute;
    private CORBA.short_var hour;

    public void init() {
        minute = new CORBA.short_var();
        hour = new CORBA.short_var();
```

9.4.2 OrbixWeb and Joe

```
public class HelloWorldApplet extends java.applet.Applet {
// OrbixWeb, Joe
    private ShortHolder minute;
    private ShortHolder hour;
```

```
public void init()
     minute = new ShortHolder();
     hour = new ShortHolder();
```

9.4.3   *Invoking the Operation*

In the method `action()`, we invoke the operation and display the result in the text field.

```
// invoke the operation
try {
    locality = new String( good_day.hello( hour, minute) );
}
// catch CORBA system exceptions
catch(CORBA.SystemException ex) {
    System.err.println(ex);
}
if( minute.value < 10 )
    text = new String("The local time in " + locality +
        " is " + hour.value + ":0" + minute.value + "." );
else
    text = new String("The local time in " + locality +
        " is " + hour.value + ":" + minute.value + "." );
text_field.setText( text );
```

When the applet is compiled and loaded into a browser via an HTML page as shown above, we see a user interface (Figure 5-3). When the button is clicked and the operation invoked we see text in a display similar to the one in the client above:

```
Hello World! The local time in Brisbane is 16:44.
```

9.5   Object Implementation

The variable declarations and the constructor are as in the class `SimpleGoodDayImpl`, but the signature of the method `hello()` has changed. There are now two `short` container objects as parameters.

We create an object `date` which holds the time information of the system. The corresponding class is defined in `java.util.Date`. We retrieve the hour and the minute by invoking the methods `getHours()` and `getMinutes()` on the object. We assign the values to the corresponding `value` variables of the container objects and return the locality as in the earlier example.

```
import java.util.Date;

class GoodDayImpl extends HelloWorld._sk_GoodDay {

    // declarations and constructor as in SimpleGoodDayImpl
```

```
            // method
            public String hello(
                // Visibroker
                    CORBA.short_var hour, CORBA.short_var minute
                // OrbixWeb, Joe
                // ShortHolder hour, ShortHolder minute
                ) throws CORBA.SystemException {

                // get local time of the server
                Date date = new Date();
                hour.value = (short) date.getHours();
                minute.value = (short) date.getMinutes();

                return locality;
            }
        }
```

The server implementation is almost unchanged. We simply substitute
`GoodDayImpl` for `SimpleGoodDayImpl`.

C H A P T E R

6

OMG IDL to Java Mapping

This chapter provides a detailed explanation of the mapping from OMG IDL to Java. There is no OMG standard for the Java language mapping, so we provide details of the mappings used by the three Java ORBs now available: Visibroker, OrbixWeb, and Joe. The chapter should be viewed mainly as a reference.

The mapping begins with the basic IDL data types, then the structured data types are presented. The final sections detail the mappings for operations and attributes, interfaces and their inheritance relationships, and finally modules.

1 Basic Data Types

The mapping for basic data types is straightforward because of the similarities between the corresponding IDL types and Java types (see Table 6-1).

TABLE 6-1. Basic data type mappings.

IDL Type	Visibroker, OrbixWeb, and Joe
boolean	boolean
char	char
octet	byte
short/unsigned short	short
long/unsigned long	int

1.1 Boolean

The IDL type boolean is mapped to the Java type `boolean`. The IDL constants True and False are mapped to the Java constants `true` and `false`.

1.2 Char

The IDL type char is mapped to the Java type `char`. The IDL char is an 8-bit type according to the ISO 8859.1 character set, and Java char is a 16-bit type according to the UNICODE character set. When a value of type `char` is passed as a parameter in IDL-defined operations, attributes, or exceptions, only the lower 8 bits are transmitted.

The OMG is in the process of defining additional basic types for *wide chars* and strings made up of these characters, called *Istring* (internationalized string).

1.3 Octet

The IDL type octet is mapped to the Java type `byte`.

1.4 Integer Types

There is a difference between OMG IDL and Java with respect to the various IDL integer types. OMG IDL defines short and unsigned short (16 bit) and long and unsigned long (32 bit). Java has types `short` (16 bit), `int` (32 bit), and `long` (64 bit), which are all signed.

Obviously there is a mismatch between unsigned integer types in IDL and the signed integer types in Java. For example, the `int` type in Java is capable of representing all the values for the signed IDL type long, but not all of the values of the IDL type unsigned long, because values from $2^{31} - 1$ to $2^{32} - 1$ cannot be represented. Nonetheless, both signed and unsigned short in IDL map to `short` in Java. The IDL signed and unsigned long types both map to Java `int`.

1.5   Floating Point Types

The IDL floating point types, `float` and `double,` are mapped to the corresponding Java floating point types `float` and `double`. Both languages have adopted the IEEE Standard for Binary Floating-Point Arithmetic (ANSI/ IEEE Std 754-1985).

2   *String Types*

OMG IDL defines bounded and unbounded strings. Both kinds of string are mapped to a Java object of the class `java.lang.String`. Since the boundary (maximum length) of a bounded string is not mapped, an application programmer has to take care of the boundary when creating the corresponding Java String object. However, the stub code generated from the IDL checks the correctness of the string boundary at run time and raises an exception if it is exceeded.

3   *Enums*

An IDL enum type is mapped to a generated Java class named after the enum type. This class defines a field of type `final int` for each enum member. The fields are named after the enum members and have the value 0 for the first enum member, 1 for the second, and so on.

Here is an example enum in IDL:

enum Slot { am9, am10, am11 };

The IDL compilers of the three Java ORBs generate the following classes.

♦ Visibroker

```
// Java - Visibroker
final public class Slot {
    public static final int am9 = 0;
    public static final int am10 = 1;
    public static final int am11 = 2;

    public static final int narrow(int i) throws CORBA.BAD_PARAM {

        if( (i >= 0) && (i < 3) )
            return i;
        else
            throw new CORBA.BAD_PARAM();
    }
}
```

◆ OrbixWeb

```
// Java - OrbixWeb
public class Slot {
    public static final int am9 = 0;
    public static final int am10 = 1;
    public static final int am11 = 2;
}
```

◆ Joe

```
// Java - Joe
public class Slot {
    public static final int am9 = 0,
                            am10 = 1,
                            am11 = 2;
    public static final int narrow(int i) throws
sunw.corba.EnumerationRangeExce
ption {
        if (am9 <= i && i <= am11) {
            return i;
        }
        throw new sunw.corba.EnumerationRangeException();
    }
}
```

Visibroker and Joe define the generated class as `final`, whereas OrbixWeb does not and hence allows subtyping of this class. Additionally, the classes generated by Visibroker and Joe have methods called `narrow` which check that a Java `int` is in the range defined by the IDL enum.

4 Struct

An IDL struct is mapped to a Java class that provides fields for the members of the struct and some constructors. The class is named after the struct. There is a constructor which has a parameter for each member of the struct and initializes the object properly. A second constructor, the null constructor, only creates the object; the values of the structure members have to be filled in later.

Here is an example IDL struct:

```
struct Equipment {
    boolean video;
    boolean audio;
};
```

The following classes are generated by the three Java ORBs:

♦ Visibroker

```
// Java - Visibroker
final public class Equipment {

    public boolean video;
    public boolean audio;

    //constructors
    public Equipment(boolean _video, boolean _audio) {
        video = _video;
        audio = _audio;
    };

    public Equipment() { };
};
```

♦ OrbixWeb

```
// Java - OrbixWeb
public class Equipment implements
    IE.Iona.Orbix2.CORBA.IDLCloneable, IE.Iona.Orbix2.CORBA.
        Marshalable {

    public boolean video;
    public boolean audio;

    public Equipment () { }

    public Equipment (boolean video, boolean audio) {
        this.video = video;
        this.audio = audio;
    }
}
```

♦ Joe

```
// Java - Joe
public final class Equipment {

    // instance variables
    public boolean video;
    public boolean audio;

    // constructors
    public Equipment() { }
    public Equipment (boolean _video, boolean _audio) {
        video = _video;
        audio = _audio;
    }
}
```

Again, Visibroker and Joe define the generated class as `final`, whereas OrbixWeb does not.

5   *Unions*

An IDL union is mapped to a Java class that provides a constructor, an accessor method for the discriminator, and accessor and modifier methods for each of the branches. The constructor is a null constructor, which means that values for the discriminator and the corresponding branch must be set explicitly by using the modifier methods.

The accessor method for the discriminator `discriminator()` returns the type defined in the switch expression. The accessor and a modifier method for a branch are both named after the branch but differ in their signature. The accessor has no parameters and returns the value of the type corresponding to the branch. The modifier method is of type `void` and has two parameters, one of the discriminator type, the other of the type of the particular branch.

Here is an example union for which Java code is generated below:

```
union Video switch (boolean) {
    case TRUE: short standard;
};
```

♦ Visibroker. Visibroker always uses the type `int` for the discriminator, whereas OrbixWeb keeps the original type, for example, `boolean`.

```
// Java - Visibroker
final public class Video {

    public Video() {};

    public boolean discriminator() {
        // get discriminator value
    };

    public short standard() {
        // get branch value
    };

    public void standard(int discriminator, short _val) {
        // set branch value
    };
}
```

♦ OrbixWeb. Note that OrbixWeb has the parameters in the modifier method in the reverse order.

```
// Java - OrbixWeb
public class Video implements
    IE.Iona.Orbix2.CORBA.IDLCloneable,
    IE.Iona.Orbix2.CORBA.Marshalable {
```

```
public Video() { }

public boolean discriminator() {
    // get discriminator value
}

public short standard()
    throws IE.Iona.Orbix2.CORBA.BAD_OPERATION {
    // get branch value
}

public void standard(short value, boolean discriminator)
    throws IE.Iona.Orbix2.CORBA.BAD_PARAM {
    // set branch value
}
```

♦ Joe. Joe uses different names for the accessor methods rather than overloading the branch name like the other ORBs. The names it uses are of the form get*branch-name*() and set*branch-name*(). It also offers static methods called create*branch-name*() for each branch. These methods act as constructors and initialize both the branch and the discriminator.

```
// Java - Joe
public class Video {

    //    constructor
    public Video() {
    }

    //    discriminator accessor
    public boolean discriminator() {
        // return discriminator value
    }

    //    branch constructors and get and set accessors
    public static Video createstandard(short value) {
        // create initialized Video object
    }

    public short getstandard() throws sunw.corba.
        UnionDiscriminant Exception
        // retrieve value
    }

    public void setstandard(short value) {
        // set value
    }

    public void setstandard(boolean discriminator, short value)
                    throws sunw.corba.UnionDiscriminantException {
        // set branch value
    }
}
```

6 *Typedef*

Typedefs in IDL provide aliasing of type names; Java does not provide aliasing. The Java ORB implementers have dealt with this problem in different ways.

IDL typedefs are ignored in Visibroker and Joe. This means that the base type has to be used where the typedef name is expected in the Java implementation.

OrbixWeb uses subtyping for typedefs where possible. Unlike the Joe and Visibroker IDL mappings, basic IDL types are not mapped by OrbixWeb to final classes and can therefore have subclasses with typedef names. IDL types that map to integral Java types, such as `int` or `string`, cannot have typedefs.

Typedefs for IDL arrays and sequences are discussed in Sections 8 and 9.

7 *Exception Type*

The mapping for exceptions is similar to that for structs. An IDL exception is mapped to a generated Java class that provides instance variables for the fields of the exception and some constructors. The class is named after the exception. User-defined exceptions are derived from an exception hierarchy, as shown in Figure 6-1.

The generated classes have two constructors. One has a parameter for each field of the exception and initializes the object properly. The other constructor is the null constructor, which only creates the object, leaving the values of the fields to be filled in later.

Here is an example exception declaration in IDL:

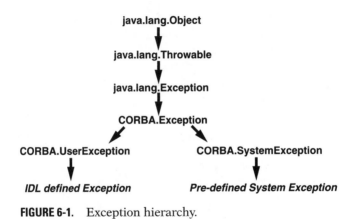

FIGURE 6-1.   Exception hierarchy.

```
exception SlotAlreadyTaken { string who; };
```

The code generated by the three Java ORBs is shown below.

♦ Visibroker

```
// Java - Visibroker
public class SlotAlreadyTaken extends CORBA.UserException {

    public String who;

    //constructors
    public SlotAlreadyTaken(String _who) {
            who = _who;
    };

    public SlotAlreadyTaken() {};
}
```

♦ OrbixWeb

```
// Java - OrbixWeb
public class SlotAlreadyTaken
    extends IE.Iona.Orbix2.CORBA.UserException
    implements IE.Iona.Orbix2.CORBA.IDLCloneable,
    IE.Iona.Orbix2.CORBA.Marshalable {

    public String who;

    public SlotAlreadyTaken() {
    }

    public SlotAlreadyTaken(String who) {
        super("ExceptionExample::SlotAlreadyTaken");
        this.who = who;
    }
}
```

♦ Joe

```
// Java - Joe
public class SlotAlreadyTaken
        extends sunw.corba.UserException {

    //  instance variables
    public String who;

    //  constructors
    public SlotAlreadyTaken() {
        super("IDL:SlotAlreadyTaken:1.0");
    }

    public SlotAlreadyTaken(String _who) {
        super("IDL:SlotAlreadyTaken:1.0");
        who = _who;
    }
}
```

8   Arrays

IDL arrays are mapped to Java arrays. That means there is no particular Java data type or class generated. An application programmer just defines a Java array of the mapped base type of the IDL array. For example, to create an instance of the following IDL array in a Java application

```
typedef long long_10_array(10);
```

a programmer using Visibroker, OrbixWeb, or Joe has to declare and allocate the array:

```
int[] long_10_array = new int[10];
```

9   Sequences

Sequences are approached quite differently by the three mappings. Visibroker and Joe deal with sequences the same way they do with arrays, that is, no data type or class is generated. The boundary of bounded sequences is checked by both Joe and Visibroker at run time and an exception is raised if the boundary is violated.

9.1   OrbixWeb

OrbixWeb generates a class for an IDL sequence. The name of the class follows the pattern _sequence_element-type-name.

The generated class is a wrapper around an array of elements. The type of the array is that of the IDL sequence. It provides two constructors, two instance variables, and a method:

- ♦ Constructors. One constructor initializes a null array, the other takes one argument of type int which specifies the size of the array.
- ♦ buffer[]. An array with elements of the type of the sequence.
- ♦ length. Indicates the current length of the sequences stored in buffer, which can be less than the size of the array. If length is less than 0 or greater than the size of the array, OrbixWeb assumes that the length of the sequence will be equal to the size of the array.
- ♦ ensureCapacity(). Manages the memory associated with a sequence. It has one argument of type int which specifies the minimum sequence size an application programmer requires. If the current size of the array is less than the argument to ensureCapacity(), the generated code allocates the appropriate memory and copies existing elements into the new array. The

allocated buffer will be of at least the specified size, but the generated code may allocate more space to avoid repeated copying of the buffer.

Here are some example sequences in IDL:

```
typedef sequence<long>long_seq;
typedef sequence<Equipment, 10>Equipment_10_seq;
```

OrbixWeb has predefined classes for arrays of basic types, for example, `IE.Iona.Orbix2.CORBA._sequence_Long`. However, because sequences of basic types must be typedefed to be used as parameter types in IDL, OrbixWeb generates classes that extend these. The derived classes are named after the type alias. They extend the base class by providing constructors that fit the name pattern.

```
// Java - OrbixWeb
public class long_seq extends IE.Iona.Orbix2.CORBA._sequence_Long {

    public long_seq() {
        super();
    }

    public long_seq(int len) {
        super(len);
    }
}
```

The code generated by OrbixWeb for the sequence of Equipment structures is defined generically, and then an appropriate subclass is defined for the typedef name.

```
public class _sequence_Equipment implements
    IE.Iona.Orbix2.CORBA.IDLCloneable,
    IE.Iona.Orbix2.CORBA.Marshalable {

    public Sequence.Equipment buffer[];
    public int length;

    public _sequence_Equipment() {
        // empty constructor
    }
    public _sequence_Equipment(int len) {
        // constructor creates a buffer of length "len"
    }

    public void ensureCapacity(int min) {
        // checks size of the buffer and increases size if necessary
    }
}
```

```
public class Equipment_10_seq extends Sequence._sequence_Equipment {

    public Equipment_10_seq() {
        super();
    }
    public Equipment_10_seq(int len) {
        super(len);
    }
}
```

This definition suggests a model whereby programmers must call ensureCapacity() with a new size if they intend to assign to buffer elements indexed higher than the current length.

10   The Any Type

The IDL Any type is a predefined type that can hold values of an arbitrary IDL type (including an Any type). It also carries type information about the contained value.

The IDL Any is mapped to the predefined class Any, which is embedded in the package structure of each product. This class provides constructors and methods to store values in and to retrieve values from an Any object.

The constructors named Any() create an Any object containing no value. OrbixWeb provides further specific constructors, such as a copy constructor which makes a copy of its argument of type Any.

OrbixWeb supports the proprietary Orbix protocol as well as GIOP/IIOP. The proprietary protocol is used by default. To enable IIOP, Any types have to be marshaled differently, and this is achieved by setting flags in the IDL compiler and in the Any constructor. The default and copy constructors take an extra argument of type int. To create Anys that can be marshaled over IIOP the constructor's argument must to be set to

```
IE.Iona.Orbix2._CORBA.IT_INTEROPERABLE_OR_KIND
```

When dealing with Anys we have to consider two different cases: IDL predefined types and user-defined types.

Inserting values into and retrieving values from an Any is very similar in all ORBs. The main difference is in the naming of the methods.

10.1   IDL Predefined Types

10.1.1   Inserting a Value

The class CORBA.Any provides methods for inserting values of IDL-defined types, that is, all basic data types, Objects, TypesCodes, and Anys.

Visibroker Visibroker has defined methods that follow the pattern

```
public Any from_type(type value) throws SystemException
```

and, for example, for type short

```
public Any from_short(short value) throws SystemException
```

For the programmer's convenience, methods return a reference to the Any the method was invoked on.

OrbixWeb OrbixWeb defines similar methods using the naming pattern:

```
public void inserttype(type value) throws SystemException
```

and, for example, for type short

```
public void insertShort(short value) throws SystemException
```

These methods have the return type void.

Joe Joe's Any class provides static constructors to create an Any from basic CORBA types. These are named according to type:

```
public static Any createAnyFromType(type x) throws SystemException
```

and, for example, for type short

```
public static Any createAnyFromShort(short x) throws SystemException
```

10.1.2   *Retrieving a Value*

The class CORBA.Any provides methods for retrieving values of predefined IDL types. These methods follow a similar pattern to the ones for storing values.

Visibroker Visibroker uses the following pattern:

```
public type to_type() throws SystemException
```

For example, for type short

```
public short to_short() throws SystemException
```

OrbixWeb OrbixWeb uses this form:

```
public type extracttype() throws SystemException
```

For example, for type `short`

```
public short extractShort() throws SystemException
```

Joe   Once again, Joe uses static methods of the following form:

```
public static synchronized type getTypeFromAny(Any a)
                        throws SystemException
```

For example, for type `short`

```
public static synchronized short getShortFromAny(Any a)
                        throws SystemException
```

10.2   User-defined types

The three products have approached the handling of user-defined types differently. Visibroker generates methods for each of the user-defined types. OrbixWeb provides a generic method for storing and retrieving all types. At the time of writing Joe did not support the insertion of user-defined types into Anys.

10.2.1   Storing a Value

Visibroker   Visibroker's IDL compiler generates code to construct Anys from user-defined data types, for example, enums, structs, and unions. This method creates and returns an Any that contains the type and value of the object it was invoked on. The method is defined as a class method in a `_var` class.

If we again take the `struct Equipment` as an example, the IDL generates a class `Equipment_var` which contains a class method `any()`.

```
// Java - Visibroker
final public class Equipment_var {

    public static CORBA.Any any(Struct.Equipment value)
        throws CORBA.SystemException {
        // creates and returns an Any containing "value"
    }
```

Using this method an Any can be constructed from an object of the class `Equipment`.

```
// construct an object of class Equipment
Equipment equipment = Equipment( true, false );
```

```
// construct an Any which contains the object equipment
CORBA.Any any_equipment = Equipment_var.any( equipment );
```

OrbixWeb   OrbixWeb provides a generic method `insert()` at the interface `CORBA.Any` which is defined as follows:

```
public void insert ( Marshalable m )
    throws SystemException;
```

The example to convert the `struct` `Equipment` into an Any would be implemented with OrbixWeb as follows.

```
// Java - OrbixWeb

// construct an object of class Equipment
Equipment equipment = Equipment( true, false );

// create Any
IE.Iona.Orbix2.CORBA.Any any_equipment = new IE.Iona.Orbix2.CORBA.Any(
    IE.Iona.Orbix2._CORBA.IT_INTEROPERABLE_OR_KIND );

// insert value from struct
any_equipment.insert( equipment );
```

10.2.2   *Retrieving a Value*

Again the approaches in the various language bindings are different.

Visibroker   Visibroker static constructors are generated in each `_var` class that extract a value from an Any and produce a new object of the corresponding class. For example:

```
final public class Equipment_var {

    public static Equipment any( CORBA.Any any )
        throws CORBA.SystemException {
        // creates and returns an instance of the class "Equipment",
        // initialised from the value of "any"
    }
```

This constructor would be used in the following way:

```
CORBA.Any any_equipment = ...; // Initialize the Any
Equipment re_equipment = Equipment_var.any( any_equipment );
```

OrbixWeb   OrbixWeb again provides only one generic method, `extract()`, on the interface `CORBA.Any` to retrieve values. This method is defined as follows:

```
public void extract( Marshalable m )
    throws SystemException
```

The parameter must be of the expected type and must be preallocated.
For our equipment example the following code needs to be written:

```
IE.Iona.Orbix2.CORBA.Any any_equipment = ...; // Initialize the Any
Equipment re-equipment = new Equipment();
any_equipment.extract( re_equipment );
```

10.3   Arrays and Sequences

Arrays and sequences are treated similarly when using Anys. We will use the
following unbounded sequence type as an example:

```
typedef sequence <Equipment> Equipment_seq;
```

10.3.1   Visibroker

Visibroker provides methods to insert arrays and sequences into and extract
them from Anys in a similar manner to other user-defined types. The corresponding _var classes contain the necessary methods.

For the example IDL above, Visibroker generates a _var class with the
following methods that are relevant to Anys:

```
final public class Equipment_seq_var {

    public static CORBA.Any any(Sequence.Equipment[] value)
        throws CORBA.SystemException {
        // creates and returns an Any containing "value"
    }

    public static Sequence.Equipment[] any(CORBA.Any any)
        throws CORBA.SystemException {
        // creates and returns an instance of the class "Equipment",
        // initialized from the values of "any"
    }
}
```

10.3.2   OrbixWeb

OrbixWeb also provides methods that support Anys for sequences in a similar
way to other user-defined data types. Because OrbixWeb maps IDL sequences
to Java classes, the methods are defined in the generated sequence classes.

There are special methods to deal with arrays of predefined IDL types. Their definition follows this pattern:

```
// insert arrays
public void insertTypeArray( type _array[], int length )
    throws SystemException;

// extract arrays
public void extractTypeArray( type _array[], int length )
    throws SystemException;
```

When retrieving arrays, the first parameter must be preallocated and of sufficient length. If the allocated array is shorter than the one contained in the Any, the CORBA system exception BAD_PARAM is raised.

The use of the second parameter, length, is not really clear since a Java array contains its size. This signature only creates a source of possible errors by allowing inconsistencies between the second argument and the actual length of the array.

To handle, for example, arrays of type long we have the following two methods:

```
// insert arrays
public void insertLongArray( int int_array[], int length )
    throws SystemException;

// extract arrays
public void extractLongArray( int int_array[], int length )
    throws SystemException;
```

Like the generic insert and retrieve methods, a couple of methods are generated for storing and retrieving arrays of each user-defined type. These methods have two arguments, the array itself and an integer specifying the length of the array.

```
// insert arrays
public void insertArray( Marshalable m_array[], int length )
    throws SystemException;

// extract arrays
public void extractArray( Marshalable m_array[], int length )
    throws SystemException;
```

The generic array methods are used in the same way as the other generic methods. The memory for the variable passed to extractArray() must be preallocated.

11 Constants

IDL constants are mapped to Java classes containing a static variable that has the value of the constant. The attributes of the generated class and its variable `value` ensure the semantics of an IDL constant:

- ◆ `final` (class) prevents further derivation of that class.
- ◆ `static` (variable) ensures that instances of that class have the same value.
- ◆ `final` (variable) ensures that the value cannot be overridden.

Here is an example IDL constant:

```
module Constant{
    const short MaxSlots = 8;
};
```

11.1 Visibroker

In Visibroker, IDL constant values are mapped to `public static final` classes in Java. The name of the IDL constant is used as the name of a Java class. The constant value is available as the class variable `value`.

This is the code generated by Visibroker for the IDL above:

```
// Java - Visibroker
final public class MaxSlots{
    final public static short value = (short)8;
}
```

11.2 OrbixWeb

OrbixWeb also creates a new class named after the module in which the constant is defined. Within the class a static final variable of the corresponding type and value is defined.

```
// Java - OrbixWeb
public class _Constant {
    public static final short MaxSlots = 8;
}
```

11.3 Joe

Joe creates a new final class containing a final static variable called `value` that is initialized to the constant value.

```
// Java - Joe
public final class MaxSlots {
    public static final short value = (short) (8L);
}
```

12   *Attributes*

IDL attributes are mapped to Java methods: an accessor method, and, if the attribute is not read only, a modifier method.

The accessor method does not have parameters and it returns a value of the attribute type (mapped to Java). The modifier method is of type `void` and has one parameter of the attribute type.

The mapping is similar for Visibroker, OrbixWeb, and Joe. It only differs in the naming of the accessor and modifier methods.

Here are two example attributes in an IDL interface:

```
attribute string purpose;
readonly attribute string participants;
```

12.1   Visibroker

Visibroker names both the accessor and modifier methods after the attribute, although the methods differ in their signatures. This is how the examples above are mapped in Visibroker:

```
// Java - Visibroker

// methods of a class representing some IDL interface

public String purpose()
    throws CORBA.SystemException {
    // accessor
}

public void purpose( String val)
    throws CORBA.SystemException {
    // modifier
}

public String participants()
    throws CORBA.SystemException {
    // accessor
```

12.2   OrbixWeb

OrbixWeb prefixes the attribute name with `get` and `set` to produce the names of the accessor and modifier methods, respectively.

```
// Java - OrbixWeb

// methods of a class representing some IDL interface
```

```
public String getpurpose()
    throws IE.Iona.Orbix2.CORBA.SystemException {
    // accessor
}

public void setpurpose(String value)
    throws IE.Iona.Orbix2.CORBA.SystemException {
    // modifier
}

public String getparticipants()
    throws IE.Iona.Orbix2.CORBA.SystemException {
    // accessor
}
```

12.3   Joe

Joe uses the same naming convention as OrbixWeb, but the declarations differ because the methods are declared in an interface rather than a class.

```
// Java - Joe
String getpurpose() throws sunw.corba.SystemException;

void setpurpose(String arg) throws sunw.corba.SystemException;

String getparticipants() throws sunw.corba.SystemException;
```

13   *Operations*

IDL operations are mapped to methods on the Java interface which corresponds to the IDL interface. The type of the operation result is mapped to Java according to the mapping for data types described above. IDL void is mapped to Java void.

13.1   Parameter Semantics

IDL defines three different parameter passing modes, indicated by the tags: in,inout, and out. The tag in defines pass-by-value semantics; a client supplies a value which is kept unchanged during the time of the invocation. The tag out defines pass-by-result semantics; the server supplies a value which will be available to the client after the invocation returns. The tag inout defines pass-by-value-result semantics; the client supplies a value which is subject to change by the server. The modified value is available to the client after the invocation returns.

Java only defines pass-by-value semantics for operation parameters. This matches the semantics for in parameters only. To map inout and out parameters additional mechanisms are needed.

When a Java client invokes a method and supplies a Java object reference as an argument, the invoked object can modify the state of the object that was referenced by the parameter. After the invocation, the client still has the reference to the object, which has been modified.

This mechanism is used to handle inout and out parameters in Java. Java objects are used as containers for these parameters. References to the container objects are passed instead of the parameters themselves. This mechanism is illustrated in Figure 6-2.

These container classes are also known as _var classes in Visibroker, or Holder classes in OrbixWeb and Joe. All container classes follow the same pattern: they have a public instance variable that holds the actual value of the parameter. These classes also provide a couple of constructors. One is a null constructor (intended for out parameters) and the other is a constructor that has a parameter of the contained type (intended for inout parameters).

The three products have slightly different approaches to the implementation of container classes. There are predefined container classes for predefined IDL types, for example, the container for short is defined as follows:

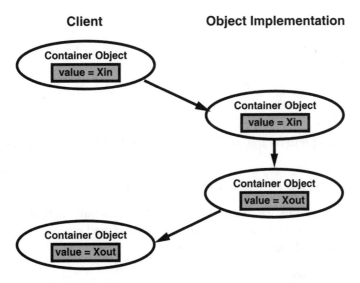

FIGURE 6-2. Parameter containers.

13.1.1 Visibroker

```
// Java - Visibroker
public final class short_var extends Object {

    public short value;

    public short_var();
    public short_var( short newValue );
}
```

13.1.2 OrbixWeb

```
// Java - OrbixWeb
public class ShortHolder {

    public short value;

    public ShortHolder( short _value ) {
        value =_value;
    };
}
```

13.1.3 Joe

```
// Java - Joe
public class ShortHolder {

    public short value;

    public ShortHolder();

    public ShortHolder(short initial) {
        value = initial;
    };
}
```

The complete listing of these predefined types is given in Appendix B.

13.2 Mapping from Operations to Methods

As an example, we use an operation that has parameters with all the different tags as well as a combination of predefined and user-defined types. The user-defined type is struct Equipment.

```
module Operation {
    struct Equipment {
```

```
        boolean video;
        boolean audio;
    };

    interface OpIf {
        short op(
            in char p1,
            inout char p2,
            in Equipment p3,
            out Equipment p4 );
    };
};
```

13.2.1   Visibroker

Visibroker's IDL compiler generates several classes and interfaces. The class generated as a container for the Equipment structure when it is passed as an out or inout parameter is called Equipment_var.

```
final public class Equipment_var {
  public Operation.Equipment value;
  public Equipment_var() {
  }
  public Equipment_var(Operation.Equipment value) {
    this.value = value;
  }
```

The operation is mapped to a method whose out and inout parameters are _var types. This class also contains a pair of methods named any() which were shown earlier in this chapter.

```
// Java - Visibroker

public interface OpIf extends CORBA.Object {
    public short op(
        char p1,
        CORBA.char_var p2,
        Operation.Equipment p3,
        Operation.Equipment_var p4
    ) throws CORBA.SystemException;
}
```

13.2.2   OrbixWeb

OrbixWeb generates a very similar Java interface. Note that OrbixWeb does not use a Holder object for parameter p4 since the struct Equipment is already mapped to a Java class. When an object of this type is used as an inout or out parameter, it already acts as a container around the encapsulated values.

```
// Java - OrbixWeb
public interface Ref extends IE.Iona.Orbix2.CORBA.Object.Ref {

    public short op(
        char p1,
        IE.Iona.Orbix2.CORBA.CharHolder p2,
        Operation.Equipment p3,
        Operation.Equipment p4)
        throws IE.Iona.Orbix2.CORBA.SystemException ;
}
```

13.2.3   Joe

Joe uses Holders consistently for predefined and user-defined types, and so generates a Holder class for the Equipment class representing the IDL struct.

```
// Java - Joe
public final class EquipmentHolder
{
    // instance variable
    public Operation.Equipment value;
    // constructors
    public EquipmentHolder() {
        this(null);
    }
    public EquipmentHolder(Operation.Equipment arg) {
        value = arg;
    }
}
```

The method generated for operation op() uses the Holder classes wherever out or inout parameters are declared.

```
public interface OpIfOperations {
    short op(char p1,
            sunw.corba.CharHolder p2,
            Operation.Equipment p3,
            Operation.EquipmentHolder p4)
            throws sunw.corba.SystemException;
}
```

14   Interfaces

IDL interfaces are mapped to Java interfaces. Although this sounds rather straightforward, it is where the major differences between the three mappings occur.

Only Visigenic's Visibroker currently provides a full server-side mapping and a corresponding ORB implementation. Joe provides the ability to do callbacks to an object reference supported in the application and so can be considered to have a partial server-side mapping. OrbixWeb has announced a server-side mapping to be released in 1997.

14.1   Visibroker

From an IDL interface, four classes and two interfaces with the following name conventions are generated. Given an IDL interface named `IfId`, the following files are generated by Visibroker's IDL compiler:

♦ `IfId.java`. Contains the Java interface `IfId` which extends `CORBA.Object`. Clients obtain references to objects that implement this interface.

♦ `_st_IfId.java`. Contains a Java class for the stub code. This class implements the interface `IfId` on the client side. This is also known as the client proxy. The stub class is not directly used by application programmers.

♦ `IfId_var.java`. Contains a class to provide container objects for inout and out parameters, the narrow operation for objects, methods for Anys, and other proprietary methods, for example, `bind()` (see Chapter 8).

♦ `_sk_IfId.java`. Contains a class for the skeleton as defined in the ORB. The skeleton class implements the interface `IfId`.

♦ `IfIdOperations.java` and `_tie_IfId.java`. Contains a Java interface similar to `IfId`, though it does not extend the interface `CORBA.Object`. The `_tie_IfId` contains a class which extends the class `_sk_IfId`. The interface `IfIdOperations` and the class `_tie_IfId` are used for the Tie mechanism.

14.1.1   Client-side Mapping

An IDL interface is mapped into a Java interface of the same name. The Java interface extends the interface `CORBA.Object`. For example, the IDL interface

```
// RoomBooking.idl
module RoomBooking {
    interface Room {};
};
```

is mapped to the Java interface

```
// Room.java
package RoomBooking;
    public interface Room extends CORBA.Object {
    };
```

A client obtains an object reference in the usual way, that is, via `string_to_object`, from a Naming or Trading Service, or from a third-party object. This referenced object is an implementation of the generated Java interface and hence clients can invoke the operations and attribute accessors and modifiers as specified in the corresponding IDL.

A stub class is also generated, but application programmers are not concerned with this class. In a client program, one only declares object references, such as

```
RoomBooking.Room myRoom;
```

and assigns a value to the variable in the manner described above. The use of the client-side mapping is explained in greater detail in Chapter 9.

14.1.2   Server-side Mapping

The IDL compiler generates a skeleton class _sk_IfId that implements the interface IfId. A CORBA object implementation extends the skeleton, overriding the methods with the appropriate application semantics.

```
class Room extends RoomBooking._sk_Room{

    // implementation of the methods
}
```

For more information, see Chapter 9. Alternatively, the Tie mechanism can be used.

14.2   OrbixWeb

OrbixWeb also creates a number of Java interfaces and classes for an IDL interface specification. It generates server-side mappings, but these were undocumented at the time of writing.

For an IDL interface IfId the following client-side files are generated:

- ♦ IfId.java. Contains the class IfId which is the client-side implementation of the Java interface IfId.Ref, the client-side proxy interface.
- ♦ IfId/Holder.java. Defines the container classes for out and inout parameter passing.
- ♦ IfId/Ref.java. The Java interface Ref corresponds directly to the IDL interface.

An application programmer uses a Java object type IfId.Ref as an object reference. For the Room interface of the above example we declare:

```
RoomBooking.Room.Ref myRoom;
```

The definition of the interface is

```
package RoomBooking.Room;

public interface Ref extends IE.Iona.Orbix2.CORBA.Object.Ref {
}
```

The class `IfId` implements the interface `IfId.Ref`, for example, `Room` implements `Room.Ref`.

14.3   Joe

The following files are generated by the Joe IDL compiler:

- ◆ `IfIdOperations.java`. Contains methods representing the IDL for inheritance into both client and server interfaces.
- ◆ `IfIdRef.java`. Contains the interface to the client-side proxy `IfIdRef`.
- ◆ `IfIdStub.java`. Contains the `IfIdStub` class which implements the proxy for `IfId` objects.
- ◆ `IfIdHolder.java`. Defines containers for use with out and inout parameters.
- ◆ `IfIdServant.java`. Contains the interface to be implemented to create a CORBA object's methods.
- ◆ `IfIdSkeleton.java`. Defines the `IfIdSkeleton` class that delegates to the Servant. Joe always uses the Tie approach.

14.3.1   Client-side Mapping

The Java interfaces that are pertinent to the client's access to a CORBA object are `IfIdOperations` and `IfIdRef`. The `IfIdOperations` interface contains the methods derived from the operations and attributes in the IDL interface.

The `IfIdRef` Java interface inherits from the `IfIdOperations` interface and from Joe's `sunw.corba.ObjectRef` interface. The `ObjectRef` interface provides all the operations on the IDL interface CORBA::Object.

The `IfIdRef` interface is implemented by the `IfIdStub` class. The `IfIdStub` class then implements all the methods declared in the `Ref` interface, making available all the operation and attribute methods from the IDL interface and all the operations defined on CORBA::Object. In addition the `IfIdStub` class implements other IDL interface-specific methods not found in the `IfIdRef` declaration available to the programmer, such as `narrow()`.

14.3.2   Server-side Mapping

An object implementation is achieved by implementing the methods defined in the `IfIdServant` interface, which are in turn inherited from the `IfIdOperations` Java interface. The `IfIdOperations` interface forms the common basis for client and server because it is inherited by the proxy interface `IfIdRef` and the servant interface.

The remaining class that is generated by the IDL compiler is `IfIdSkeleton`. This class implements the abstract interface `sunw.orb.Skeleton`. The Joe approach to associating the implementation object with the skeleton is essentially the same as the Tie approach, except that the CORBA object is created by static methods that take a reference to an implementation object (an instance of a subclass of `IfIdServant`). For more information, see Chapter 10.

15 *Inheritance*

OMG IDL defines multiple inheritance for interfaces; an IDL interface can extend any number of interfaces. Java defines only single inheritance for classes; a class can extend only one superclass (see Chapter 3). The Java language designers have deliberately made this decision to avoid semantic problems caused by the inheritance of implementations. Java interfaces consist only of signatures, and hence multiple inheritance for interfaces does not imply implementation inheritance and is allowed in Java.

As IDL interfaces are mapped to Java interfaces, the mapping of inheritance is straightforward. A Java interface representing a derived IDL interface (D) extends all the Java interfaces representing the base interfaces of D.

The following example illustrates inheritance by using a diamond inheritance structure (see Figure 6-3).

```
module InheritanceExample {
    interface Base {};
    interface Left : Base {};
    interface Right : Base {};
    interface Derived : Left, Right {};
};
```

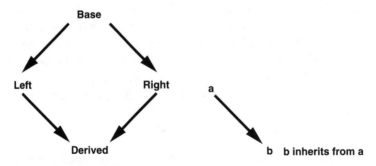

FIGURE 6-3. Diamond inheritance.

15.1 Visibroker

Visibroker generates the Java interfaces shown in the following code:

```
// Java - Visibroker

// Base.java
package InheritanceExample;
    public interface Base extends CORBA.Object { };

// Left.java
package InheritanceExample;
    public interface Left extends InheritanceExample.Base { };

// Right.java
package InheritanceExample;
    public interface Right extends InheritanceExample.Base { };

// Derived.java
package InheritanceExample;
    public interface Derived extends
        InheritanceExample.Left, InheritanceExample.Right { };
```

15.2 OrbixWeb

OrbixWeb's IDL compiler generates the following Java interfaces:

```
// Java - OrbixWeb

// Base.java
package InheritanceExample.Base;
    public interface Ref extends IE.Iona.Orbix2.CORBA.Object.Ref {
    }

// Left.java
package InheritanceExample.Left;
    public interface Ref extends
        InheritanceExample.Base.Ref,
        IE.Iona.Orbix2.CORBA.Object.Ref {
    }

// Right.java
package InheritanceExample.Right;
    public interface Ref extends
        InheritanceExample.Base.Ref,
        IE.Iona.Orbix2.CORBA.Object.Ref {
    }
```

```
// Derived.java
package InheritanceExample.Derived;
    public interface Ref extends
        InheritanceExample.Left.Ref, InheritanceExample.Right.Ref,
        IE.Iona.Orbix2.CORBA.Object.Ref {
    }
```

15.3   Joe

Joe uses the following interfaces to represent the IDL above:

```
// Java - Joe

// BaseRef.java
package InheritanceExample;

public interface BaseRef
    extends sunw.corba.ObjectRef,
            InheritanceExample.BaseOperations {
}

// LeftRef.java
package InheritanceExample;

public interface LeftRef
    extends sunw.corba.ObjectRef,
            InheritanceExample.BaseRef,
            InheritanceExample.LeftOperations {
}

// RightRef.java
package InheritanceExample;

public interface RightRef
    extends sunw.corba.ObjectRef,
            InheritanceExample.BaseRef,
            InheritanceExample.RightOperations {
}

// DerivedRef.java
package InheritanceExample;

public interface DerivedRef
    extends sunw.corba.ObjectRef,
            InheritanceExample.LeftRef,
            InheritanceExample.RightRef,
            InheritanceExample.DerivedOperations {
}
```

16 *Modules*

Modules scope identifiers in IDL specifications to prevent clashes with identifiers used in other specifications. Java provides packages for scoping identifiers. IDL modules are mapped to Java packages of the same name, with that package corresponding to a directory in the file system. The IDL compiler creates a subdirectory named after the IDL module. All generated files containing interfaces and classes according to this mapping are put into this directory. The files created contain a corresponding package declaration.

Modules can be nested, that is, one can define modules within modules. Nested module definitions result in a corresponding nesting of subpackages and subdirectories.

Additional packages are created for type definitions within the scope of an interface. They are added to the package that corresponds to the module in which the interface is defined.

Figure 6-4 illustrates these mapping rules.

The following IDL, when compiled, generates the directories, files, and corresponding package structure listed for each ORB below.

```
module Outer {
  module Inner {
    interface If {
```

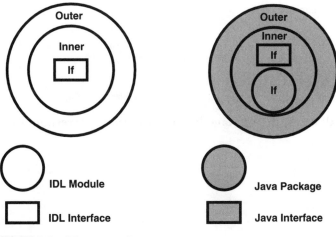

FIGURE 6-4. Name scoping.

```
    struct Equipment {
        boolean video;
        boolean audio;
    };
};
};
};
```

Below are the package structures generated by the three Java ORBs.

◆ Visibroker

```
Outer:
Inner/

Outer/Inner:
If.java            _If/            _sk_If.java    _tie_If.java
IfOperations.java  If_var.java     _st_If.java

Outer/Inner/_If:
Equipment.java     Equipment_var.java
```

◆ OrbixWeb

```
Outer:
Inner/

Outer/Inner:
If/                IfOperations.java       IfStub.java
IfHolder.java      IfRef.java

Outer/Inner/If:
Equipment.java     EquipmentHolder.java
```

◆ Joe

```
Inner/

Outer/Inner:
If/                IfOperations.java       IfStub.java
IfHolder.java         IfRef.java

Outer/Inner/If:
Equipment.java              EquipmentHolder.java
```

In all cases, the package hierarchy directly corresponds to the IDL module structure.

ORB Run-time System

The CORBA2.0 specification defines the ORB run-time system in the form of the pseudo-objects ORB, BOA, and Object. They are called pseudo-objects because they provide interfaces like normal objects, but the operations on those interfaces are implemented in libraries and do not usually result in a remote invocation. Interfaces of pseudo-objects are specified in OMG IDL, which is commented as "Pseudo-IDL (PIDL). In this chapter we explain the implementation of these pseudo-objects for Java ORBs, that is, their corresponding Java APIs.

Besides the three pseudo-objects, we introduce the Java mapping for TypeCodes, the DII, the DSI, and Contexts.

This chapter contains mappings for the following interfaces:

- CORBA::Object
- CORBA::ORB
- CORBA::BOA
- TypeCode
- DII

♦ DSI
♦ CORBA::Context

1 Object Interface

All CORBA objects, that is, objects that have been specified in OMG IDL and implemented in a CORBA environment, are extensions of CORBA::Object. The interface CORBA::Object defines operations that are applicable to any object. These operations are implemented by the ORB itself instead of being passed to the implementation of the derived object.

In this section we will discuss the implementation of these operations within each of the Java ORBs. The mappings will be presented in the following format:

♦ IDL interface   CORBA::Object
♦ Visibroker interface   CORBA.Object
♦ OrbixWeb interface   CORBA.Object.Ref
♦ Joe interface   corba.ObjectRef

1.1 get_implementation()

The Implementation Repository contains information that allows the ORB to locate and activate object implementations. This information is accessible from an object with an IDL interface CORBA::ImplementationDef. Note that the specification of CORBA::ImplementationDef is left to the particular ORB implementation since it deals with operating system-specific information. The operation returns an object that can then be queried about details of the object implementation.

IDL operation   ImplementationDef get_implementation();
Visibroker method   Not mapped
OrbixWeb method   String _get_implementation()
Joe method   Not mapped

1.2 get_interface()

The interface repository contains type information of IDL-defined types. Although the IR can be modified directly through an IDL-defined interface, the type information is usually created and stored by the IDL compiler, with the appropriate options switched on.

The type information is kept in objects with the IDL interface CORBA::InterfaceDef. Operations on this interface allow the query of type information in the IR. The operation get_interface() returns an ImplementationDef object that represents the interface type of the object it was called on.

- ♦ IDL operation   ImplementationDef get_implementation();
- ♦ Visibroker method   `CORBA.InterfaceDef _get_interface()`
- ♦ OrbixWeb method   `InterfaceDef.Ref _get_interface()`
- ♦ Joe method   Not mapped

The use of this method is demonstrated in Chapter 10.

1.3   `is_nil()`

An object reference can be tested for this value by the operation is_nil(). This operation returns TRUE if the value of the reference is nil, otherwise FALSE. The result is determined by the ORB; the implementation of the object is not involved. Visibroker uses the Java `null` type as a nil object reference, so a test like

```
if( obj == null )
```

can be used in place of is_nil().

- ♦ IDL operation   boolean is_nil ();
- ♦ Visibroker method   Not mapped
- ♦ OrbixWeb method   `boolean CORBA.is_nil()`
- ♦ Joe method   `boolean isNil()`

1.4   `duplicate()` **and** `release()`

There is no need to map the operations duplicate() and release(), since Java provides memory management for object references as it does for any other object or data type. However, Joe does provide these operations for completeness.

IDL operations   Object duplicate();   void release();
Visibroker methods   Not mapped
OrbixWeb methods   Not mapped
Joe methods   `ObjectRef duplicate()`   `void release()`

1.5   `is_a()`

The operation is_a() tests if the object the operation is called on is of the interface type supplied as an argument. This string argument to is_a() is interpreted as an IR identifier (see Chapter 2 for an explanation). It returns

TRUE if the object is of the type identified. This means either that the object's type and the identified type are the same, or that the identified type is a base type of the object's type. A FALSE return value does not necessarily mean that the object is not substitutable.

IDL operation	boolean is_a(in string logical_type_id);
Visibroker method	`boolean is_a(String repId)`
OrbixWeb method	Not mapped
Joe method	`boolean isA(String RepositoryIdentifier)`

1.6 `non_existent()`

The operation non_existent() can be used to test if an object has been destroyed. It returns TRUE if the ORB can authoritatively determine that the referenced object does not exist. Otherwise it returns FALSE. Note that the FALSE may not mean that the object still exists.

IDL operation	boolean is_a(in string logical_type_id);
Visibroker method	`boolean _non_existent()`
OrbixWeb method	Not mapped
Joe method	Not mapped

1.7 `is_equivalent()`

The operation is_equivalent() determines if two object references are equivalent, that is, are identical or refer to the same object. The operation returns TRUE if the object reference on which the object was called and the reference other_object are known to be equivalent, otherwise it returns FALSE. Note that the FALSE does not mean that the object could not possibly be the same.

IDL operation	is_equivalent(in Object other_object);
Visibroker method	`boolean _is_equivalent(Object other_object)`
OrbixWeb method	Not mapped
Joe method	Not mapped

1.8 `hash()`

The operation hash() is used to effectively manage large numbers of object references. It generates a hash value for the object reference on which the operation is called. The hash value relates to an ORB-internal identifier. As usual with hash functions, different object references can result in the same hash value and further operations such as the operation is_equivalent() need to be called.

IDL operation	unsigned long hash(in unsigned long maximum);
Visibroker method	`int _hash(int maximum)`
OrbixWeb method	Not mapped
Joe method	Not mapped

1.9 `create_request()`

The operation create_request() is used to create a dynamic invocation Request when using the DII. It is discussed in this context in Chapter 10.

♦ IDL operation

```
Status create_request(
    in Context ctx,
    in Identifier operation,
    in NVList arg_list,
    inout NamedValueresult,
    out Requestrequest,
    in Flags req_flags );
```

♦ Visibroker method

```
public abstract Request _create_request(
    Context ctx,
    String operation,
    NVList arg_list,
    NamedValue result )
throws SystemException;
```

♦ OrbixWeb method

```
public int _create_request(
    IE.Iona.Orbix2.CORBA.Context ctx,
    String operation,
    IE.Iona.Orbix2.CORBA.NVList arg_list,
    IE.Iona.Orbix2.CORBA.NamedValue result,
    IE.Iona.Orbix2.CORBA.Request.Holder
                                    hrequest,
    IE.Iona.Orbix2.CORBA.Flags req_flags)
throws IE.Iona.Orbix2.CORBA.SystemException;
```

♦ Joe method   Not mapped

2   *ORB Interface*

The ORB interface provides operations to bootstrap a CORBA application. This requires the initialization of an Object Adapter, the conversion of object references into strings and vice versa, and the resolution of initial references.

There are more operations defined on the ORB pseudo-interface that are concerned with TypeCodes, Contexts, the DII, and the DSI. The mappings for these operations are explained in the appropriate sections.

The ORB interface is mapped as follows:

- ♦ IDL interface   CORBA::ORB
- ♦ Visibroker class   `CORBA.ORB`
- ♦ OrbixWeb class   `CORBA.ORB`
- ♦ Joe class   `corba.OrbRef`

2.1 ORB Initialization

Before an application can use the operations on the ORB interfaces it needs a reference to an ORB pseudo-object. ORBs in Java applications and Java applets require different initializations to overcome applet security restrictions.

2.1.1 Initialization for Java Applications

- ♦ IDL operation   ORB ORB_init(inout arg_list argv, in ORBid orb_identifier);
- ♦ Visibroker method   `ORB init()` is a static method in the `ORB` class
- ♦ OrbixWeb object   The `_CORBA.Orbix` object is preinitialized
- ♦ Joe method   `corba.OrbStub.ORBInit(String orbIdentifier)`

2.1.2 Initialization for Java Applets

- ♦ IDL operation   ORB ORB_init(inout arg_list argv, in ORBid orb_identifier);
- ♦ Visibroker method   `ORB init(Applet applet)` is a static method in the ORB class
- ♦ OrbixWeb object   The `_CORBA.Orbix` object contains only static methods and so requires no instantiation
- ♦ Joe method   `corba.OrbStub.ORBInit(Applet app,`
                                      `String orbIdentifier)`

The Visibroker and Joe methods initialize an applet-aware ORB environment that uses HTTP tunneling for remote method invocations. In the case of Joe, the use of HTTP depends on the ORB identifier argument.

2.2 Converting Object References into Strings and Vice Versa

Object references can be externalized by converting them into strings. A stringified object reference can be conveniently stored in a file or passed around by means other than CORBA, for example, by e-mail. Of course, a stringified object reference must be reconvertible into a real object reference, which refers to the same object as the original one.

There are two operations at the ORB interface which stringify and destringify object references. The object_to_string() operation converts an interoperable object reference (IOR) into a string.

- ◆ IDL operation   string object_to_string(in Object obj);
- ◆ Visibroker method   `String object_to_string(Object obj)`
- ◆ OrbixWeb method   `String Orbix.object_to_string(Object.Ref oref)`
- ◆ Joe method   `String objectToString(ObjectRef obj)`

The operation string_to_object() converts a stringified object reference back into an IOR.

- ◆ IDL operation   Object string_to_object(in string obj);
- ◆ Visibroker method   `Object string_to_object(String ior)`
- ◆ OrbixWeb object   `Object.Ref string_to_object(String s)`
- ◆ Joe method   `ObjectRef stringToObject(String str)`

It is guaranteed that a stringified IOR that has been produced by object_to_string() is reconvertible by string_to_object() independent of which ORB the operations have been invoked on.

Note that the result of string_to_object() is of type CORBA::Object and must be narrowed to the object type expected.

2.3 BOA Initialization

Besides initializing an ORB, a server also needs to initialize an Object Adapter. The only Object Adapter that has been standardized by the OMG is the Basic Object Adapter (BOA). The concept of the BOA was introduced in Chapter 2.

The ORB pseudo-interface provides the operation BOA_init():

- ◆ IDL operation   BOA BOA_init(inout arg_list argv, in OAid boa_identifier);
- ◆ Visibroker method   `BOA BOA_init()`
- ◆ OrbixWeb object   Not mapped
- ◆ Joe method   Not mapped

3   *Basic Object Adapter*

Earlier we introduced the operation BOA_init(), which initializes a BOA and provides a server with a pseudo-object reference to a BOA. In this section we will introduce the operations specified in BOA pseudo-interface and their mapping to Java. Since the server-side was not fully supported by OrbixWeb and Joe at the time of writing, we will only discuss Visibroker for Java in this section.

The IDL-specified BOA pseudo-interface CORBA::BOA is mapped to the Java interface CORBA.BOA.

3.1 Activation and Deactivation

The operation object_is_ready() makes the specified object available for clients.

- ♦ IDL operation   `void object_is_ready( in Object obj,`
                                                `in ImplementationDef impl );`
- ♦ Visibroker method   `void obj_is_ready(Object object)`

Although an object reference can be passed to clients, for example, via a Naming or Trading Service, or externalized with object_to_string() as soon as an object is created, methods can only be invoked after `obj_is_ready()` has been called for this particular object.

The operation deactivate_object() deactivates the specified object. Once an object has been deactivated it is no longer accessible to clients. An attempt to invoke a method on a deactivated object will raise the exception CORBA.NO_IMPLEMENT.

- ♦ IDL operation   `void deactivate_object( in Object obj );`
- ♦ Visibroker method   `void deactivate_obj(Object object)`

The operation impl_is_ready() activates objects on a per-server basis, that is, all objects that have been created by a particular server are made accessible to clients.

- ♦ IDL operation   `void impl_is_ready(in ImplementationDef impl);`
- ♦ Visibroker method   `void impl_is_ready()`

Visibroker, however, implements the method with slightly different semantics. Visibroker requires a call to `obj_is_ready()` for each object. The method `impl_is_ready()` makes a program listen for requests to the objects it has created. Calling this method is optional. It can be omitted if there is another thread running, for example, an event loop controlling a GUI.

3.2 Other Operations

There are other operations defined in the BOA interface. These are outlined in Appendix A, but they have not been mapped and implemented within Visibroker.

4   *TypeCodes*

TypeCodes represent IDL type definitions at run time. They can be created and examined at run time. TypeCodes are defined in the CORBA specification by the pseudo-IDL interface CORBA::TypeCode. They are used in the following contexts:

- ◆ The Any type—describing the type of the value which is contained by the Any object.
- ◆ DII—used to determine the type of the parameters of a Request.
- ◆ Interface Repository—representing type specifications stored in the Interface Repository.
- ◆ IORs—representing the type of the referenced object.

4.1   Interface TypeCode

The pseudo-IDL interface is mapped to Java interfaces or classes:

◆ IDL interface	CORBA::TypeCode
◆ Visibroker interface	CORBA.TypeCode
◆ OrbixWeb class	CORBA.TypeCode
◆ Joe	Only supports predefined TypeCodes. No dynamic creation or query.

4.1.1   TCKind

The CORBA module defines a pseudo-IDL definition of an enum, TCKind. This enum defines constants to determine various "kinds" of TypeCodes. Different operations are allowed on different kinds of TypeCodes.

◆ IDL type	CORBA::TCKind
◆ Visibroker class	CORBA.TCKind
◆ OrbixWeb class	CORBA.TCKind

See Appendix B for the complete definition of the CORBA.TCKind classes.

4.1.2   *General Methods*

The operation equal() returns TRUE if the TypeCode is structurally equivalent to tc, FALSE otherwise.

◆ IDL operation	boolean equal(in TypeCode tc);
◆ Visibroker method	boolean equal(TypeCode tc)
◆ OrbixWeb method	boolean equals(java.lang.Object _obj)

The operation kind() returns the kind of the TypeCode as defined in `CORBA.TCKind`.

- ◆ IDL operation   TCKind kind();
- ◆ Visibroker method   `int kind()`
- ◆ OrbixWeb method   `int kind()`

The operation id() returns a RepositoryId for a type in the Interface Repository (see Appendix A).

- ◆ IDL operation   RepositoryId id() raises (BadKind);
- ◆ Visibroker method   `String id() throws SystemException, BadKind`
- ◆ OrbixWeb method   Not mapped

The operation name() returns the unscoped name of the type as specified in IDL. This is only valid for `tk_objref`, `tk_struct`, `tk_union`, `tk_enum`, `tk_alias`, `tk_except`.

- ◆ IDL operation   Identifier name() raises (BadKind);
- ◆ Visibroker method   `String name() throws SystemException, BadKind`
- ◆ OrbixWeb method   Not mapped

4.1.3 Methods for Structured Types

The operation member_count() returns the number of members in the type description. It is only valid for the following TypeCode kinds: `tk_struct`, `tk_union`, `tk_enum`, `tk_except`.

- ◆ IDL operation   unsigned long member_count() raises (BadKind);
- ◆ Visibroker method   `int member_count()`
              `throws SystemException, BadKind`
- ◆ OrbixWeb method   `int param_count()`

The operation member_name() returns the name of the indexed member. It is only valid for the following TypeCode kinds: `tk_struct`, `tk_union`, `tk_enum`, `tk_except`.

IDL operation   Identifier member_name(in unsigned long index)
                      raises (BadKind, Bounds);

Visibroker method   `String member_name(int index)`
                   `throws SystemException, BadKind, Bounds`

OrbixWeb method   Not mapped

The operation member_type() returns the type of the indexed member, only valid for the following TypeCode kinds: `tk_struct`, `tk_union`, `tk_except`.

- ◆ IDL operation   TypeCode member_type(in unsigned long index)
                         raises (BadKind, Bounds);

* Visibroker method   TypeCode member_type(int index)
                                    throws SystemException, BadKind, Bounds

* OrbixWeb method   Not mapped

OrbixWeb uses the CORBA1.1 operation parameter(), which was mapped to the following method: Any parameter(int index) throws Bounds
    Visibroker also implements this method for backward compatibility. The "parameters" include the names of members in structured types, and the value of the Any that is returned can be a name string, a TypeCode, a sequence bound value, and so on. This arrangement eliminates the need for different methods to deal with different structured types. Therefore we only consider the Visibroker mappings of the operations below.

4.1.4   Methods for Unions

The operation member_label() returns the label of member index (of a case statement). It is only valid for the tk_union TypeCode kind.

* IDL operation   any member_label(in unsigned long index)
                                    raises (BadKind, Bounds);
* Visibroker method   Any member_label(int index)
                                    throws SystemException, BadKind, Bounds

    The operation discriminator_type() returns the type of the union discriminator (only valid for tk_union).

* IDL operation   TypeCode discriminator_type() raises (BadKind);
* Visibroker method   TypeCode discriminator_type()
                                    throws SystemException, BadKind

    The operation default_index() returns the default index of the union (only valid for tk_union).

* IDL operation   long default_index() raises (BadKind);
* Visibroker method   int default_index()
                                    throws SystemException, BadKind

4.1.5   Methods for Template Types

The operation length() returns the number of elements contained by the type. It returns zero for unbounded strings and sequences. It is only valid for the following TypeCode kinds: tk_string, tk_sequence, tk_array.

* IDL operation   unsigned long length() raises (BadKind);
* Visibroker method   int length()
                                    throws SystemException, BadKind

The operation `content_type()` returns the base type of the template types (`tk_sequence`, `tk_array`) or the aliased type (`tk_alias`).

- ◆ IDL operation   TypeCode content_type() raises (BadKind);
- ◆ Visibroker method   `TypeCode content_type()`
              `throws SystemException, BadKind`

4.2   Creating TypeCodes

TypeCodes are created using operations in the CORBA::ORB interface. Visibroker for Java is currently the only Java ORB to support the standard TypeCode creation mechanism, and since Visigenic has provided a faithful language mapping of these operations we will provide only the method signatures in this section.

All the TypeCode creation methods follow a similar pattern. The result of the method is the newly created `TypeCode` object. These methods must be recursively applied for TypeCodes of recursive types.

4.2.1   Structured and Flat Types

The methods to create TypeCodes for structured and flat types, that is, structs, unions, enums, alias, exception, and interface, have the same first two parameters. The first parameter is a Repository Identifier specifying the type in IDL. The second parameter is the unscoped type name of the type. Further parameters determine specific components depending on the kind of TypeCode. This will be explained below.

The method `create_struct_tc()` creates a TypeCode describing an IDL struct. The parameter `members` determines an array of structures defining the members of the type.

```
public static TypeCode create_struct_tc(
    String repository_id,
    String type_name,
    StructMember members[]) throws SystemException
```

The method `create_union_tc()` creates a TypeCode describing an IDL union. The parameter `discriminator_type` determines the type of the discriminator, for example, the type used in the switch statement. The parameter `members` determines an array of structures defining the members of the type.

```
public static TypeCode create_union_tc(
    String repository_id,
    String type_name,
    TypeCode discriminator_type,
    UnionMember members[]) throws SystemException
```

The method `create_enum_tc()` creates a TypeCode describing an IDL enum. The parameter `members` determines an array of strings defining the members of the type.

```
public static TypeCode create_enum_tc(
    String repository_id,
    String type_name,
    String members[]) throws SystemException
```

The method `create_alias_tc()` creates a TypeCode describing an IDL typedef alias. The parameter `original_type` determines the aliased type.

```
public static TypeCode create_alias_tc(
    String repository_id,
    String type_name,
    TypeCode original_type) throws SystemException
```

The method `create_exception_tc()` creates a TypeCode describing an IDL exception. The parameter `members` determines an array of structures defining the members of the type.

```
public static TypeCode create_exception_tc(
    String repository_id,
    String type_name,
    StructMember members[]) throws SystemException
```

The method `create_interface_tc()` creates a TypeCode describing an IDL interface.

```
public static TypeCode create_interface_tc(
    String repository_id,
    String type_name) throws SystemException
```

4.2.2 *Template Types*

The methods to create TypeCodes for template types, that is, strings, sequences, and arrays, have the same first parameter, `length`. This parameter specifies the length of bounded types. A zero value determines an unbounded type.

The method `create_string_tc()` creates a TypeCode describing an IDL string.

```
public static TypeCode create_string_tc(
    int length) throws SystemException
```

The method `create_sequence_tc()` creates a TypeCode describing an IDL sequence. The parameter `element_type` determines the type of the elements contained by the sequence.

```
public static TypeCode create_sequence_tc(
    int length,
    TypeCode element_type) throws SystemException
```

The method `create_recursive_sequence_tc()` creates a TypeCode describing an IDL sequence. The parameter `offset` determines how many levels up in the type hierarchy the TypeCode's definition can be found.

```
public static TypeCode create_recursive_sequence_tc(
    int length,
    int offset) throws SystemException
```

The method `create_array_tc()` creates a TypeCode describing an IDL array. The parameter `element_type` determines the type of the elements contained in the array.

```
public static TypeCode create_array_tc(
    int length,
    TypeCode element_type) throws SystemException
```

5 Dynamic Invocation Interface

The DII enables clients to invoke operations on objects without compile-time knowledge of their IDL type, that is, without the stub code generated by the IDL compiler. Currently Joe does not support the DII, so we only show Visibroker and OrbixWeb mappings in this section.

A client creates a *Request,* which is the dynamic equivalent of an operation. A Request contains an object reference, an operation name, and type information and values of the arguments which are supplied by the client. Eventually a Request can be invoked that has the same semantics as invoking the operation using stub code.

In this section we will explain common data structures, the Request interface, and the NVList interface. The use of the DII is explained with an example in Chapter 10.

5.1 Common Data Structures

There are a number of common data structures to be used in the context of the DII and elsewhere in the ORB. In this section we introduce *Named Values* and *Named Value Lists* and their respective mapping to Java.

Named Values are usually used to describe results and parameters of operations. A Named Value List is used to describe a parameter list of an operation.

5.1.1 Named Values

A Named Value is specified as

```
struct NamedValue {
  Identifier name;
    any     argument;
    long    len;
    Flags   arg_modes;
};
```

where name determines the name of the parameter. The argument carries the value of the parameter encapsulated in an Any. Note that the argument does not only carry the value but also the type (in the form of a TypeCode) of a value. The len parameter determines the length of the value (argument) in bytes. The arg_modes can have the value CORBA::ARG_IN, CORBA::ARG_INOUT, or CORBA::ARG_OUT to determine if the parameter is in, inout, or out.

The type NamedValue is mapped as follows:

- ◆ IDL interface   CORBA::NamedValue
- ◆ Visibroker interface   `CORBA.NamedValue`
- ◆ OrbixWeb class   `CORBA.NamedValue`

Its members are mapped to the following methods:

- ◆ Visibroker method   `String name() throws SystemException`
- ◆ OrbixWeb method   `String name()`

- ◆ Visibroker method   `public abstract Any value()`
                              `throws SystemException`
- ◆ OrbixWeb method   `Any value()`

- ◆ Visibroker method   `public abstract int flags()`
                              `throws SystemException`
- ◆ OrbixWeb method   `Flags flags()`

The `Flags` returned by the OrbixWeb method are encapsulated in a class `CORBA.Flags` which is also used for Context operations.

There is no need for the mapping of len because Anys are objects in Java and consequently all values are of the same length.

Note that Visibroker objects implementing the NamedValue interface cannot be created directly. Instead, they must be obtained via the NVList interface as shown below.

5.2 Creating an NVList

An NVList can be created by using the operation create_list() provided on the ORB pseudo-interface.

- ♦ IDL operation
- ♦ Visibroker method
- ♦ OrbixWeb object

```
Status create_list(
   in long count,
   out NVList new_list );
NVList create_list(int length)
NVList(), NVList(int size)
```

The operation create_list() creates a pseudo-object of type NVList where count determines the length of the list. The return type Status can be defined as either

```
typedef unsigned long Status
```

(intended to describe a status code rather than raising an exception) or

```
typedef void Status
```

5.3   NVList Interface

The Interface NVList is defined in pseudo-IDL in the module CORBA. It provides the operations in the following subsections.

5.3.1   Adding Elements to NVLists

The pseudo-IDL operation add_item() incrementally adds arguments of type NamedValue to the list. It is implemented by three methods, add_item(), add_value(), and add(), in both Visibroker and OrbixWeb.

- ♦ IDL operation

```
Status add_item(
   in Identifier item_name,
   in TypeCode   item_type,
   in void       *value,
   in long       value_len,
   in Flags      item_flags
);
```

- ♦ Visibroker methods

```
void add_item(
   String name,
   int flags
) throws SystemException
void add_value(
   String name,
   Any any,
   int flags
) throws SystemException
void add(int Flags)
   throws SystemException
```

♦ OrbixWeb methods

```
NamedValue add_item(
        String item_name,
        Flags item_flags
)
NamedValue add_value(
        String item_name,
        Any value,
        Flags item_flags
)
NamedValue add(Flags item_flags)
```

The flags parameter can take the values ARG_IN, ARG_OUT, or ARG_INOUT, which correspond to the parameter tags in, out, and inout. The Visibroker defines values for these `flags` in the `CORBA` class. The OrbixWeb `item_flags` parameter requires an object of type `Flags` whose class has a constructor which takes values defined in the `_CORBA` class. OrbixWeb also maps two other flags values which Visibroker does not:

♦ `IN_COPY_VALUE`. This causes the production of a copy of the `NamedValue` parameter, which is then added to the list instead of the original.
♦ `DEPENDENT_LIST`. This must be specified if the added item is a list structure. It causes the sub-list to be freed when the parent list is freed.

The OrbixWeb methods always return a reference to the updated `NamedValue` object from each method.

The `add()` method adds a `NamedValue` item to the list. This item can only be initialized with a parameter mode.

The `add_item()` method adds a `NamedValue` item to the list. This item can only be initialized with a parameter mode and a name.

The `add_value()` method adds a `NamedValue` item to the list. This item can be initialized with a parameter mode, a name, and a value of type `Any`.

The TypeCode and the value pointer parameters in the IDL are replaced by the `Any` in the methods. There is also no need for the length parameter because the `void *` is replaced by a reference to a Java Any object, and hence is of known length.

5.3.2 *Freeing Lists*

The IDL interface provides two operations to handle garbage collection. The operations free() and free_memory() are not mapped into Java because memory management is performed by the run-time system.

5.3.3 *List Management*

The pseudo-IDL interface provides the operation get_count() which returns the total number of items in the list.

♦ IDL operation	Status get_count(out long count);
♦ Visibroker method	`int count() throws SystemException`
♦ OrbixWeb method	`int count()`

A number of other useful operations are provided by Visibroker and OrbixWeb.

The `item()` method returns the indexed element from the list. Visibroker throws BAD_PARAM if the index is out of range and OrbixWeb throws Bounds.

♦ Visibroker method	`NamedValue item(int index)` `throws SystemException`
♦ OrbixWeb method	`NamedValue item(int index)` `throws Bounds`

The `remove()` method removes the indexed element from the list. Visibroker throws BAD_PARAM if the index is out of range and OrbixWeb throws Bounds.

♦ Visibroker method	`void remove(int index) throws SystemException`
♦ OrbixWeb method	`int remove(int index) throws Bounds`

5.4 DII Request

Request is a pseudo-IDL interface that provides the mechanism to dynamically invoke operations on objects. Requests are created by the ORB.

5.5 Creating a Request

The pseudo-interface CORBA::ORB provides an operation to create Request objects. The operation create_request() returns a new Request pseudo-object. Visibroker and OrbixWeb provide the equivalent method on the object reference, CORBA.Object.

♦ IDL operation	Status create_request(in Context ctx, in Identifier operation, in NVList arg_list, inout NamedValueresult, out Requestrequest, in Flags req_flags);
♦ Visibroker method	`Request _create_request(` `Context ctx,` `String operation,` `NVList arg_list,` `NamedValue result` `) throws SystemException`

♦ OrbixWeb method

```
int _create_request(
    Context ctx,
    String operation,
    NVList arg_list,
    NamedValue result,
    CORBA.Request.Holder hrequest,
    Flags flags
) throws SystemException
```

The `ctx` parameter specifies the context of the Request. The `operation` parameter determines the name of the operation to be invoked. The `arg_list` parameter provides the arguments to that operation. The `result` parameter provides a type expected as the result of the operation. The `req_flags` and `flags` parameters indicate the memory management required for the out parameters. If set to `CORBA::OUT_LIST_MEMORY`, all memory associated with out parameters can be freed by the ORB when freeing the `arg_list`, otherwise it has to be freed explicitly. The newly created `Request` object is returned as the result of the Visibroker method, and in the `hrequest` parameter by the OrbixWeb method.

There is an additional pair of operations to create partially initialized `Request` objects:

♦ Visibroker method

```
Request _request(String operation)
        throws SystemException
```

♦ OrbixWeb method

```
Request _request(String operation)
```

All other parameters of the `Request` object must be set through the object's interface as described below.

5.6 Request Interface

The pseudo-interface Request is defined in the module CORBA. It is mapped to the Java interface `CORBA.Request`. The pseudo-interface defines the following operations. The add_arg() operation incrementally adds arguments of type NamedValue to the Request's parameter list (of type NVList).

♦ IDL operation

```
Status add_arg(
    in Identifier name,
    in TypeCode arg_type,
    in void     *value,
    in long     len,
    in Flags    arg_flags
);
```

♦ Visibroker method

```
NVList arguments() throws SystemException
```

♦ OrbixWeb method

```
int add_arg(
    String name,
    Any a,
```

```
        Flags arg_flags
) throws SystemException
```

OrbixWeb maps the operation in a straightforward way, using an Any to provide the argument's type and value. In addition OrbixWeb provides helper methods of the form insert*Type*() and extract*Type*() for basic types and template types containing basic types. These helper methods allow the programmer to avoid building NVLists and dealing with Anys. Visibroker, however, returns a reference to the NVList that the Request will use, and allows direct manipulation of the list using the NVList methods.

When the Request is correctly initialized it can be invoked by calling the invoke() operation:

◆ IDL operation	Status invoke(in Flags arg_flags);
◆ Visibroker method	void invoke() throws SystemException
◆ OrbixWeb method	int invoke() throws CORBAException

If the operation returns successfully, the result is set in the result field of the Request and the inout and out parameters have been modified in the Request's parameter list by the object implementation.

The operation delete() destroys the Request object. It is not mapped in Java, because it is not needed due to automatic garbage collection.

The operation send() allows an asynchronous Request to be made. The semantics are that the operation returns without waiting for the target object to invoke the operation. It is paired with the operation get_response() which allows the caller to check for results at a later time. The invoke_flags parameter may contain the flag CORBA::INV_NO_RESPONSE to indicate that operation is oneway, or that the caller expects no results in any case.

The send() operation is mapped to a pair of methods. The method send_oneway() is mapping for send() with the flag CORBA::INV_NO_RESPONSE. The method send_deferred() is the mapping for send() without this flag set.

◆ IDL operation	Status send(in Flags invoke_flags);
◆ Visibroker methods	void send_oneway() throws SystemException
	void send_deferred() throws SystemException
◆ OrbixWeb methods	int send_oneway() throws CORBAException
	int send_deferred() throws CORBAException

The operation result and any inout or out parameters won't be valid until the operation get_response() has been invoked and has returned. The operation get_response() receives the result as well as inout and out parameters from an operation invocation initiated by the send() operation.

◆ IDL operation	Status get_response(in Flags arg_flags);
◆ Visibroker methods	void get_response() throws SystemException
◆ OrbixWeb methods	int get_response() throws CORBAException

The methods block until the operation invocation initiated by the Request is complete.

Visibroker and OrbixWeb provide an additional method, `poll_response()`, which returns a boolean indicating whether or not the operation invocation is complete.

- ♦ Visibroker methods

```
boolean poll_response() throws
SystemException
```

- ♦ OrbixWeb methods

```
boolean poll_response() throws CORBAException
```

It returns `true` if the response to the asynchronous invocation is available, `false` otherwise. Note that `get_response()` must be called even if `poll_response()` returns `true`, since `get_response()` reads in the result values.

The CORBA specification provides an operation for making multiple Requests, send_multiple requests(), and a corresponding response operation get_next_response(). These operations are defined in C syntax.

The operations are mapped to the following Java methods provided in the `CORBA.ORB` class in both Visibroker and OrbixWeb. The method `send_multiple_requests_oneway()` sends all the Requests in its argument array, and the method `send_multiple_requests_deferred()` sends all of the Requests provided to it and returns.

- ♦ Visibroker methods

```
void send_multiple_requests_oneway(
    Request reqs[] ) throws SystemException
void send_multiple_requests_deferred(
    Request reqs[] ) throws SystemException
```

- ♦ OrbixWeb methods

```
int send_multiple_requests_oneway(
    Request reqs[] ) throws CORBAException
int send_multiple_requests_deferred(
    Request reqs[] ) throws CORBAException
```

The method `get_next_response()` blocks until a response to a deferred Request is available. The method `poll_next_response()` informs the caller if any invocations have completed.

- ♦ Visibroker methods

```
Request get_next_response()
    throws SystemException
boolean poll_next_response()
    throws SystemException
```

- ♦ OrbixWeb methods

```
int get_next_response(
    CORBA.Request.Holder
) throws CORBAException
boolean poll_next_response()
    throws CORBAException
```

The Visibroker method returns the Request on which a response has been received as the result of the `get_next_response()` method and OrbixWeb returns it in a Holder object.

6 *Dynamic Skeleton Interface*

The DII provides a mechanism to invoke operations from a client without compile-time knowledge about the interface. The DSI provides a similar mechanism for the other side, that is, the ORB can invoke an object implementation without compile knowledge about the interface, that is, without the skeleton. For an object implementation, calls via a compiler-generated skeleton and the DSI are not distinguishable.

The idea behind the DSI is to invoke all object implementations via the same general operation. This operation is provided by an interface of a pseudo-object, called `ServerRequest`, which is similar to the `Request` pseudo-object of the DII.

At the time of writing Visibroker for Java was the only Java ORB that supported this interface. All methods provided below are in the Visibroker `CORBA.ServerRequest` class.

6.1   ServerRequest Interface

The pseudo-IDL specification of `ServerRequest` provides the following operations. The operation op_name() returns the name of the operation that was invoked.

- ♦ IDL operation   Identifier op_name();
- ♦ Visibroker method   `String op_name() throws SystemException`

The operation ctx() provides the invocation Context of the operation.

- ♦ IDL operation   Context ctx();
- ♦ Visibroker method   `Context ctx() throws SystemException`

The params() operation returns the list of parameters passed to the invocation.

- ♦ IDL operation   void params(inout NVList params);
- ♦ Visibroker method   `void params(NVList params)`
  `            throws SystemException`

The result() operation returns the Any in which the result is to be placed.

- ♦ IDL operation   Any result();
- ♦ Visibroker method   `void result(Any result) throws`
  `SystemException`

Additionally, the Java interface provides the method

`void exception( Any exception ) throws SystemException,`

which allows the invocation to return an exception instead of a result.

7   *Context Interface*

A Context object contains a list of properties, pairs of names, and values. CORBA restricts values to type `string`. The intended role of context objects is similar to that of environment variables in various operating systems, which can determine a user's or an application's preferences. They could be defined for a system, for a user, or for an application. Context objects can be manipulated by concatenating their property lists or by arranging them into context trees.

Operations can be declared with a context by adding a context clause after the raises expression. A context is made available to the server by an additional argument to the stub and skeleton interfaces. When an operation with a context is invoked through either the stub or the DII, the ORB will insert the values of the properties of the specified context.

7.1   Creating a Context Object

Contexts are organized in trees. Each context has an internal reference to its parent context. The root context is the global default context. The pseudo-interface Context is mapped to Java interfaces and classes.

- ♦ IDL pseudo-interface   CORBA::Context
- ♦ Visibroker interface   CORBA.Context
- ♦ OrbixWeb class   CORBA.Context

The ORB pseudo-interface provides the operation get_default_context() to obtain the root context. The equivalent method in Visibroker and OrbixWeb is provided by the Java class CORBA.ORB.

- ♦ IDL operation   Status get_default_context(out Context ctx);
- ♦ Visibroker method   Context get_default_context()
                                      throws SystemException
- ♦ OrbixWeb method   Context get_default_context()

7.2   Manipulating a Context Object

The pseudo-IDL interface CORBA::Context provides operations to manipulate a context object. The operation set_one_value() sets the value of the named property.

- ♦ IDL operation
```
Status set_one_value(
    in Identifier prop_name,
    in string value
);
```

♦ Visibroker method

```
void set_one_value(
    String prop_name,
    Any value
) throws SystemException
```

♦ OrbixWeb method

```
int set_one_value(
    String prop_name,
    Any value
)
```

The value is supplied as an Any rather than a `String`. Note that NamedValues also have values of type `Any`.

The operation set_values() sets the values of those properties that are named in the `values` parameter.

♦ IDL operation

```
Status set_values( in NVList values );
```

♦ Visibroker method

```
void set_value( NVList values )
            throws SystemException
```

♦ OrbixWeb method

```
int set_value( NVList values )
```

Note that the flags of the items of the `NVList` must be 0 and that the TypeCode field of the values of the items must be `TC_String`.

Values can be read with the operation get_values().

♦ IDL operation

```
Status get_values(
    in Identifier start_scope,
    in Flags op_flags,
    in Identifier prop_name,
    out NVList value
);
```

♦ Visibroker method

```
NVList get_values(
    String start_scope,
    int op_flags,
    String prop_name
) throws SystemException
```

♦ OrbixWeb method

```
get_values(
    String start_scope,
    Flags op_flags,
    String prop_name,
    NVList.Holder hvalues
)
```

The prop_name parameter specifies the name of the returned properties. A string can specify multiple property names by using a naming convention with a wildcard "*" similar to the notations used in various operating system shells. The parameter start_scope determines the scope of this query within the context hierarchy. The naming of scopes is implementation dependent. The op_flags parameter can have the value CORBA::CTX_RESTRICT _SCOPE, which limits the scope to the specified start_scope. An empty flag uses the whole context tree. The `value` parameter carries the named properties, including their values contained in Anys. The output value is mapped as a return value in Visibroker and as a Holder object in OrbixWeb.

The operation delete_values() deletes the named properties from the Context object.

♦ IDL operation   `Status delete_values( in Identifier prop_name );`

♦ Visibroker method   `void delete_values( String name )`
                          `throws SystemException`

♦ OrbixWeb method   `int delete_values( String name )`
                          `throws SystemException`

Visibroker and OrbixWeb provide an additional method that returns the name of the context object.

♦ Visibroker method   `String context_name() throws SystemException`

♦ OrbixWeb method   `String context_name()`

7.3   Manipulating the Context Object Tree

There are additional operations on the context object to manipulate the context tree. The operation create_child() creates a new context object that is a child of the object on which the operation is invoked.

♦ IDL operation   `Status create_child(`
                        `in Identifier ctx_name,`
                        `out Context child_ctx`
                `);`

♦ Visibroker method   `void create_child(`
                    `String context_name,`
                    `Context parent`
              `) throws SystemException`

♦ OrbixWeb method   `int create_child(`
                    `String ctx_name,`
                    `Context.Holder hctx`
              `)`

The methods mapping this operation assign a parent context to an existing context which is obtained through the get_default_context() operation.

The operation delete() deletes the context object on which it is invoked. The del_flags parameter can take the value CORBA::CTX_DELETE_DESCENTS. If this flag is specified it causes the deletion of all descendent objects. If the flag is not specified and the object has children, an exception is raised.

♦ IDL operation   `Status delete( in Flags del_flags );`

Because of the garbage collection mechanisms in Java there is no need to implement this operation for Java ORBs.

There is, however, an additional method provided by both Visibroker and OrbixWeb that returns the parent context of the object. It returns `null` if the context is the global default context.

- ♦ Visibroker method   `Context parent() throws SystemException`
- ♦ OrbixWeb method   `Context parent()`

C H A P T E R

8

Discovering Services

This chapter provides an overview of the two most important CORBA Services for locating objects: the Naming Service, which finds objects by name, and the Trading Service, which finds objects by type and properties. This chapter also explains how ORBs name and locate servers and objects by using mechanisms proprietary to each ORB.

1 The CORBA Naming Service

The Naming Service locates object implementations and thus is a fundamental service for distributed object systems. This section is organized as follows:

- ♦ An overview and explanation of how to use the Naming Service
- ♦ An explanation of the interface specification in detail
- ♦ A programming example

1.1 Overview of the Naming Service

The Naming Service provides a mapping between a name and an object reference. Storing such a mapping in the Naming Service is known as *binding an object* and removing this entry is called *unbinding*. Obtaining an object reference that is bound to a name is known as *resolving the name*.

Names can be hierarchically structured by using contexts. Contexts are similar to directories in file systems and they can contain names as well as subcontexts.

The use of object references alone to identify objects has two problems. Object references are difficult for human users because they are opaque data types and their string form is a long sequence of numbers. When a service is restarted, its objects typically have new object references. However, in most cases clients want to use the service repeatedly without needing to be aware that the service has been restarted.

The Naming Service solves these problems by providing an extra layer of abstraction for the identification of objects. It provides

♦ *Readable object identifiers for the human user.* Users can assign names that look like structured file names.
♦ *A persistent identification mechanism.* Objects can bind themselves under the same name regardless of their object reference.

The typical use of the Naming Service involves object implementations binding to the Naming Service when they come into existence and unbinding before they terminate. A client resolves names, producing objects on which they subsequently invoke operations. Figure 8-1 illustrates this typical usage scenario.

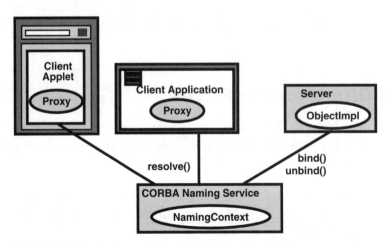

FIGURE 8-1. Typical use of the CORBA Naming Service.

1.2 Interface Specification

The central interface is called NamingContext and it contains operations to bind names to object references and to create subcontexts. Names are sequences of NameComponents. Naming Contexts can resolve a name with a single component returning an object reference. They resolve names with more than one component by resolving the first component to a subcontext and passing the remainder of a name on to that subcontext for resolution.

1.2.1 The Name Type

```
module CosNaming {

    typedef string Istring;

    struct NameComponent {
        Istring id;
        Istring kind;
    };

    typedef sequence <NameComponent> Name;
```

The type Istring is used to define the Name type for future compatibility with internationalized strings. At the time of writing this type was defined to be string. A NameComponent has two fields: id contains the string that will actually be matched when a name is resolved; kind is available for application-specific purposes and is not interpreted by the Naming Service.

The Name type is a sequence of component, or atomic, names and no syntax is given for the textual representation of names. This allows application programs to use separators such as the UNIX file system "/" character to separate components when printing names for users.

1.2.2 Bindings

```
// module CosNaming

enum BindingType {nobject, ncontext};

struct Binding {
    Name binding_name;
    BindingType binding_type;
};

typedef sequence <Binding> BindingList;
```

The type CosNaming::Binding provides a name and a flag of type BindingType. The value ncontext indicates that an object bound to a name is a NamingContext at whose interface further name resolution can take place. The value nobject means that the binding, even if to a NamingContext, cannot be used for further resolution.

1.2.3 Adding Names to a Context

There are two operations for binding an object to a name in a context, and two for binding another context to a name.

```
// module CosNaming

interface NamingContext {

// we elide the exceptions declared here

void bind(in Name n, in Object obj)
  raises(NotFound, CannotProceed, InvalidName, AlreadyBound);
void rebind(in Name n, in Object obj)
  raises(NotFound, CannotProceed, InvalidName);

void bind_context(in Name n, in NamingContext nc)
  raises(NotFound, CannotProceed, InvalidName, AlreadyBound);
void rebind_context(in Name n, in NamingContext nc)
  raises(NotFound, CannotProceed, InvalidName);
```

The bind() and bind_context() operations associate a new name with an object. In the case of bind_context() the object must be of type NamingContext. We will see how to create new contexts below. If the name used has more than one component, the NamingContext will expect that all but the last component refers to a nested context, and it will make the binding in the context which is resolved by the first part of the name. For example, consider Figure 8-2.

We use the "/" character as a separator for NameComponents. In our example we invoke the bind() operation on the NamingContext object we have called

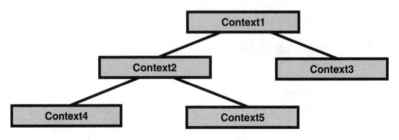

FIGURE 8-2. Naming context structure—before binding.

Context1 with the parameters Context2/Context5/MyName and some object reference. This results in a new atomic name, MyName, being bound to the object in the Context5 context (see Figure 8-3). The BindingType of the resulting binding will be nobject.

If we had invoked bind_context with the same parameters (although the object reference must be to a NamingContext) then the same situation would result. However, the BindingType will be ncontext, and the Context5 context will now be able to resolve names like MyName/x/y/z by passing the remainder, x/y/z, to the new MyName context.

The rebind() and rebind_context() operations act the same as bind() and bind_context(), but rather than raising an exception if the name already exists, they simply replace the existing object reference.

1.2.4   Removing Names from a Context

```
void unbind(in Name n)
   raises(NotFound, CannotProceed, InvalidName);
```

The single operation unbind() will remove a name and its associated object reference from a context or one of its subcontexts.

1.2.5   Name Resolution

```
Object resolve (in Name n)
   raises(NotFound, CannotProceed, InvalidName);
```

The resolve() operation behaves as follows:

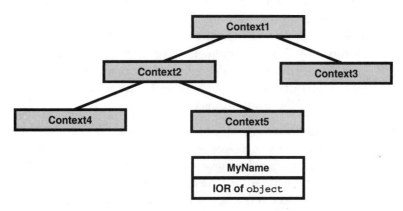

FIGURE 8-3.   Naming context structure—after binding.

- ♦ It resolves the first component of the name, n, to an object reference.
- ♦ If there are no remaining components then it returns this object reference to the caller.
- ♦ Otherwise it narrows the object reference to a NamingContext and passes the remainder of the name to its resolve() operation.

Implementations of the Naming Service will probably optimize this process so that the narrow() and resolve() operations are not called repeatedly. However, the result will logically be the same as that produced by the algorithm above.

1.2.6   Exceptions

Here are the exceptions elided above:

```
// interface NamingContext

enum NotFoundReason {missing_node, not_context, not_object};

exception NotFound {
  NotFoundReason why;
  Name rest_of_name;
};

exception CannotProceed {
  NamingContext cxt;
  Name rest_of_name;
};

exception InvalidName{};
exception AlreadyBound {};
exception NotEmpty{};
```

The NotFound exception may be raised by any operation that takes a name as an argument. It indicates that the name does not identify a binding. The Naming Service specification does not explain the meaning of the why member of this exception, but we make the following interpretation: At some stage of tracing the leading name components down to the context in which the final component is bound to a (possibly noncontext) object reference one of these situations occurs:

- ♦ A NameComponent does not exist in the context expected (missing_node).
- ♦ A leading NameComponent is bound to an object with a binding type of nobject rather than ncontext, or an ncontext binding is bound to an object of a type other than NamingContext (not_context).
- ♦ The object reference bound to a NameComponent denotes a destroyed object (not_object).

If this happens, the rest_of_name member returns the rest of the sequence from the unresolvable name onward. This is not explicitly specified in the Naming Service.

The CannotProceed exception returns a NamingContext object reference and a part of the original name. It indicates that the resolve() operation has given up, for example, for security or efficiency reasons. However, the client may be able to continue at the returned context. The rest_of_name member returns the part of the name that should be passed to the returned ctx context for resolution.

InvalidName indicates that the name is syntactically invalid. For example, it might contain a zero length NameComponent. The Names acceptable to different Naming Services may vary.

The AlreadyBound exception may be raised by bind operations. It informs the caller that a name is already used and cannot be overridden without using a rebind operation.

NotEmpty is an exception raised by the destroy() operation defined below. Contexts that still contain bindings cannot be destroyed.

1.2.7 Context Creation

There are operations to create new contexts defined with the NamingContext interface.

```
// interface NamingContext

NamingContext new_context();
NamingContext bind_new_context(in Name n)
    raises(NotFound, AlreadyBound, CannotProceed, InvalidName);
```

New NamingContexts may be created and later used alone or bound into other contexts using bind_context(). They can also be created with a particular name and bound in a single operation. The operation new_context() produces an empty NamingContext that can be used anywhere. The operation bind_new_context() also creates a new context, but binds it to a name in the context on which the operation is invoked. It can raise the usual exceptions for an operation that takes a name as an argument.

1.2.8 Context Destruction

When a context is no longer used and all the bindings it contained have been unbound it can be destroyed.

```
// interface NamingContext

void destroy()
    raises(NotEmpty);
```

The destroy() operation deletes a context as long as it contains no bindings. Be sure at the same time to remove any bindings that may refer to this context.

1.2.9 Browsing Contexts

NamingContexts support browsing of their contents by use of the list() operation.

```
// interface BindingIterator; has been forward declared

// interface NamingContext

void list ( in unsigned long how_many,
        out BindingList bl, out BindingIterator bi);

}; // end of interface NamingContext
```

The parameters of the list() operation allow the caller to specify how many bindings to return in a BindingList sequence. The rest will be returned through an iterator object referred to by the bi parameter, which will be a nil object reference if there are no further bindings.

1.2.10 Binding Iterators

A BindingIterator object will be returned if the number of bindings in a context exceeds the how_many argument value of the list() operation invoked on the context.

```
// module CosNaming

interface BindingIterator {
    boolean next_one(out Binding b);
    boolean next_n( in unsigned long how_many,
                    out BindingList bl);
    void destroy();
};
}; //end of module CosNaming
```

The next_one() operation returns a binding and TRUE if there are remaining bindings. The Naming Service specification is ambiguous about whether it will return FALSE if this is the last binding in the iterator or whether it will return FALSE on the next call.

The next_n() operation returns a sequence of at most how_many bindings in the out parameter bl. It also returns FALSE if there are no further bindings to be iterated over. It is not specified whether the FALSE value is returned with the last binding or on the next call.

The destroy() operation allows the iterator to deallocate its resources and it renders the object reference invalid. Iterators may sometimes be implemented so that they time out or are deleted on demand for resource recovery.

1.2.11   The Names Library

The Naming Service also defines some Pseudo-IDL for a names library. This is a set of operations intended to ease the creation and manipulation of names. To our knowledge it has not been implemented in any Naming Service product, and so we will omit details of this part of the specification.

We have found that users typically type in strings to nominate objects. In our examples we use a Java class library, which allows the use of strings in a convenient syntax to access the Naming Service.

1.3   Using the Naming Service from a Java Client

This subsection contains some of the methods for an EasyNaming class that will be used in Chapter 9. This class allows applications to obtain a stringified object reference to a NamingContext and then to use string arguments with the "/" character as a name separator to identify objects relative to that context. This example is implemented using the Visibroker language binding.

First let's look at the declaration of the class, its private fields, and constructor:

```
public class EasyNaming {

    private CosNaming.NamingContext root_context;

EasyNaming( CORBA.ORB orb, String ior_string ) {

    try {
        CORBA.Object obj = orb.string_to_object( ior_string );
        root_context = CosNaming.NamingContext_var.narrow( obj );
        System.out.println("Root context:");
        System.out.println( orb.object_to_string( root_context ));
        System.out.println("");
    }
    catch(CORBA.SystemException corba_exception) {
        System.err.println(corba_exception);
    }

}
```

We expect an ORB reference and a stringified object reference as constructor arguments. The reference is then turned into a live object reference, and after narrowing this is stored in the `root_context` private field. We then output the stringified form of the context IOR or any exception which is raised.

We define a method called `str2name()` that takes a UNIX file name string format (always starting with a "/" character, as all names are relative to our root context) and produces a CosNaming::Name, which is mapped to a Java array of `CosNaming.NameComponent`. The method's signature is defined below, and the implementation of the class `EasyNaming` can be found in Appendix C.

```
public CosNaming.NameComponent[] str2name( String str )
    throws CosNaming._NamingContext.InvalidName
```

The `EasyNaming` class provides methods equivalent to the operations on naming contexts, but accepts string arguments. The `bind_from_string()` and `rebind_from_string()` methods also allow the use of names that refer to nonexistent contexts and create subcontexts as necessary. This allows us to exercise the bind() or rebind() operations, as well as resolve(), to check the existence of a subcontext, and bind_new_context() to create the subcontexts that don't already exist. This is how we implement `bind_from_string()`:

```
public void bind_from_string( String str, CORBA.Object obj )
    throws
    CosNaming._NamingContext.InvalidName,
    CosNaming._NamingContext.AlreadyBound,
    CosNaming._NamingContext.CannotProceed,
   CosNaming._NamingContext.NotFound, CORBA.SystemException {

 CosNaming.NameComponent[] name = str2name( str );
 CosNaming.NamingContext context = root_context;
 CosNaming.NameComponent[] _name = new CosNaming.NameComponent[1];

   try {
       root_context.bind( name, obj );
   }

catch( CosNaming._NamingContext.NotFound not_found ) {
  // bind step by step

  // create and bind all non-existent contexts in the path
  for( int i = 0; i < name.length - 1; i++ ) {
    _name[0] = name[i];
    try {
       // see if the context exists
       context = CosNaming.NamingContext_var.narrow(
         context.resolve( _name ) );
       System.out.println("Resolved " + _name[0].id);
    }
```

```
catch( CosNaming._NamingContext.NotFound nf ) {
    System.out.println("Creating " + _name[0].id);
    // if not then create a new context
    context = context.bind_new_context( _name );
}
// let other exceptions propagate to caller
}

    // bind last component to the obj argument
    _name[0] = name[ name.length - 1 ];
    context.bind( _name, obj );
}
// let other exceptions propagate to caller
}
```

First the `str` argument is converted to a Naming Service name and an attempt is made to bind the `obj` argument using the bind() operation. If one of the contexts in the name path is not found, the method bind_from_string() descends the context hierarchy one NameComponent at a time. If a component resolves correctly to a context then that context is used to test the name of the next component. If the resolve() operation fails then the name component is used to create a new subcontext. This continues until the final component, which is then bound in the final subcontext to the referenced object passed as an argument.

2   *Trading Service*

The Trading Service has its basis in the ISO Open Distributed Processing (ODP) standards. The trader work in this group had reached a Draft International Standard (DIS) level within ISO when responses were due for OMG's Object Services RFP 5. The submitters to the RFP were mostly people who had been working on the ODP standard, which enabled the convergence of the trading standards from both groups. Even though ODP uses OMG IDL as an interface specification language, implementations of ODP standards may use any technology. However, the common underlying semantics of the two efforts greatly enhances the prospects for future cross-platform interworking.

2.1   Overview of Trading

Traders are repositories of object references that are described by an interface type and a set of property values. Such a description of an interface is known as a *service offer.* Each service offer has a *service type,* which is a com-

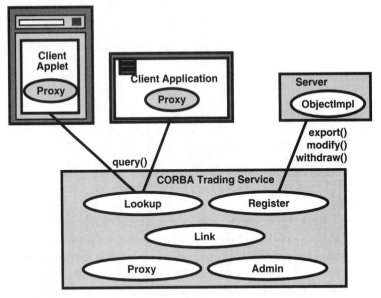

FIGURE 8-4. Typical use of a CORBA Trading Service.

bination of the interface type of the object being advertised and a list of properties that a service offer of this service type should provide values for.

An *exporter* is a service, or some third party acting as an agent for the service, that places a service offer into a trader. That service offer can then be matched by the trader to some client's criteria. A client that queries a trader to discover a service is called an *importer*. An importer provides the trader with a specification of a service type and a constraint expression over the properties of offers of the type which describes the importer's requirements.

A long-standing example of a trading scenario is that of printing services. Currently system administrators configure new printers in a network by providing a unique name for a new device and then notifying potential users by e-mail, news, or notice board. Each user must then remember the printer's name and type it into a dialog box in an application. A better way to discover new printers is to allow applications or users to provide their requirements to the application, which then sends the print job to the most appropriate printer. This is achieved as follows:

♦ We must first assume that new printers are provided with an implementation of a standard printing interface, specified in IDL, for example,

```
interface Printer {
    typedef string filename;
```

```
        exception PrinterOffLine {};

        void print_file(in filename fn)
            raises(PrinterOffLine);

        short queue_length()
            raises(PrinterOffLine);
    };
```

♦ This simple interface will be replaced by CORBA's Printing Common Facility once its RFP process is completed.

♦ Then we must define a service type, *PrinterST*, that nominates the Printer interface and a number of property names and types. For example, the printer's location, its language (ASCII, PostScript, HP Laser Jet, etc.), its resolution in DPI, its color properties, its print queue length, and its name.

♦ Each printer is then advertised by exporting a service offer to the trader. For convenience we will refer to the example printers below by their "name" property:

Property	*Value*
building	"A Block"
floor	2
language	postscript
resolution	150
color	black
queue_len	——> [PrinterObjectRef]->queue_length
name	"12ps"

Property	*Value*
building	"A Block"
floor	3
language	postscript
resolution	300
color	black
queue_len	——> [PrinterObjectRef]->queue_length
name	"monster"

Property	*Value*
building	"A Block"
floor	7
language	postscript
resolution	150
color	256color
queue_len	——> [PrinterObjectRef]->queue_length
name	"rib"

♦ Applications now configure print requests based on user preferences from a user's environment, a dialog box, or a text query. This results in a constraint expression that can be passed to the trader in an import query. For example,

```
building == "A Block" && floor <= 5 && language == postscript.
```

♦ This query would result in matching two printers ("12ps" and "monster"). The query can ask for the resulting service offers to be ordered according to a *preference expression*. This provides the matched service offers in order based on some minimal, maximal, or boolean expression. For example,

```
max resolution.
```

The `queue_len` property is what is called a *dynamic property*, which means that its value is not stored but looked up each time a query is made. So we would probably have a default preference criterion of `min queue_len`. This would sort the printers that are returned so that we print to the one that matches the constraint expression *and* has the shortest queue.

Let's imagine that a new color printer is installed in block A and that it is higher in resolution than the "rib" printer. All users who want high resolution will have this maximized in their preferences, and when they next require a color printer the new printer is automatically selected when their application does an import. If, on the other hand, a new printer is installed on floor 1 of the building, then people who used to walk upstairs to collect printouts will have their ordinary black-and-white postscript print jobs directed to the new printer on their floor, without having to change their environment, or even know the name of the printer. In this way they will be informed of a new device as soon as they trade for a printer and the new one meets their requirements.

Of course it is hard to set requirements and preferences when you don't know what is available. Some applications that regularly use the Printer interface will have browsers built in to allow users to see all available printers and their properties by querying the trader with a simple constraint such as `building == "A Block"`.

2.1.1 Service Types and Service Offers

Service types are templates from which service offers are created. They ensure that groups of services that offer the same interface and have the same nonfunctional considerations are grouped together. This allows efficient searching and matching of service offers in the trader. Most importantly, it allows exporters and importers to use the same terminology (property names) to describe a common set of features so that expressions written in terms of those properties will always be evaluated correctly.

2.1.2   *Export and Lookup of Service Offers*

Any program may export a service offer to a trader if it has an object reference to some application object and knowledge of the implementation behind the reference so that it can describe the properties of that object. Often services will advertise themselves by exporting a service offer.

Any client that is complied using a set of IDL stubs for a particular interface may assign any valid object reference to a variable at run time and execute operations on that object. As new implementations of servers become available, a client may wish to select objects based on proximity, quality of service, or other characteristics. To do this, it formulates a constraint expression in terms of the property names of a service type. This expression determines which service offers of that type match the client's requirements.

A client may also ask a trader to sort the matching service offers based on some preference expression that emphasizes the values of particular properties. The trader will return a sorted list of matching service offers and the client will then use the object reference extracted from one of these.

2.1.3   *Trader Federation*

Each trader contains a database of service offers which it searches when it receives an import request. It may also store a number of *links* to other traders to which it can pass on queries to reach a larger set of service offers. Links are named within a trader and consist of an object reference to the Lookup interface of another trader, as well as some rules to determine when to use the link to satisfy an importer's request. Traders that are linked in this manner are said to be interworking or *federated*.

Federated queries are import requests passed from one trader via its links to other traders, and perhaps by them to other traders and so forth. These queries can be constrained by policies passed in by the initial importer, by the policies of each trader, and by the rules stored in the links themselves.

2.2   Overview of the Trading Service Interfaces

In this section we give an overview of the specification of the CORBA Trading Service. The specification includes the following interface definitions:

- Service Type Repository
- Trader Components
- Lookup
- Iterators
- Register
- Link
- Admin
- Proxy
- Dynamic Properties

2.2.1   Service Type Repository

We have seen the importance of service types in the scenario presented earlier in this chapter. If a service offer does not provide an object reference of a known type then it is impossible for an importer to invoke operations on the object references it gets back. If a service offer's property names and types vary then the constraint and preference expressions that express the requirements of an importer will fail to match relevant service offers. For example, if one service offer for a Printer described its floor via the property (`"Floor"`, `"ground"`), and another as the property (`"level"`, `4`), then it would be impossible to compare them for proximity.

Service types are stored in the Service Type Repository. A service type consists of a name, an interface type, and a set of property specifications. A property specification gives the name and TypeCode of properties that will occur in service offers of this type. Properties are also given modes which allow them to be specified as read-only and/or mandatory. Read-only properties may not be modified after export. Mandatory properties must be included in a service offer to be accepted as an instance of this service type.

The data types and operations for the Service Type Repository are contained in the CosTradingRepos::ServiceTypeRepository interface. We will list the data types, but omit the definitions of the operations to add, remove, and look-up service types in the repository. Most traders will implement a compiler for a service type language (for which there is no standard syntax) and browsing tools to enable importers to compose queries to a trader without needing to write clients to the Service Type Repository. The only type needed when actually using a trader is ServiceTypeName, which is a string.

```
typedef sequence <CosTrading::ServiceTypeName> ServiceTypeNameSeq;
```

```
enum PropertyMode {
    PROP_NORMAL, PROP_READONLY,
    PROP_MANDATORY, PROP_MANDATORY_READONLY
};
```

```
struct PropStruct {
    CosTrading::PropertyName name;
    CORBA::TypeCode value_type;
    PropertyMode mode;
};

typedef sequence <PropStuct> PropStructSeq;

typedef CosTrading::Istring Identifier; //IR::Identifier

struct IncarnationNumber {
    unsigned long high;
    unsigned long low;
};

struct TypeStruct {
    Identifier if_name;
    PropStructSeq props;
    ServiceTypeNameSeq super_types;
    boolean masked;
    IncarnationNumber incarnation;
};
```

Substitutability of Service Types   Service types, like IDL interfaces, are substitutable via an inheritance relationship. For IDL interfaces this simply means that all the attributes and operations defined in the base interface become part of the derived interface. However, in service types there are three aspects to substitutability:

◆ The interface type of a derived service type may be a subtype of the interface type in the base service type.
◆ The property set may be extended in a derived service type with new property names (and their associated type and mode specifications).
◆ Inherited properties may be "strengthened." That is, nonmandatory properties may be made mandatory, and modifiable properties may be made read-only. However, the data type of an inherited property must remain the same.

When an importer queries the trader it may receive service offers of a subtype of the requested service type, in the same way that object references to subtypes of a required interface type may be passed where a base type is required.

The masked member of the TypeStruct allows service types to be declared as abstract base service types. The incarnation member is assigned an increasing index so that queries on service type definitions can be restricted to those that were defined after some other service type which has a lower incarnation number.

2.2.2 TraderComponents—Finding the Right Interface

The trader defines five separate interfaces:

- ◆ Lookup, where importers make queries.
- ◆ Register, where exporters advertise new service offers.
- ◆ Link, where links to federated traders are administered.
- ◆ Admin, where policies of the trader are administered.
- ◆ Proxy, where legacy mechanisms for advertising services are added so that they look like service offers.

A single interface TraderComponents is inherited by all the interfaces listed above. This allows users to locate the other interfaces supported by a particular trader implementation.

```
interface TraderComponents {
    readonly attribute Lookup lookup_if;
    readonly attribute Register register_if;
    readonly attribute Link link_if;
    readonly attribute Proxy proxy_if;
    readonly attribute Admin admin_if;
};
```

2.2.3 Lookup

The Lookup interface is used by importers to find service offers that meet their needs. It offers a single operation, query(), that requires a specification of the service type and matching constraint expression and returns a list of service offers. The signature for query() is significantly more complex than this simple explanation would indicate:

```
void query (
    in ServiceTypeName type,
    in Constraint constr,
    in Preference pref,
    in PolicySeq policies,
    in SpecifiedProps desired_props,
    in unsigned long how_many,
    out OfferSeq offers,
    out OfferIterator offer_itr,
    out PolicyNameSeq limits_applied
) raises (
    IllegalServiceType,
    UnknownServiceType,
    IllegalConstraint,
    IllegalPreference,
    IllegalPolicyName,
    PolicyTypeMismatch,
    InvalidPolicyValue,
```

```
    IllegalPropertyName,
    DuplicatePropertyName,
    DuplicatePolicyName
);
```

The third parameter, pref, is a minimizing, maximizing, or boolean sorting expressing that tells the trader which matched offers to return first.

The policies parameter allows the importer to influence the way in which the trader searches its service offers and the way in which it propagates the query to other traders. Often query invocations will be given an empty PolicySeq because the trader administrator will configure the trader to allow a trade-off between search space and resource usage that will deliver appropriate services to users.

A desired_props argument must be provided so that the trader knows whether to return properties of the service offers that matched or simply the object references to the services. The SpecifiedProps type is defined as follows:

```
enum HowManyProps { none, some, all };

union SpecifiedProps switch ( HowManyProps ) {
    case some: PropertyNameSeq prop_names;
};
```

Sometimes a service type will contain many properties that do not interest a particular importer. In this case the importer will need to specify in the prop_names field of the desired_props which property values to return. In many cases the choice to ignore the property values or to require all the values is sufficient.

The how_many parameter specifies that the importer wishes to receive a certain number of offers back in the form of a sequence (in the offers out parameter). The remainder of the offers will be obtained through an iterator, whose object reference is returned in the offer_itr out parameter. Typically importers are interested in one of these:

◆ Getting back a small number of offers so that they can ensure that one service is actually available at the time.
◆ Examining a large number of service offers for direct comparison outside the trader.

In the first case an importer may save the trader the time and resources of creating an iterator by specifying a policy called return_card. This policy instructs the trader only to return the number of matching service offers specified by the policy. If its value is the same as the how_many argument no iterator will be created. The creation of policies is dealt with later in this chapter.

2.2.4 Iterators

An iterator is an object that controls a logical list of objects or data items and can return them to a client a few at a time. We use the term logical list because the object supporting the iterator may produce new items for the list as they are required. This is a common style used in many OMG specifications. In the trader two iterators are specified:

- OfferIterator is used when a large number of service offers are returned from the Lookup::query operation.
- OfferIdIterator is used to return all of the OfferIds held in a particular trader from the Admin::list_offers operation.

They have essentially the same interface, so we will look at only one of them here.

```
interface OfferIterator {

    unsigned long max_left (
    ) raises (
        UnknownMaxLeft
    );

    boolean next_n (
        in unsigned long n,
        out OfferSeq offers
    );

    void destroy ();
};
```

The max_left() operation provides an upper bound on the number of offers that the iterator contains. If the offers are being constructed a few at a time, then the upper bound may not be easily calculated, so the UnknownMaxLeft exception will be raised. The next_n() operation will return up to *n* offers in the offers out parameter, and a return value of FALSE indicates that no other offers are contained in the iterator. Although the trader may clean up iterators from time to time to reclaim resources, responsible clients will call destroy() on iterators as soon as they have extracted enough offers.

2.2.5 Register

The Register interface provides operations for advertisers of services. The most important operations are

- export()—advertises a service offer in the trader and returns an identifier for it.

- withdraw()—removes an identified service offer from the trader.
- describe()—returns the properties of an identified service offer.
- modify()—allows an exporter to change the values of non-read-only properties of a service offer.

The other operations allow exporters to withdraw all service offers matching a particular query and to obtain the Register interface of a linked trader by name.

```
OfferId export (
        in Object reference,
        in ServiceTypeName type,
        in PropertySeq properties
) raises (
        InvalidObjectRef,
        IllegalServiceType,
        UnknownServiceType,
        InterfaceTypeMismatch,
        IllegalPropertyName, // e.g. prop_name = "<foo-bar"
        PropertyTypeMismatch,
        ReadonlyDynamicProperty,
        MissingMandatoryProperty,
        DuplicatePropertyName
);
```

The export() operation takes three parameters that describe a service and places that service offer in the trader's database for return as a result of an importer's query. The reference parameter must contain an object reference of the type specified in the service offer named by the second parameter, type. The properties parameter must contain a value for each mandatory property in the service type and may contain values for other properties. All values provided for property names specified in the service type must be of the property type specified, and additional properties of any other name and type may also be included. Any non-read-only property value may be replaced by a structure of the following type:

```
struct DynamicProp {
        DynamicPropEval eval_if;
        TypeCode returned_type;
        any extra_info;
};
```

This will cause the property's value to be determined at import time, which means that the constraint will be evaluated on up-to-date information. The printer example above has a property that reflects the length of the current print queue. The eval_if member is an object reference to a standard interface that has a single operation to return an Any. The returned_type member is the type of the value expected in that Any and must match the type specified for this property in the service type.

The exceptions that may be returned are mostly self-explanatory. The ReadonlyDynamicProperty exception indicates that it is illegal for a read-only property to change after export.

The withdraw() operation passes the trader an OfferId returned from a previous export() and the trader removes the corresponding service offer from its database.

```
void withdraw (
    in OfferId id
) raises (
    IllegalOfferId,
    UnknownOfferId,
    ProxyOfferId
);
```

The other withdraw operation, withdraw_using_constraint(), will remove all service offers that match a particular expression. This should generally only be used by the administrator.

The describe() operation returns an OfferInfo structure corresponding to the id parameter. OfferInfo contains exactly the same information as the three parameters to export(): an object reference, a service type, and a sequence of properties.

```
struct OfferInfo {
    Object reference;
    ServiceTypeName type;
    PropertySeq properties;
};

OfferInfo describe (
    in OfferId id
) raises (
    IllegalOfferId,
    UnknownOfferId,
    ProxyOfferId
);
```

The modify() operation allows exporters to change the properties contained in a particular service offer. Some traders do not allow the modification of service offers and will raise the NotImplemented exception. Traders that implement this operation must succeed on all modifications, or fail on all. Properties listed in the del_list parameter will be deleted if possible, and property values in modify_list will replace current values in the identified service offer, if this is allowed. The reasons the operation may fail are reflected in its long raises clause. In short, the two list parameters may be inconsistent, or the caller may be trying to modify something read-only or delete something mandatory.

```
void modify (
    in OfferId id,
    in PropertyNameSeq del_list,
    in PropertySeq modify_list
) raises (
    NotImplemented,
    IllegalOfferId,
    UnknownOfferId,
    ProxyOfferId,
    IllegalPropertyName,
    UnknownPropertyName,
    PropertyTypeMismatch,
    ReadonlyDynamicProperty,
    MandatoryProperty,
    ReadonlyProperty,
    DuplicatePropertyName
);
```

The resolve() operation is for obtaining a reference to the Register interface of another trader, to which this trader has a named link. This is how one exports service offers to and withdraws them from federated traders.

```
Register resolve (
    in TraderName name
) raises (
    IllegalTraderName,
    UnknownTraderName,
    RegisterNotSupported
);
```

2.2.6 Link

Links can be considered a specialization of service offers. They advertise other traders that can be used to perform federated queries. The Link interface therefore looks much the same as the Register interface, with operations to add and remove as well as describe and modify links. Each link has four associated pieces of information: its name, its object reference (to a Lookup interface), and two policies on link following. Most users of traders do not need to know what links a trader has or how they are followed. The trader administrator sets up link policies and trader defaults.

2.2.7 Admin

The Admin interface contains a large number of operations to set the policies of a trader and operations to list the OfferIds of service offers contained in the trader. Ordinary trader users can query the attributes of the other interfaces to determine the current policies of a trader, but will never need to use the Admin interface. Some traders will not even offer this interface since all policies are determined by the implementation.

2.2.8 *Proxies and Dynamic Properties*

Proxies are objects that sit alongside service offers but hide some legacy mechanism of service creation or discovery. Most traders will not support the Proxy interface. Traders that do return identical results from a proxy as from a normal service offer.

Dynamic properties are a mechanism to allow a service to provide a property value at import time that reflects the current state of the service. We have seen in the explanation of the export operation above that the value of a non-read-only property may be replaced by a DynamicProp structure. This will cause the trader to call back to an interface supported by the service (or some associated server) to obtain the property value when the constraint expression of a query is being evaluated. The object reference provided in that structure must be of the following interface type:

```
interface DynamicPropEval {

    any evalDP (
        in CosTrading::PropertyName name,
        in TypeCode returned_type,
        in any extra_info
    ) raises (
        DPEvalFailure
    );
};
```

When evaluating a dynamic property, the trader invokes the evalDP() operation of the eval_if member of the DynamicProp, passing the property name and the returned_type and extra_info members of the structure. It receives an appropriate value in return.

The evaluation of a query that involves calling back to several services to determine the dynamic value of a property can be very costly, and some traders will not support dynamic properties, as indicated by the SupportAttributes::supports_dynamic_properties boolean attribute. However, for some services the information is invaluable for determining their suitability for a purpose. For example, a printer that is one floor up from me and has a zero-length queue is much more useful than one in the same room that has thirty jobs queued or is out of toner.

2.3 Finding an Object using a Trader

In this section we use OrbixWeb to implement a simple Java application client that trades for a suitable Printer interface to send its print job to. We have used the DSTC trader implementation. Since it was not incorporated into ORB products at the time of writing, the ORB bootstrap resolve_initial_reference() could not be used to obtain a reference to a trader by passing it the string TradingService. Instead, the application uses a helper class called IORFile that reads an IOR from a file and produces a string that we can pass the ORB::string_to_object() operation. The implementation of the IORFile class can be found in Appendix C. The application is implemented as a class PrintClient, in which we implement a single method, main(). The application expects two mandatory and two optional arguments:

♦ A name of the file where the IOR to a CosTrading::Lookup object is stored.
♦ The name of the file we wish to print.
♦ A constraint expression to select suitable printers.
♦ A preference expression to order the printer service offers returned.

The structure of the application is as follows:

♦ The class usage is checked for the appropriate number of arguments.
♦ We obtain a reference to a Lookup.Ref object.
♦ The command-line arguments to the application are processed.
♦ Some basic policies for a trader query are established.
♦ The query is made.
♦ The returned Printer.Ref objects are tried in order until one successfully prints the file.

Let's look at the code starting with the imported classes, the PrintClient class definition, and command line argument check:

```
import IE.Iona.Orbix2._CORBA;
import IE.Iona.Orbix2.CORBA.*;
import IE.Iona.Orbix2.CORBA.UserException;
import IE.Iona.Orbix2.CORBA.SystemException;
import IE.Iona.Orbix2.CORBA.Any;
import IE.Iona.Orbix2.CORBA.Object.*;
import java.lang.String;

public class PrintClient {

  private static final boolean IIOP = true;

  public static void main(String args[]) {
```

```
if( args.length < 2 || args.length > 4 ) {
    System.out.println( "usage: PrintClient trader_ior_file \
printfile [constraint [preference]]");
    System.exit( 1 );
}
```

The variable IIOP is declared so that OrbixWeb's Any class can be initialized to marshal its contents for IIOP rather than the Orbix protocol. The application exits if it has not been run with the two mandatory arguments.

The next piece of code declares some variables and then obtains a reference to the trader's Lookup interface.

```
// some general purpose variables
Any policy_any;
if(IIOP)
    policy_any = new Any(_CORBA.IT_INTEROPERABLE_OR_KIND);
else
    policy_any = new IE.Iona.Orbix2.CORBA.Any();
IE.Iona.Orbix2.CORBA.Object.Ref obj;

// get reference to trader lookup interface
CosTrading.Lookup.Ref my_lookup = null;
try {
    IORFile ior_file = new IORFile( args[0] );
    obj = _CORBA.Orbix.string_to_object( ior_file.get_ior_string() );
    my_lookup = CosTrading.Lookup._narrow( obj );
}
catch(IE.Iona.Orbix2.CORBA.SystemException se) {
    System.err.println("CORBA System Exception: " + se);
    System.exit(1);
}
```

The IORFile class opens and reads the file given as a command-line argument and produces a string for use with the ORB's string_to_object() method. In the case of OrbixWeb, this is a static method of the Orbix class. We then narrow the reference obtained and catch any exceptions.

The next step is to prepare the query for a printer. We use any constraint and preference strings received from the command line and provide suitable defaults when they are not provided.

```
// determine the constraint
String constr;
if( args.length > 2 )
    constr = args[2];
else
    constr = "";

// determine the prefs
String prefs;
```

```
if (args.length > 3 )
    prefs = args[3];
else
    // if no preference, compare the offers for shortest queue
    prefs = "min queue_len";
```

An empty constraint string will match all service offers of the right type. If the user does not supply a preference, then we use a default that orders the returned printers by shortest queue length. Now we set parameter values and some policies which will ensure that we get a reasonable result.

```
// set some basic policies
CosTrading.PolicySeq query_pols = new CosTrading.PolicySeq(2);

//declare variables needed in the query()

short num_offers = 3;
String service_type = "PrinterST";
CosTrading.PolicyValue policy_value;
CosTrading.PropertyNameSeq desired_prop_names;
CosTrading.Lookup.SpecifiedProps desired_props = null;
CosTrading.OfferSeq return_offers = new CosTrading.OfferSeq();
CosTrading.OfferIterator.Holder iter =
    new CosTrading.OfferIterator.Holder();
CosTrading.PolicyNameSeq limits =
    new CosTrading.PolicyNameSeq();
```

We will ask for at most three offers, as this provides a reasonable likelihood of one being operational. This value is used in the policy return_card, which specifies the maximum number of service offers to return from a query. If we then pass the same value to the query() operation's how_many parameter we can ensure that all of the results will come back in the offers out parameter and we will not have to process an iterator. Because the initialization of the policy values requires the use of Anys, we must use a try block to catch CORBA System Exceptions:

```
try {
    // we want at most 3 offers back
    policy_any.insertShort( num_offers );
    policy_value = new CosTrading.PolicyValue(policy_any);
    query_pols.buffer[0] =
        new CosTrading.Policy("return_card", policy_value);
```

The other policy we will pass to the trader is use_dynamic_properties, which tells the trader to evaluate the queue_len property dynamically so that the value used is up to date.

```
    // we want to use dynamic props to find printer queue length
    policy_any.insertBoolean(true);
```

```
policy_value = new CosTrading.PolicyValue(policy_any);
query_pols.buffer[1] =
    new CosTrading.Policy("use_dynamic_properties", policy_value);
```

The desired_props parameter to query() lists the property names whose values we want returned with the query result. For easy processing in this example we will ask for only the printer name, which assumes that users of our application know their printers by name. A more advanced printing application would probably ask for all the properties and provide the user with information on the location of printers, which would enable new printers to be discovered by location.

```
    // we want back only the name property
    desired_prop_names = new CosTrading.PropertyNameSeq(1);
    desired_prop_names.buffer[0] = "name";
    desired_props = new CosTrading.Lookup.SpecifiedProps();
    // the value of CosTrading.Lookup.HowManyProps.some is 1
    desired_props.prop_names(desired_prop_names, (int) 1);
}
catch (IE.Iona.Orbix2.CORBA.SystemException se) {
    System.err.println("Query param initialization failed: " + se);
    System.exit(1);
}
```

The SpecifiedProps type is a union, so we must initialize its value and discriminator. The enum value CosTrading.Lookup.HowManyProps.some is the discriminator used when specifying a partial list of properties to be returned. We use the method prop_names() to set the value of this field of the union, providing the discriminator value at the same time. As usual we catch any System Exceptions.

Having created objects or variables for each of the parameters to the query() method, we can now invoke it:

```
// make a query
try {
    my_lookup.query( service_type,
                     constr,
                     prefs,
                     query_pols,
                     desired_props,
                     num_offers,
                     return_offers,
                     iter,
                     limits);
}
```

Since we have set the value in policy return_card to the value of num_offers (the size of the sequence we are prepared to accept back in the out `return_offers` object) we can ignore the iterator. We also ignore the feedback from the trader about what policy restrictions it applied to our query, which are returned in the `limits` object. This time we must catch the user exceptions as well as any System Exceptions. Rather than catching each of the ten possible user exceptions that the query() operation could raise, we will catch the base class of all of these, `CORBA.UserException`.

```
// catch exceptions
catch (IE.Iona.Orbix2.CORBA.UserException ue) {
    System.err.println("Query failed - User Exception: " + ue);
    System.exit(1);
}
catch (IE.Iona.Orbix2.CORBA.SystemException se) {
    System.err.println("Query failed: " + se);
    System.exit(1);
}
```

Having received a response from the trader we will now attempt to use the service offers to print the file. This is done by entering a loop that exits once the print_file() operation has successfully been invoked on one of the objects returned in a service offer. First we declare and initialize some variables, including a string and an Any to extract the printer's name from the single returned property in each service offer.

```
// send job to printer
int i = 0;
boolean printed = false;
String pname = "";

Any return_any;
if(IIOP)
    return_any = new Any(_CORBA.IT_INTEROPERABLE_OR_KIND);
else
    return_any = new IE.Iona.Orbix2.CORBA.Any();
```

Then we enter the loop.

```
// we'll try all the returned printers until one works
while (i < return_offers.length - 1 && !printed) {
    try {
        return_any =
            return_offers.buffer[i].properties.buffer[0].value;
        pname = return_any.extractString();
        Printer.Ref printer =
            Printer._narrow(return_offers.buffer[i].reference);
        printer.print_file( args[1] );
        printed = true;
        System.out.println("File " + args[1] +
          " sent to printer " + pname);
    }
```

If the string extraction from `return_any` and the narrow of the reference are both successful, we attempt to print the file named in the second command-line argument. If the `print_file()` call succeeds, the termination variable is set to true, a message is printed, and the loop will exit. Other possibilities are that the printer is off-line or that the invocation fails for some other reason.

```
catch (Printer.PrinterOffLine pol) {
    System.out.println("Printer " + pname + " offline!");
}
catch (IE.Iona.Orbix2.CORBA.SystemException se) {
    System.out.println("Printer " + pname +
                            " raised: " + se);


}
i++;
}
}
}
```

Any failures to print are notified to the user and the next printer is tried.

This is an example of how we might run the application:

```
.../Print> java PrintClient trader.ior myfile.ps \
    'language == "postscript" && floor < 4'
```

Our constraint expression expresses our need for a postscript printer somewhere on the lower floors of our building. We do not specify a preference, as the default preference for the shortest print queue length is suitable. The execution above may result in the following output:

```
Printer 12ps offline!
File myfile.ps sent to printer monster
```

2.3.1 Possible Enhancements to the PrintClient

The example exercises the query() operation, demonstrates how to pass policies and how to specify the properties we want back, and shows how to extract the returned property values. However, it does not deal with the situation where no service offers match the constraint expression.

A more sophisticated printer query might look up the user's default printer constraint expression and preferences from a file if none were supplied on the command line. It could also check that at least one working printer offer is returned, and if not, it could make a less-specific query with an empty constraint string to match all available offers of the service type.

In the case where the first attempt fails, it could query for all printers and ask for all of their properties to be returned, then display a list and allow the user to select an appropriate printer. This would require that the `return_card` policy not be set and that an iterator be used, since the number of offers returned would be unpredictable. When making a query that might match a large number of offers it is often best to set the how_many argument to zero and to have a single loop to process the iterator. This avoids having two loops, one for the returned sequence of offers and other to invoke the next_n() operation on the returned iterator reference.

3 *Proprietary Object Location*

Each of the three Java ORBs considered in this book has a nonstandard way of naming and locating objects. Since most ORBs do not yet implement the bootstrap operations list_initial_services() and resolve_initial_references() in the CORBA::ORB interface, it may be necessary for CORBA clients to use one of the following mechanisms to obtain an object reference to a Naming Service context or a trader Lookup interface. However, in the interest of vendor independence and portability of application code we recommend that their use be kept to a minimum.

The remainder of this section introduces the naming mechanisms of Visibroker, OrbixWeb, and Joe. Since the mechanisms introduced here are uniform across the product suites of the vendors that implement them, Java ORB access to CORBA objects implemented in other languages will rely on using the equivalent mechanism in another ORB in the same family. We do not provide any details on how this is achieved, and the reader is referred to the product documentation.

3.1 Visibroker

Visibroker's mechanism for naming objects requires the object implementer to assign names at instantiation time, which registers the object implementation with Visibroker's Smart Agents. The client of the object can then use knowledge of these names to *bind* to the objects.

The Visibroker-generated skeleton classes all have a constructor that accepts a string called _iName, which is the implementation name for a particular object, assigned by the object implementer. This name is then used by object clients to obtain a reference to an object of a particular type by using the bind() methods generated in the _var class for that interface type. Let's have a look at an example constructor for an implementation of an interface X:

```
class Ximpl extends _sk_X {
    // constructor
    Ximpl( String bind_name ) {
        super( bind_name );
    }
```

The object created using this constructor will now be accessible to any client that uses the X_var class. The client has to pass the same name to a bind() method on that class. There are four variants of the bind() method,

```
public static X bind() throws CORBA.SystemException.
```

The first, parameterless, version will select an object of the correct type at random.

```
public static X bind(String name) throws CORBA.SystemException
```

The second version finds an object of type X which registered itself under the name name.

```
public static X bind(String name, String host)
    throws CORBA.SystemException
```

This bind() method works the same as the second version but is restricted to finding implementations on the host machine.

```
public static X bind(String name,
                     String host,
                     CORBA.BindOptions options)
    throws CORBA.SystemException
```

The final version allows the client to specify options by creating an object of class CORBA.BindOptions and updating its boolean fields:

- ♦ defer_bind—do not make a connection to the target object until the first invocation.
- ♦ enable_rebind—reconnect to the target object if the connection is lost.

3.2 OrbixWeb

OrbixWeb also has a *bind* mechanism, which is a way of allowing clients access to servers by names assigned to them in the Implementation Repository. Servers can also name their objects by assigning *markers* to them. These become a part of their object references.

The Orbix Implementation Repository is maintained by the *Orbix daemon,* which is responsible for launching servers as their objects are required. The daemon supports an IDL interface, IT_daemon, which allows servers' names to be associated with executable code. Iona supplies utility programs which invoke its operations. The most important of these utilities is called putit. An example C++ server registration for a server that creates objects of type x with markers listed on the command line is as follows:

```
putit Xserver "/local/orbix_servers/bin/Xserver myObject"
```

OrbixWeb also supplies a utility called jrunit which allows Java servers to be launched. It takes a class name, a class path, and class arguments from its command line and runs the class on a Java virtual machine. Here is an example of how to register a similar Java server for x objects.

```
putit JXserver "/OrbixWeb/bin/jrunit X \
        /local/orbix_servers/classes:/local/classes myObject"
```

Orbix servers create object references by storing the following components into the *reference data* (or *object key*) section of an IOR or an Orbix native object reference:

♦ The server name (as registered with the Implementation Repository).
♦ A unique identifier, or *marker,* for the individual object to which the reference refers.

The combination of a server name and marker uniquely identify each object that an Orbix daemon is responsible for activating. The machine name and port number through which the daemon is contacted is also stored in an IOR.

Orbix then makes servers and objects available to clients by generating an extra static method on each object reference (*interface-name*.Ref) class. This method is called _bind(), and has three signatures. For example, for interface X the following methods are generated in class X.Ref.

```
public static final X.Ref _bind()
    throws IE.Iona.Orbix2.CORBA.SystemException
```

The simplest version of _bind() will use the local Orbix configuration to find a server of the same name as the interface type on which the method is called. Its use is not recommended.

```
public static final X.Ref _bind(String markerServer)
    throws IE.Iona.Orbix2.CORBA.SystemException
```

The second version, which has a single parameter named markerServer, expects a string with a colon separating the name of an object's marker and the name of a server in the implementation repository.

```
public static final X.Ref _bind(String markerServer, String host)
    throws IE.Iona.Orbix2.CORBA.SystemException
```

The final version of `_bind()` is the same as the second, except that it may contact the Orbix daemon on a remote machine.

There are a number of ways of using the `markerServer` parameter. If the marker is left empty this allows any object of the correct type to be selected. Here are some example `markerServer` arguments and the objects they denote:

markerServer argument	*Description*
`":Xserver"`	Any object of the correct type that runs in "Xserver"
`"myObject:JXserver"`	The object with the marker "myObject" in the same server
`"Xserver"`	An error

The Orbix Naming Service has not yet been integrated into Orbix, and so the CORBA::ORB::resolve_initial_references operation does not yet return a NamingContext when given the parameter `CosNaming`. However, there is a distinguished marker/server name, `root:NS`, for a starting context for use with the `CosNaming.NamingContext._bind()` method.

3.3 Joe Proprietary Naming

Joe provides a number of methods in its applet class `sunw.joe.JoeApplet` that access the NEO Naming Service. A discussion of all the proprietary features of the NEO naming service is outside the scope of this book. It is a full implementation of the CORBA Naming Service, but it duplicates the functionality with different argument types used to describe object names. This interface is similar to the UNIX file system interface using string names instead of the CosNaming::Name type. It also has a current naming context, which can also be set using a string.

The two methods of interest in class `sunw.joe.JoeApplet` are called `find()` and `resolve()`. They have a number of overridden definitions for different levels of complexity.

3.3.1 The `find()` Method

The `find()` method is used to search for an atomic name in a number of predefined NEO naming contexts. The method `find()` has two definitions as follows:

```
public ObjectRef find(String serviceName)
      throws SystemException, UserException

public ObjectRef find( String serviceName,
                       int searchType,
                       boolean developmentMode)
      throws SystemException, UserException
```

First let's look at the possible arguments to the second version of `find()`:

- `serviceName`–the string name of the desired object.
- `searchType`–controls the order of search in the workspace. One of
  `MERGE`–tries a sequence of contexts to find the name requested.
  `MACHINE`–tries a context dedicated to per-machine services.
  `USERS`–tries a context dedicated to per-user services.
  `CUSTOM`–allows the user to set a search path using the `setSearchPath()` method.
- `developmentMode`–a Boolean flag indicating whether development status is active. A `true` value for this flag makes `find()` look in development subcontexts of the contexts it would otherwise look in.

Calling the simpler version of `find()` with a name string `nstr` is equivalent to calling `find(nstr, MERGE, false)`.

Be warned that the nondevelopment mode is not a useful default, as the NEO environment uses the development mode unless directed otherwise. This means that NEO servers are likely not to be found with a call to the simple `find()`.

3.3.2   The `resolve()` Method

The `resolve()` method in the `sunw.joe.JoeApplet` class allows access to objects in the NEO naming service by specifying a UNIX-style string path name relative to the current context. This context is set by the `setContext()` method, which assumes a NEO root context. The resolve method has two signatures, which differ only in allowing separators between names in a path to be something other than the default "/" character.

```
public ObjectRef resolve(String serverPath)
    throws SystemException, UserException

public ObjectRef resolve(String serverPath,
                         String separator)
    throws SystemException, UserException
```

This method is equivalent to the CosNaming operation of the same name, except that the name to be resolved is in string form and the starting context is part of the state of the JoeApplet object, set by the setContext() method.

The NEO Naming Service supports all of the standard functionality of the CORBA Naming Service, but these are used from the class CosNaming.NamingContextRef.

C H A P T E R

9

Building Applications

In this chapter we will explain how to build applications using Java ORBs. We have selected a simple room-booking system as an example. Since we want to demonstrate CORBA features rather than to prove that we can implement a sophisticated booking system, we have kept the application-specific semantics simple. But as will be seen in the IDL specification, we have chosen a very fine-grain object model which allows the creation of many CORBA objects and the demonstration of invocations between them. We will also demonstrate the use of the CORBA Naming Service.

We chose to use Visibroker for Java to implement this example because, at the time of writing, it was the only ORB providing a full Java language binding including the server side.

The chapter covers the development of an entire application including:

♦ Interface specification
♦ Implementing objects
♦ Implementing a server
♦ Implementing a factory
♦ Clients as applications and applets

1 *Application Specification*

The room-booking system allows the booking of rooms and the cancellation of such bookings. It operates over one-hour time slots from 9 AM to 4 PM. To keep things simple we do not consider time notions other than these slots, that is, days or weeks. The rooms available to the booking system are not fixed; the number of rooms and the names of the rooms can change. When booking a room, a purpose and the name of the person making the booking should be given. We do not consider security issues and anyone can cancel any booking.

The following key design decisions were made:

◆ A Room is a CORBA object.
◆ A Meeting object defines a purpose and the person responsible for the meeting.
◆ A Meeting Factory creates meeting objects.
◆ A Room stores Meetings indexed by time slots.
◆ Rooms have a name and register themselves under this name with the naming service.

Figure 9-1 illustrates a typical configuration of the Room-Booking system. There are three room servers which all have a Room object implementation. There is also a Meeting Factory server which has created a Meeting Factory object. The meeting factory has created several Meeting objects which are in the same process space (controlled by the meeting factory server). There is also a Naming Service which has various Naming Context objects forming a context tree. The Room and the Meeting Factory object implementations are registered with the Naming Service.

1.1 IDL Specification

The IDL specification of the room-booking system is contained in a module. It contains a number of interface specifications: Meeting, MeetingFactory, Room.

The interface Meeting has only two attributes: purpose and participants which are both of type string and both readonly. The attributes describe the semantics of a meeting.

Meeting objects are created at run time by a Meeting Factory which is specified in the interface MeetingFactory. It provides a single operation, CreateMeeting(), that has parameters corresponding to the attributes of the Meeting object and returns an object reference to the newly created Meeting object.

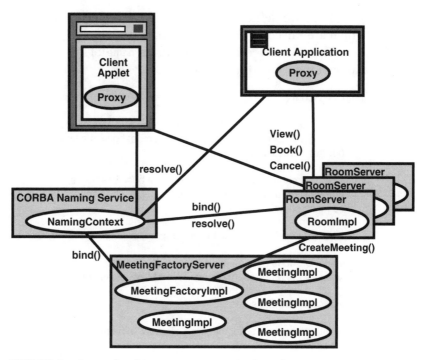

FIGURE 9-1.   Room-booking system—a typical configuration.

```
module RoomBooking {

    interface Meeting {

        // A meeting has two read-only attributes which describe
        // the purpose and the participants of that meeting.

        readonly attribute string purpose;
        readonly attribute string participants;
    };

    interface MeetingFactory {
        // A meeting factory creates meeting objects.
            Meeting CreateMeeting( in string purpose, in string participants);
    };
```

Within the specification of the interface Room, we start with the definition of some data types and a constant. There is the enum Slot which defines the time slots in which meetings can be booked. The constant MaxSlots, of type short, defines the number of the slots. The following typedef Meetings defines an array of length MaxSlots of meeting objects.

Then we define two exceptions, NoMeetingInThisSlot and SlotAlreadyTaken, which are raised by the specified operations.

There is also a readonly attribute name of type string which carries the name of the room, for example, `Board Room`.

```
interface Room {

    // A Room provides operations to view, make and cancel bookings.
    // Making a booking means associating a meeting with a time-slot
    // (for this particular room).

    // Meetings can be held between the usual business hours.
    // For the sake of simplicity there are 8 slots at which meetings
    // can take place.

    enum Slot { am9, am10, am11, pm12, pm1, pm2, pm3, pm4 };

    // since IDL does not provide means to determine the cardinality
    // of an enum, a corresponding constant MaxSlots is defined.

    const short MaxSlots = 8;

    // Meetings associates all meetings of a day with time slots
    // for a room.

    typedef Meeting Meetings( MaxSlots );

    exception NoMeetingInThisSlot {};
    exception SlotAlreadyTaken {};

    // The attribute "name" names a room.
```

There are three operations defined in the interface Room. The operation View() returns Meetings, the previously defined array of meeting objects. The meaning is that a meeting object reference indicates that this meeting is booked into the indexed slot. A null object reference means that the indexed slot is free.

The operation Book() books the meeting a_meeting in the slot a_slot of the room object on which the operation is invoked. The operation raises the SlotAlreadyTaken exception if there is already a meeting booked into the specified slot.

The operation Cancel() removes the meeting at the slot a_slot. It raises the NoMeetingInThisSlot exception if there is no meeting in the slot.

1.2 Compiling the IDL Specification

When we compile the IDL specification with Visibroker's compiler, idl2java, the compiler generates the following files containing Java interfaces and classes. There are six files per IDL interface containing two interfaces and four classes. Additionally, there are classes for constants, data types, and exceptions defined within the IDL interface Room which are in the Java package _Room. The files and directories are

```
RoomBooking:

Meeting.java                        _sk_Meeting.java
Meeting_var.java                    _st_Meeting.java
MeetingOperations.java              _tie_Meeting.java

MeetingFactory.java                 _sk_MeetingFactory.java
MeetingFactory_var.java             _st_MeetingFactory.java
MeetingFactoryOperations.java       _tie_MeetingFactory.java

Room.java                           _sk_Room.java
Room_var.java                       _st_Room.java
RoomOperations.java                 _tie_Room.java

RoomBooking/_Room:

SlotAlreadyTaken.java               SlotAlreadyTaken_var.java
NoMeetingInThisSlot.java            NoMeetingInThisSlot_var.java
MaxSlots.java                       Slot.java
Meetings_var.java
```

2 *Implementing Objects*

The objects we have to implement are Meeting and Room. We use the inheritance approach, that is, an object implementation class extends the skeleton class generated by the compiler.

2.1 Implementing the Meeting Object

We implement the meeting object in a class MeetingImpl which extends the skeleton class RoomBooking._sk_Meeting. We define two private variables purpose and participants which correspond to the attributes with the same names. The constructor has two parameters that are used to initialize those two private variables.

```
// MeetingImpl.java

class MeetingImpl extends RoomBooking._sk_Meeting{

    private String purpose;
    private String participants;
```

```
// constructor
MeetingImpl( String _purpose, String _participants) {

    // initialize private variables
    purpose = new String( _purpose );
    participants = new String( _participants );
}
```

IDL attributes are mapped to Java methods, an accessor method, and a modifier method (if not readonly). Since the attributes of the interface Meeting are readonly we only have to implement the accessors. Their implementation is straightforward; they just return the value of the corresponding private variable.

```
// attributes
public String purpose() throws CORBA.SystemException {
    return purpose;
}

public String participants() throws CORBA.SystemException {
    return participants;
}
}
```

2.2   Implementing the Room Object

The Room object is implemented in the class RoomImpl, again extending the corresponding skeleton class RoomBooking._sk_Room. We declare two private variables, name to hold the name of the Room object, and meetings to hold the array of booked meetings.

Within the constructor we copy the constructor's only parameter, determining the name of the room to be created, into our private variable room.

```
// RoomImpl.java

class RoomImpl extends RoomBooking._sk_Room {

    private String name;
    private RoomBooking.Meeting[] meetings;

    // constructor
    RoomImpl( String name ) {
        this.name = new String( name );
        meetings =
            new RoomBooking.Meeting[ RoomBooking._Room.MaxSlots.value ];
    }
```

As introduced in Chapter 6, Visibroker's language binding maps IDL bounded arrays to Java arrays. However, it is the application programmer's responsibility to initialize the array with the length defined in the IDL. The ORB only provides a run-time check to ensure that the specified boundaries hold. Our variable meetings is such a bounded array. We use the constructor to initialize it appropriately. The length of the array is defined in the specification of the interface Room as a constant MaxSlots. This constant is mapped to a class variable value of the class MaxSlots.

```
// MaxSlot.java

package RoomBooking._Room;

final public class MaxSlots{
    final public static short value = (short)8;
}
```

The package RoomBooking._Room indicates that the constant is defined within the interface Room in the module RoomBooking.

The attribute name is read-only and hence only the accessor method needs to be implemented. It returns the value of the corresponding private variable.

```
// attributes
public String name() throws CORBA.SystemException {
    return name;
}
```

The operations of the IDL interface are mapped to Java methods. The implementation of the method View() is rather straightforward. It returns the array meetings which holds the object references to the currently booked meetings.

```
// methods
public RoomBooking.Meeting[] View() throws CORBA.SystemException {
    return meetings;
}
```

The method Book() has two parameters, one of which determines the slot in which a meeting should be booked and the second of which determines the meeting. Note that elements of an IDL enum are mapped to type int.

We check if the slot is empty, that is, if the object reference indexed by the slot is nil. This is defined in CORBA as Object_NIL and the pseudo-interface CORBA::Object provides a corresponding operation is_nil() as introduced in Chapter 7. Visibroker, however, does not implement this operation directly. Instead, a comparison with the Java nil object null can be made. If the slot is empty we assign the meeting to the slot, otherwise we raise the exception `RoomBooking._Room.SlotAlreadyTaken`. The class for the exception is defined in the package `RoomBooking._Room` since the corresponding IDL exception was defined in the interface Room.

```
public void Book( int slot, RoomBooking.Meeting meeting )
    throws CORBA.SystemException,
    RoomBooking._Room.SlotAlreadyTaken {

    if( meetings[slot] == null ) {
            meetings[slot] = meeting;
    }
    else {
        throw new RoomBooking._Room.SlotAlreadyTaken();
    }
    return;
}
```

The method `Cancel()` is implemented similarly. We check if the slot is not empty and if not we assign a null object to the slot. Otherwise we raise the exception `RoomBooking._Room.NoMeetingInThisSlot`.

```
  public void Cancel( int slot )
      throws CORBA.SystemException,
      RoomBooking._Room.NoMeetingInThisSlot {

      if( meetings[slot] != null ) {
          meetings[slot] = null;
      }
      else {
          throw new RoomBooking._Room.NoMeetingInThisSlot();
      }
  }
}
```

3 Building Servers

To instantiate the object implementations and to make them available to clients we have to implement a server. A server is the operating system process in which object implementations exist. There can be one server per object or a server can handle multiple objects. A server has four fundamental tasks:

- ♦ Initialize the environment, that is, get references to the pseudo-objects for the ORB and the BOA
- ♦ Create objects
- ♦ Notify the BOA about the existence of those objects
- ♦ Execute the dispatch loop to wait for invocations

Additional tasks can include the registration of the objects with the Naming Service or the Trading Service. Alternatively, those tasks can be done by the objects themselves, for example, within the constructor.

The server `RoomServer` does the four fundamental tasks and registers the newly created room with the Naming Service. This is achieved by defining a class `RoomServer` and implementing its method `main()`. We define two strings that are used when registering the room object with the Naming Service. Then we check that the number of arguments is correct and exit the program if it is not. We expect one argument determining the name of the room object.

To use the naming service successfully, objects that want to share information via the naming service have to agree on a naming convention. For this example we use the following convention, which is also illustrated in Figure 9-2. Under a root context we have a context "BuildingApplications" which contains two contexts called "Rooms" and "MeetingFactories", respectively. We bind room objects into the context `Rooms` and the meeting factory object into the context "MeetingFactories". Following this convention will ensure that clients can locate the appropriate objects. Note that the Trading Service provides a more formal approach to categorization based on service types (see Chapter 8).

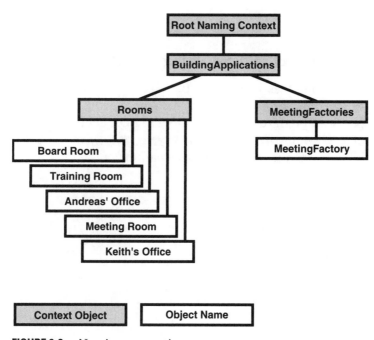

FIGURE 9-2. Naming convention.

According to this naming convention we initialize the variable `context_name` with a corresponding string version of the room context name.

3.1 Initializing the ORB

The first task is to initialize the ORB and the BOA. To get a reference to the ORB with Visibroker for Java, we call the class method `init()` on the class `CORBA.ORB`. We call `BOA_init()` on the ORB pseudo-object `orb`. This returns a reference to a BOA object.

```
// RoomServer.java

import java.io.*;

public class RoomServer {

    public static void main(String[] args) {

        String context_name, str_name;

        if( args.length != 1 ) {
            System.out.println("Usage: java RoomServer room-name");
            System.exit( 1 );
        }

        context_name = new String("/BuildingApplications/Rooms/");
```

3.2 Creating an Object and Notifying the BOA

The second task is to create the object. We create an instance of the class `RoomImpl` and provide the name as a parameter to the constructor. Then we perform the third task; we notify the BOA about the existence of the room object. We invoke the method `obj_is_ready()` on the BOA and provide the reference to the room object as a parameter.

```
try {
    //initialise ORB
    CORBA.ORB orb = CORBA.ORB.init();

    // initialise BOA
    CORBA.BOA boa = orb.BOA_init();

    // create the Room object
    RoomImpl room = new RoomImpl( args[0] );

    // notify the BOA
    boa.obj_is_ready(room);
```

3.3 Registering with the Naming Service

The next step is to register the object with the Naming Service. To do this we need a reference to a Naming Service, that is, to a root context. The CORBA way to get this reference, in the Visibroker Java language binding, is

```
CosNaming.NamingContext initial_context =
    CosNaming.NamingContext_var.narrow(
    orb.resolve_initial_reference("NamingService") );
```

which returns a reference to an initial NamingContext as `CORBA.Object`, which is then narrowed to the right interface type.

At the time of writing, Visibroker had not yet implemented this method for `NamingService` (only for `InterfaceRepository`). So we need to use a poor man's approach to bootstrap the access to a Naming Service. When starting our Naming Service it writes its stringified IOR to standard output and is then stored in a file named `CosNaming.ior`. By standardizing the file name we achieve a similar effect to `resolve_initial_reference()`. We hide all the file handling in a class `IORFile`. Its constructor reads the stringified object reference from the file. The only method in this class, `get_ior_string()`, returns the stringified IOR.

The class `EasyNaming` provides a convenient interface to the Naming Service, as explained in detail in Chapter 8. Its constructor obtains an initial context of a Naming Service via a stringified IOR. The class `EasyNaming` handles simple names including contexts in a notation similar to the notation of file names in various operating systems:

```
/<context1>/<context2>/.../<contextn>/<name>
```

It parses strings in this format and creates proper names of type **CosNaming::Name**, which maps to `CosNaming.NameComponent[]` in Visibroker. We initialize such a string in the variable `str_name`, for example, with a value `/BuildingApplications/Rooms/Board Room`. We bind the room object to the name corresponding to this string by calling `bind_from_string()` on the object `easy_naming`.

```
// register with naming service
// get IOR for Naming Service from file
IORFile ior_file = new IORFile("CosNaming.ior");

EasyNaming easy_naming =
    new EasyNaming( orb, ior_file.get_ior_string() );

str_name = context_name + args[0];

easy_naming.bind_from_string( str_name, room );
```

3.4 Entering the Dispatch Loop

The fourth task of the server is to enter an infinite loop by calling `impl_is_ready()` on the BOA to wait for incoming invocations.

Finally, we catch exceptions. If an exception of type `CosNaming._NamingContext.AlreadyBound` is raised, we realize that a room with our room's name is already registered with the Naming Service. For any exception that is raised we print the exception and exit.

```
      // wait for requests
      boa.impl_is_ready();
  }
  catch( CosNaming._NamingContext.AlreadyBound already_bound ) {
      System.err.println("Room " + context_name + args[0] +
          " already bound.");
  }
  catch(CORBA.UserException ue) {
      System.err.println(ue);
  }
  catch(CORBA.SystemException se) {
      System.err.println(se);
  }
  System.err.println("exiting ...");
  }
}
```

4 Building Factories

A factory is an object implementation running in a server. The difference from ordinary objects is the special semantics of a factory; it provides methods to dynamically create objects. It performs the same initialization of new objects as a server's `main()` method, that is, it creates objects and notifies the BOA about their existence.

The process of building factories contains the following same steps as building any other server:

◆ Implementing the object
◆ Implementing the server

4.1 Meeting Factory Object Implementation

The meeting factory implementation, the class `MeetingFactoryImpl` is an extension of the corresponding skeleton class `RoomBooking._sk_MeetingFactory`. We declare two private variables for the ORB and the BOA references. The constructor initializes the ORB and BOA.

```
// MeetingFactoryImpl.java

class MeetingFactoryImpl extends RoomBooking._sk_MeetingFactory {

    private CORBA.ORB orb;
    private CORBA.BOA boa;

    // constructor
    MeetingFactoryImpl() {

        try {
            // initialise ORB
            orb = CORBA.ORB.init();

            // initialise BOA
            boa = orb.BOA_init();
        }
        catch(CORBA.SystemException e) {
            System.out.println(e); }
    }
```

The only method of the meeting factory `CreateMeeting()` is shown below. Its parameters correspond to those of the constructor of the meeting object `MeetingImpl()`. We pass the parameters to this constructor which creates a new instance of a meeting object, `new_meeting`. Once the object is created we notify the BOA of its existence and return the reference of the created object.

```
    // method
    public RoomBooking.Meeting CreateMeeting(
        String purpose, String participants )
        throws CORBA.SystemException {

        MeetingImpl new_meeting =
            new MeetingImpl(purpose, participants);

        try {
            boa.obj_is_ready( new_meeting );
        }
        catch(CORBA.SystemException e) {
            System.out.println(e); }
        return new_meeting;
    }
}
```

4.2 Meeting Factory Server

The meeting factory server follows the same pattern as the room server. We initialize the ORB and the BOA, create the meeting factory object, and notify the BOA.

```
// MeetingFactoryServer.java

import java.io.*;

public class MeetingFactoryServer {

    public static void main(String[] args) {

        String str_name;

        if( args.length != 0 ) {
        System.out.println("Usage: java MeetingFactoryServer");
        System.exit( 1 );
        }

        str_name = new String(
            "/BuildingApplications/MeetingFactories/MeetingFactory");

        try {
            //initialise ORB
            CORBA.ORB orb = CORBA.ORB.init();

            // initialise BOA
            CORBA.BOA boa = orb.BOA_init();

            // create the MeetingFactory object
            MeetingFactoryImpl meeting_factory =
                new MeetingFactoryImpl();

            // notify the BOA
            boa.obj_is_ready(meeting_factory);
```

In the meeting factory server we use the Naming Service differently from how we use it in the room server. Instead of binding a name to the object reference we *rebind* it. This means that when there is already an object bound to the name we have chosen, we override the old binding. We use the method `rebind_from_string()` of the class `EasyNaming` which calls `rebind()` on the naming context.

```
// register with Naming Service
// get IOR for Naming Service from file
IORFile ior_file = new IORFile("CosNaming.ior");

EasyNaming easy_naming =
    new EasyNaming( orb, ior_file.get_ior_string() );

// rebind the new meeting factory
easy_naming.rebind_from_string( str_name, meeting_factory );
```

We finish by calling `impl_is_ready()` to wait for incoming invocations and catch exceptions.

```
        // wait for requests
        boa.impl_is_ready();
    }
    catch(CORBA.UserException ue) {
        System.err.println(ue);
    }
    catch(CORBA.SystemException se) {
        System.err.println(se);
    }
  }
}
```

5   Bootstrap Support

As we have already mentioned, the CORBA bootstrap mechanism provided by the operation resolve_initial_references() had not been fully implemented by Visibroker at the time of writing. We have implemented a helper server which does the bootstrapping. It is the CORBA version of the Java class IORFile that we introduced earlier. It allows access to a stringified object reference beyond file system boundaries. Figure 9-3 illustrates the two approaches.

Our bootstrap application is specified in the IDL interface RemoteIORFile:

```
module IORFile {

    interface RemoteIORFile {

        string get_ior_string();
    };
};
```

The implementation is straightforward: the named file is opened, the stringified object reference is read, and it is returned by the operation get_ior_string(). The complete code is listed in Appendix C.

Clients will use Visibroker's bind mechanism to connect to an object implementing the RemoteIORFile interface.

6   Starting Servers

Starting the server requires the following steps:

♦ *Start helper server for applet client bootstrapping.*
```
> java RemoteIORFileServer CosNaming.ior &
```
♦ *Start meeting factory server.*
```
> java MeetingFactoryServer &
```

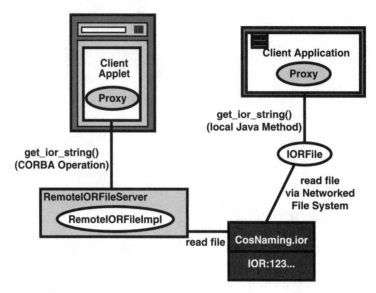

FIGURE 9-3. Bootstraping mechanisms.

♦ *Start room servers.*

```
> java RoomServer "Board Room" &
> java RoomServer "Training Room" &
> java RoomServer "Meeting Room" &
> java RoomServer "Andreas' Office" &
> java RoomServer "Keith's Office" &
```

7 *Building Clients*

Clients can be implemented as Java applications or applets. The differences between the two kinds of client are

- ♦ *Different initialization of GUI.* When using Java's AWT classes to build a GUI, the class `java.awt.Component` is the base class from which any GUI class is derived. The Applet class `java.applet.Applet` is an extension of the Component class and can be used directly to create a user interface. The GUI for an application is based on the class `java.awt.Frame`, which is also an extension of the Component class. An application programmer, however, has to take care of the thread control by implementing the interface `java.lang.Runnable`.
- ♦ *Different initialization of the ORB.* As we discussed in Chapter 4, Java applications use IIOP directly. Because of the current applet security model, Applets can only use IIOP when communicating with objects

running on the same host as the HTTP server from where the applet
was downloaded. Visibroker provides HTTP tunneling (see Chapter 4)
and the GateKeeper to communicate with objects regardless of their
location and to overcome firewall restrictions.

◆ *Access of the classes.* An application accesses application-specific and
CORBA classes from the local file system, for example, as specified by
the environment variable CLASSPATH. Applets and CORBA classes are
loaded via a network. Netscape browsers from Netscape ONE have
built in Visibroker's CORBA classes.

The parts of a client that are independent of the kind of client are separated into a class RoomBookingClient which is implemented later in this chapter. That leaves the tasks of creating an object of the class RoomBookingClient
and catching and processing user events to the applet and application
classes. In the following subsections we have a look at the applet- and
application-specific classes and explain the class RoomBookingClient. The
implementation of the applet and the client as application are presented later
in this chapter.

Figures 9-4 to 9-7 illustrate our GUI in various stages of its use. The figures will help you understand the code in the following subsections.

Figure 9-4 shows the initial state of a client that is viewing a booking
system containing four bookings made previously by other clients. The figure shows the applet client.

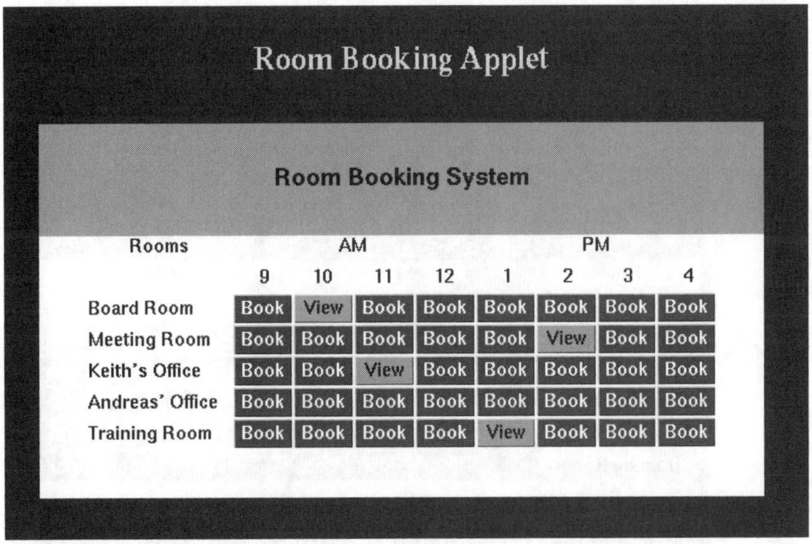

FIGURE 9-4. Applet—initial state.

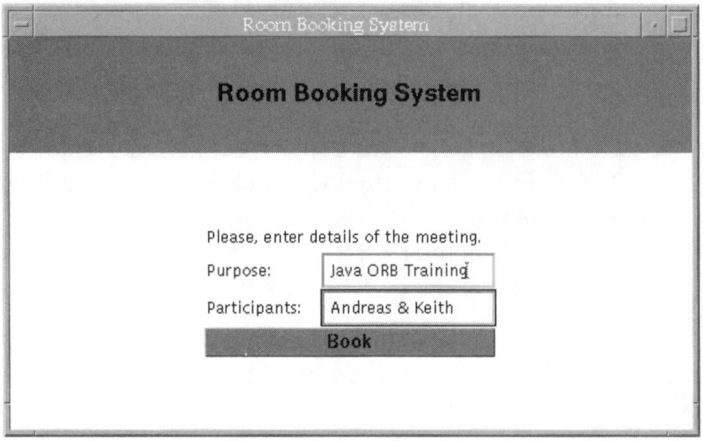

FIGURE 9-5. Application—booking form.

Figure 9-5 shows the action that takes place after the user has clicked a button labeled "Book" for the Training Room's 9 AM time slot. The user has entered the relevant data into the text fields. This is a view of the Java application version of the client.

Figure 9-6 shows the application after the booking is made.

Figure 9-7 shows the form produced by clicking the "View" button for the same meeting slot.

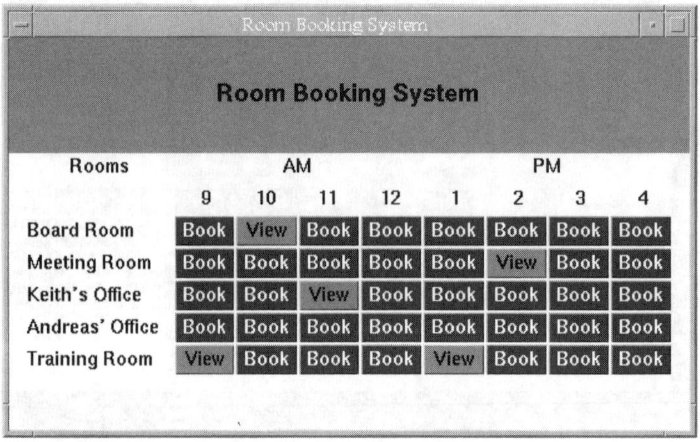

FIGURE 9-6. Application—view after booking.

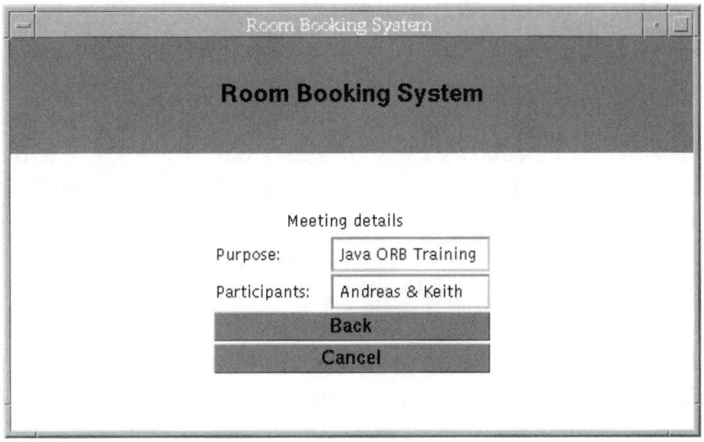

FIGURE 9-7. Application—cancel form.

7.1 Client as Applet

The first thing we have to do to develop the applet is to write an HTML page that anchors it. We give the page a title and a header and put the applet in the middle of the page. The applet class is RoomBookingApplet and we reserve a display area of a certain size.

```
<html>
<header>
<title>
Room Booking Applet
</title>
<BODY BGCOLOR=15085A TEXT=FFD700 LINK==FFFFFF VLINK=FFFFFF ALINK=FFFFFF>
<center>
<pre>

</pre>
<h1>
Room Booking Applet
</h1>
</center>
<pre>

</pre>
<center>
<applet code=RoomBookingApplet.class width=600 height=300>
</applet>
</center>
</body>
</html>
```

The structure of an applet is based on the structure of its base class `java.applet.Applet`. We override the method `init()` of the class `java.applet.Applet`. We declare a variable as a reference to an object of the class `RoomBookingClient`. Then we create the object within the method `init()`. We have two constructors for the class `RoomBookingClient` which are similar to the two kinds of constructors for the ORB: one to be used by applets, the other by applications. As you will see later, these constructors use the appropriate ORB constructor and get a root context of the Naming Service using the proprietary bind methods.

We initialize the GUI with method `init_GUI()` on the object `client` of class `RoomBookingClient`. To do this we have to provide an object of class `java.awt.Container`. The Applet class extends the Container class.

After having initialized the Naming Service by calling the method `init_from_ns()` on the `client` object, we invoke the method `view()`. The implementation of the `view()` method obtains the available rooms from the Naming Service and invokes the operation View() on each of these room objects.

```java
import java.awt.*;

public class RoomBookingClientApplet extends java.applet.Applet {

private RoomBookingClient client;

    // override init method of Class Applet
    public void init() {

        // create a RoomBookingClient object -
        // using the applet constructor
        client = new RoomBookingClient( this );

        // initialize the GUI
        client.init_GUI( this );

        // initialise Naming Service
        client.init_from_ns();

        // view existing bookings
        client.view();
    }
```

The object also has to handle the catching and processing of events locally. The events we expect are the clicking of the various buttons defined in the GUI. A convenient way of catching events is to override the method `action()` of the class `java.awt.Component`. As illustrated in Figure 9-8, the Applet class extends this class. This method is called when an event occurs in the component, that is, in the applet.

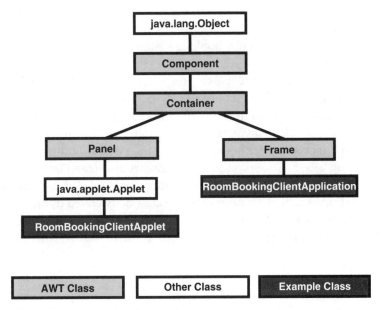

FIGURE 9-8. AWT class hierarchy.

In our implementation of the method `action()` we compare the event target with the various buttons that are defined as public variables in the class `RoomBookingClient`. When we find the event that has occurred we invoke the corresponding method on the object `client`.

```
// catch and process events
public boolean action(Event ev, java.lang.Object arg) {

    if(ev.target == client.view_button)
        return client.view();
    if(ev.target == client.book_button)
        return client.book();
    if(ev.target == client.cancel_button)
        return client.cancel();

    // look for free/book button pressed
    for( int i = 0; i < client.no_of_rooms(); i++ ) {
        for( int j = 0; j < RoomBooking._Room.MaxSlots.value; j++ ) {
            if( ev.target == client.slot_button[i][j] ) {
                return client.process_slot( i, j );
            }
        }
    }
    return false;
}
}
```

7.2 Client as Application

To implement the room-booking system client as a Java application we implement a class `RoomBookingClientApplication`. This class extends `java.awt.Frame`, a specialization of the class `java.awt.Component`. The application class also implements the Java interface `java.lang.Runnable`.

The implementation of the constructor of the `RoomBookingClient Application` class invokes the constructor of the superclass (`java.awt.Frame`). The only parameter sets the title of the corresponding window. We pass the string `Room Booking System` to the constructor (see Figure 9-6).

The Runnable interface defines a parameterless method `run()`, which we implement. The method is automatically called upon creation of a thread which is associated with an object implementing the Runnable interface. We implement the method in its simplest form, that is, with an infinite loop.

```
import java.awt.*;

public class RoomBookingClientApplication
    extends Frame implements Runnable {

    private static RoomBookingClient client;

    // constructor
    RoomBookingClientApplication() {
        super( "Room Booking System" );
    }

    // implement method run() of interface Runnable
    public void run() {
        while( true ) { ; }
    }
}
```

We also implement the `main()` method of the class, which is similar to the `init()` method of the applet class. The `main()` method must create an object of the application class. We call this object `gui` because it plays the role of our GUI. We again create an object of the class `RoomBookingClient`. However, here we use a different constructor, one suitable for applications rather than applets. Then we again initialize the GUI and the Naming Service and invoke the method `view()` on the client object.

```
public static void main( String args[]) {

    // create an object of its own class
    RoomBookingClientApplication gui =
        new RoomBookingClientApplication();

    // create a RoomBookingClient object -
```

```
    // using the application constructor
    client = new RoomBookingClient();

    // initialise the GUI
    client.init_GUI( gui );

    // initialise the Naming Service
    client.init_from_ns();

    // view existing bookings
    client.view();
}
```

Again we have to catch and process events, which we do exactly as in the applet case.

```
    // catch and process events
    public boolean action(Event ev, java.lang.Object arg) {

        if(ev.target == client.view_button)
            return client.view();
        if(ev.target == client.book_button)
            return client.book();
        if(ev.target == client.cancel_button)
            return client.cancel();

        // look for free/book button pressed
        for( int i = 0; i < client.no_of_rooms(); i++ )
            for( int j = 0; j < RoomBooking._Room.MaxSlots.value; j++ )
                if( ev.target == client.slot_button[i][j] ) {
                    return client.process_slot( i, j );
                }
        return false;
    }
}
```

7.3 Independent Client Code

In this subsection we explain the independent client code, that is, the client code that makes calls to the various object implementations. This code is encapsulated in a class RoomBookingClient. Unfortunately, the code of the class is rather voluminous, mainly due to the necessity of managing the GUI. We will partition the code to aid understanding.

7.3.1 Overview of Methods

The class RoomBookingClient implements the following methods.

♦ public int no_of_rooms(). Returns the number of rooms, that is, the length of the private array rooms.

- `public void init_GUI( java.awt.Container gui )`. **Initializes the GUI.**
- `public void init_from_ns()`. **Gets the room context from the root context and obtains a reference to the meeting factory by resolving it from a predefined name.**
- `public boolean view()`. **Queries all rooms and displays the result at the user interface.**
- `public boolean cancel()`. **Cancels a selected booking.**
- `public boolean process_slot( int _selected_room, int _selected_slot )`. **Processes the event of clicking a button to book or view a meeting. It decides if the room is free and a booking can be made or if the booking details should be displayed.**
- `public boolean meeting_details()`. **Queries and displays the details of a meeting. The method deals mainly with GUI programming and hence the code is only shown in Appendix C.**
- `public void booking_form()`. **Produces a booking form for a user to enter meeting details. As this is pure GUI programming we have omitted its explanation in the following text. The complete code is in Appendix C.**
- `public boolean book()`. **Creates a meeting and books it into a selected slot.**

7.3.2   *Variable Declarations*

We start the implementation of the class with a number of local variables. The buttons are defined as `public` because they are used by the applet and application objects to compare event targets. Instead of importing the packages CORBA and RoomBooking, we use fully scoped names to increase the readability of the code.

```
import java.awt.*;

public class RoomBookingClient {

    public Button view_button;
    public Button book_button;
    public Button cancel_button;
    public Button[][] slot_button;

    private TextField participants_tf;
    private TextField purpose_tf;

    private Panel main_panel;
    private Panel title_panel;

    private boolean[][] booked;

    private int selected_room;
    private int selected_slot;
```

```
private CORBA.ORB orb;
private CosNaming.NamingContext room_context;
private EasyNaming easy_naming;

private RoomBooking.MeetingFactory meeting_factory;
private RoomBooking.Room[] rooms;
private RoomBooking.Meeting meetings[];

private String ior;

Color green = new Color( 0, 94, 86 );
Color red = new Color( 255, 61, 61 );
```

7.3.3 Constructors

The class `RoomBookingClient` has two constructors, one each for applets and applications.

Constructor for Applets   The constructor for applets has a single parameter of type `java.applet.Applet`. It initializes the ORB for applets, that is, it makes the ORB use the HTTP tunneling mechanism introduced in Chapter 3.

The ORB initialization routine `resolve_initial_references()` is not yet implemented for the Naming Service. Consequently we use Visiboker's proprietary bind mechanism (as explained in Chapter 8) to connect to our bootstrap object of type RemoteIORFile from which we get an initial reference to a root context of the Naming Service.

```
// constructor for applets
// using bind mechanism to get a root context
RoomBookingClient( java.applet.Applet applet ) {

    try {
        // initialize the ORB
        orb = CORBA.ORB.init( applet );

        // proprietary bind to a remote IOR file server
        RemoteIORFile remote_ior_file =
            RemoteIORFile_var.bind("CosNaming.ior");
        easy_naming = new EasyNaming(
            remote_ior_file.get_ior_string() );
    }
    catch(CORBA.SystemException system_exception ) {
        System.err.println( "constructor RoomBookingClient: " +
            system_exception );
    }
}
```

Constructor for Applications   The constructor for Java applications initializes the ORB to use IIOP directly. Since an application can access the local file system, it can use our class IORFile to get an initial reference to the Naming Service.

```
// constructor for applications
// using a stringified IOR to get a root context
RoomBookingClient() {

    try {
        // initialize the ORB
        orb = CORBA.ORB.init();

        IORFile ior_file = new IORFile("CosNaming.ior");
        easy_naming = new EasyNaming( orb, ior_file.get_ior_string() );
    }
    catch(CORBA.SystemException system_exception ) {
        System.err.println( "constructor RoomBookingClient: " +
            system_exception );
    }
}
```

7.3.4   no_of_rooms()

The method no_of_rooms() is implemented to allow us to keep the variable room private.

```
public int no_of_rooms() {
    return rooms.length;
}
```

7.3.5   init_GUI()

The method init_GUI() defines the principal layout of our GUI. It takes one argument, which is of type java.awt.Container. Depending on where we call the method from, we supply either an object of type Applet or of type Frame, which are both extensions of the Container class.

After having set the background and created some button objects, we create two panels, one for the title and another one where we display information from the room-booking system. For the layout we use the Java layout manager and a border layout.

```
// initialize widgets

gui.setBackground( Color.white );

view_button = new Button("Back");
view_button.setFont(new Font("Helvetica", Font.BOLD, 14));
view_button.setBackground( red );
```

```
book_button = new Button("Book");
book_button.setFont(new Font("Helvetica", Font.BOLD, 14));
book_button.setBackground( red );

cancel_button = new Button("Cancel");
cancel_button.setFont(new Font("Helvetica", Font.BOLD, 14));
cancel_button.setBackground( red );

main_panel = new Panel();
title_panel = new Panel();

title_panel.setLayout( new GridLayout(3,1));
title_panel.setFont(new Font("Helvetica", Font.BOLD, 20));
title_panel.setBackground( red );
title_panel.add( new Label("", Label.CENTER) );
title_panel.add( new Label("Room Booking System", Label.CENTER) );
title_panel.add( new Label("", Label.CENTER) );

gui.setLayout(new BorderLayout());
gui.add( "North", title_panel );
gui.add( "Center", main_panel );
gui.resize( 500, 300 );
gui.show();
```

7.3.6 `init_from_ns()`

We have determined a naming convention for the room-booking system as illustrated in Figure 9-2. Room objects are bound to names in the context `/BuildingApplications/Rooms`, and the meeting factory object is bound to the name `/BuildingApplications/MeetingFactories/MeetingFactory`. The method `init_from_ns()` resolves the `Rooms` context and obtains an object reference to the meeting factory using methods from the class `EasyNaming()`.

```
public void init_from_ns()

    // initialize from Naming Service
    try {
        // get room context
        room_context = CosNaming.NamingContext_var.narrow(
            easy_naming.resolve_from_string(
            "/BuildingApplications/Rooms" ) );
        if( room_context == null ) {
            System.err.println( "Room context is null," );
            System.err.println( "exiting ..." );
            System.exit( 1 );
        }

        // get MeetingFactory from Naming Service
        meeting_factory = RoomBooking.MeetingFactory_var.narrow(
            easy_naming.resolve_from_string(
```

```
            "/BuildingApplications/MeetingFactories/MeetingFactory") );
        if( meeting_factory == null ) {
            System.err.println(
                "No Meeting Factory registered at Naming Service" );
            System.err.println( "exiting ..." );
            System.exit( 1 );
        }
    }
    catch(CORBA.SystemException system_exception ) {
        System.err.println( "Initialize ORB: " + system_exception );
    }
    catch(CORBA.UserException naming_exception) {
        System.err.println( "Initialize ORB: " + naming_exception );
    }
}
```

7.3.7 view()

The method view() displays information about the current availability of
rooms. Therefore it has to find out about all existing rooms and calls the
View() operation on all of them.

Object references for the available rooms can be obtained from the
Naming Service. We have already initialized a room context in which,
according to our convention, room objects are bound.

We query the room context by using the method list() defined in the
interface CosNaming::NamingContext. As explained in Chapter 8, the operation
list() has three parameters:

♦ in int length. The maximum length of the list returned by the second
  parameter.
♦ out CosNaming::BindingList. A sequence of names. Since it is an out parameter we use a _var object in the Visibroker for Java language binding.
♦ out CosNaming::BindingIterator. A binding iterator, that is, an object from
  which further names can be obtained. It is also an out parameter and
  hence we use a _var object.

In our implementation, we ignore names possibly held by the iterator.
We create the array rooms with the right size, that is, the actual length of the
binding list bl_var.value.length and initialize it with object references of the
rooms. We obtain those references from the room context via the resolve()
operation. We then narrow the resulting object to the right type.

```
public boolean view() {

    try {
        // list rooms
        // initialise binding list and binding iterator
```

```
            // _var objects for out parameter
            CosNaming.BindingList_var bl_var =
                    new CosNaming.BindingList_var();
            CosNaming.BindingIterator_var bi_var =
                    new CosNaming.BindingIterator_var();

            // we consider only 20 rooms although there could
            // be more in the binding iterator
            room_context.list( 20, bl_var, bi_var );

            // create an array of Room and initialise it by resolving
            // the entries in the Room context of the Naming Service
            rooms = new RoomBooking.Room[ bl_var.value.length ];
            for( int i = 0; i < bl_var.value.length; i++ ) {
                System.out.println( "Room " + i + " : " +
                bl_var.value[i].binding_name[0].id );
                rooms[i] = RoomBooking.Room_var.narrow(
                    room_context.resolve( bl_var.value[i].binding_name ));
            }
```

We create an array of labels, one for each room, which eventually displays the names of the rooms. We also create an array of type `boolean` for internal use to store information about whether each slot is already booked or not.

```
// create labels and slots according to the number of rooms
Label[] r_label = new Label[rooms.length];
slot_button =
    new Button[rooms.length][RoomBooking._Room.MaxSlots.value];
booked =
    new boolean[rooms.length][RoomBooking._Room.MaxSlots.value];
main_panel.removeAll();
```

Then we define the layout of the rest of table.

```
// define layout for the table
GridBagLayout gridbag = new GridBagLayout();
GridBagConstraints c = new GridBagConstraints();
main_panel.setLayout(gridbag);

c.fill = GridBagConstraints.BOTH;

c.gridwidth = 2;
c.gridheight = 1;
Label room_label = new Label("Rooms", Label.CENTER );
room_label.setFont(new Font("Helvetica", Font.BOLD, 14));
gridbag.setConstraints( room_label, c);
main_panel.add( room_label );

// and so on for the header of the table
```

Next we initialize the elements of the label array by creating objects of type java.awt.Label. The constructor we use takes a string argument, which we set to the name of a room. We obtain the name by invoking the accessor method for the attribute name of the interface Room.

```
// show the label with the room name
for( int i = 0; i < rooms.length; i++ ) {
    c.gridwidth = 2;
    c.gridheight = 1;
    r_label[i] = new Label( rooms[i].name() );
    r_label[i].setFont(new Font("Helvetica", Font.BOLD, 14));
    gridbag.setConstraints( r_label[i], c );
    main_panel.add( r_label[i] );
```

For each of the rooms we invoke the operation View(), which returns an array of meeting objects. The semantics of such arrays are that a valid object reference identifies a meeting object which is booked into the indexed slot; a nil object reference means an empty slot. We go through the array and create either a green or red button depending on whether the slot is empty or not.

```
    meetings = rooms[i].View();

    // create book or free button
    c.gridheight = 1;
    for( int j = 0; j < meetings.length; j++ ) {
        if( j == meetings.length - 1 )
            c.gridwidth = GridBagConstraints.REMAINDER;
        else
            c.gridwidth = 1;
        if( meetings[j] == null ) {
            // slot is free
            slot_button[i][j] = new Button("Book");
            slot_button[i][j].setBackground( green );
            booked[i][j] = false;
        }
        else {
            // slot is booked - view or cancel
            slot_button[i][j] = new Button("View");
            slot_button[i][j].setBackground( red );
            booked[i][j] = true;
        }
        gridbag.setConstraints( slot_button[i][j], c );
        main_panel.add( slot_button[i][j] );
    }
}
// some more laying out
main_panel.layout();
}

catch(CORBA.SystemException system_exception) {
```

7.3.8 `cancel()`

To cancel a meeting, the method `cancel()` invokes the operation Cancel() on the appropriate room, providing the selected slot as an argument. If the selected slot does not contain a meeting object reference, the operation Cancel() raises an exception of type `RoomBooking._Room.NoMeetingInThisSlot`. This can only happen when there are multiple clients running which attempt to cancel the same meeting in overlapping time intervals. A more sophisticated approach would be to use the CORBA Transaction Service.

```
public boolean cancel() {
    try {
        rooms[selected_room].Cancel( selected_slot );
    }
    catch(RoomBooking._Room.NoMeetingInThisSlot no_meeting ) {
        System.err.println("Cancel :" + no_meeting );
    }
    catch(CORBA.SystemException system_exception) {
        System.err.println("Cancel :" + system_exception);
    }

    // show bookings of all rooms
    return view();
}
```

The method `process_slot()` sets state variables and determines whether a red or a green button has been pressed and how to proceed in each case. If a green button has been pressed it invokes the method `booking_form()`, allowing the user to enter meeting details. If a red button has been pressed it invokes the method `booking_details()`, which displays the meeting details of the selected meeting and provides buttons to cancel the meeting or to return to the main view. The implementation of both methods is omitted, but the complete code is in Appendix C.

```
public boolean process_slot( int _selected_room, int _selected_slot ) {

    selected_room = _selected_room;
    selected_slot = _selected_slot;

    if( booked[selected_room][selected_slot] ) {
        // view the meeting details, potentially cancel
        meeting_details();
    }
    else {
        // get meeting details and book
        booking_form();
    }
    return true;
}
```

7.3.9 book()

The booking of a meeting, managed by the method book(), involves two tasks: creation of the appropriate meeting object, and booking of the selected meeting. We create the meeting object using the meeting factory. This is done by invoking the operation CreateMeeting(). Its two parameters are obtained from two text fields.

The newly created meeting is then booked by calling the operation Book() on the selected room object. It is again possible that someone else has booked the slot in the meantime. If so, we catch an exception of type RoomBooking._Room.SlotAlreadyTaken.

```
public boolean book() {
    try {
        // create the meeting
        RoomBooking.Meeting meeting =
            meeting_factory.CreateMeeting(
                purpose_tf.getText(),
                participants_tf.getText() );

        // book the meeting in the selected slot of the selected room
        rooms[selected_room].Book( selected_slot, meeting );
    }
    catch(RoomBooking._Room.SlotAlreadyTaken already_taken ) {
        System.out.println( "book :" + already_taken );
    }
    catch(CORBA.SystemException system_exception ) {
        System.out.println( "book :" + system_exception );
    }

    // show bookings of all rooms
    return view();
    }
}
```

8 Extensions to the Example Application

The application can be extended, for example, to include various other CORBA Services. We outline possible extensions below.

The Object Trading Service can be an alternative to the Naming Service for locating objects. The server classes would *register* objects with the Trading Service and a client would *query* the Trading Service to search for room and meeting factory objects.

To make the implementation of room and meeting objects more robust, the Persistence Service could be used to store the state of those objects in a persistent manner.

The Transaction Service could be used to ensure ACID properties to booking and cancel operations. In the current implementation we do not explicitly roll back the creation of a meeting object when it cannot be booked into a particular slot.

The Security Service could be used to authenticate users and to authorize a user to execute certain operations. For example, only a user who originally booked a meeting should be allowed to cancel it.

The Event Service could be used to notify certain users that a meeting in which they are participating is now starting.

C H A P T E R

10

Advanced Features

In this chapter we explain and give examples of how to use some advanced CORBA features. The features that are explained in detail here have already been introduced in Chapters 6 and 7. They are

- ◆ TypeCodes
- ◆ Any
- ◆ Interface Repository
- ◆ Dynamic Invocation Interface
- ◆ Applet Server

In addition we will introduce a widely accepted object implementation mechanism known as *Tie*.

Some of these features are implementable using any Java ORB, but only Visibroker provides the complete set of features. We will therefore use the Visibroker language mapping for all of the code examples.

To demonstrate these advanced features we will adapt the Hello World example from Chapter 4. For the implementation of objects in applets we present a more appropriate example.

1 The Any Type and TypeCodes

In this section we want to demonstrate the use of Anys as parameters of IDL-defined operations. We use a variant of the Hello World example in Chapter 5.

1.1 Interface Specification

In the IDL below, although we have changed the signature of the interface specification we retain the semantics of the hello() operation. Both the result of the operation and the only parameter are of type Any. As before, the operation will return the locality of the object implementation as a string, this time contained in an Any. This is an example of the use of a predefined data type within an Any.

The any_time parameter is an example of passing a user-defined data type in an Any. The parameter will contain a structure with two fields, both short integers, representing the minute and hour of the local time at the object implementation. Although this structure is not directly used in the specification of the operation, its definition needs to be available to the client and the server. Hence we define the Time structure within the module.

```
module HelloWorldAny {

    struct Time {
      short hour;
      short minute;
    };

    interface GoodDay {
      any hello( out any any_time );
    };
};
```

1.2 Object Implementation

The object implementation follows the usual structure. The implementation class GoodDayImpl extends the skeleton class HelloWorldAny._sk_GoodDay which is generated by the IDL compiler. We also keep the same private variable any_locality and the constructor.

The signature of the method hello() corresponds to the IDL mapping for Anys as explained in Chapter 6. We have an Any for the result and declare a variable of type Any_var for the out parameter.

We create a date object as in the original example. In the next step we create an object of the class HelloWorldAny.Time, which is the Java representation of the IDL type definition struct Time. We use the default constructor of this class, which takes two parameters corresponding to the fields of the structure. We provide values for the parameters by invoking methods on the object date to obtain the current time in hours and minutes. Again we have to cast the integer values to type short.

Java objects that correspond to user-defined IDL data types have a method any() to construct an Any that contains the value of the object the method was invoked on. For example, we invoke any() on the object struct_time, which creates an Any and initializes it with the value of the structure. We assign the resulting Any to the public variable value of the container object any_time. Figure 10-1 illustrates the object any_time.

```
// method
public CORBA.Any hello(
        CORBA.Any_var any_time
    ) throws CORBA.SystemException {

    // get local time of the server
    Date date = new Date();

    // create time-structure assign hour and minute to it
    HelloWorldAny.Time struct_time = new HelloWorldAny.Time(
        (short) date.getHours(), (short) date.getMinutes() );

    // insert structure into any
    any_time.value = struct_time.any();

    // create any and insert locality into it
    CORBA.Any any_locality = new Any();
    any_locality.from_string( m_locality );

    return any_locality;
    }
}
```

The operation result is stored in the variable any_locality, an Any holding a string value. Since string is a predefined IDL type, we construct the Any with the standard parameterless constructor Any() which creates an Any

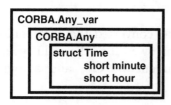

FIGURE 10-1. Any_var object.

containing no value. Then we initialize the Any with the string by calling the method `from_string()` using the private variable `m_locality` as its argument. There are similar methods defined in the class `CORBA.Any` for other predefined data types. Appendix B gives a complete listing of those methods. The last task of the implementation is to return the Any `any_locality`.

The server class implementation is the same as in Chapter 5. We name the class `HelloWorldAnyServer`.

1.3   Client Implementation

The client implementation also follows the same structure that we used before.

1.3.1   Initialization and Invocation

We declare two variables `any_locality` and `any_time` of type `CORBA.Any` and `CORBA.Any_var` for the method's result and its parameter, respectively.

```
import java.util.*;
import java.io.*;

public class HelloWorldAnyClient {

    public static void main(String args[]) {

        CORBA.Any_var any_time = new CORBA.Any_var();
        CORBA.Any any_locality;

        try {
            // initialise the ORB.
            CORBA.ORB orb = CORBA.ORB.init();

            // get object reference ..
            CORBA.Object obj = orb.string_to_object( args[0] );

            // and narrow it to "HelloWorldAny.GoodDay"
            HelloWorldAny.GoodDay good_day =
                HelloWorldAny.GoodDay_var.narrow( obj );

            // invoke the operation
            any_locality = good_day.hello( any_time );
```

Having initialized the ORB, converted the command-line argument into an object reference, and narrowed it to the right type, we invoke the method `hello()` with the argument `any_time` and assign the result to `any_locality`.

1.3.2 Obtaining TypeCodes

TypeCodes are a run-time representation of IDL types. They are explained in detail in Chapter 7. In the following example we obtain type information about the values contained in the Anys. First we declare a variable tc of type CORBA.TypeCode. Then we obtain the TypeCode of the value held in the container variable any_time. The container object's public variable value stores the Any that was returned as an out parameter. The Any object referred to by value has a method type() which returns the TypeCode of the stored value. In this example the value is a Java object representing an IDL struct.

A TypeCode represents an attributed type tree. It provides various methods to obtain the values of the attributes. For example, we query the IR identifier of the type by calling the method id() on the TypeCode object. Similarly, we get the name of the type by invoking the method name().

Since we are expecting the Any to contain an IDL structure, we need to traverse the type tree to obtain type information about the fields of the struct. The method member_count() returns the number of fields and member_name() returns the name of the indexed field.

As type definitions differ in their structure, operations on TypeCode objects are only valid for particular kinds of TypeCodes. If an inappropriate method is invoked, the exception CORBA._TypeCode.BadKind is raised. The method member_name() raises CORBA._TypeCode.Bounds when the index is out of bounds.

```
// declare a TypeCode
        CORBA.TypeCode tc;

        // get type of any_time.value and print type information
        tc = any_time.value.type();
        try {
            System.out.println("IfRepId of any_time: " + tc.id() );
            System.out.println("Type code of any_time: " + tc.name() );
            for( int i = 0; i < tc.member_count(); i++ )
                System.out.println("\tname: " + tc.member_name(i) );
        }
        catch(CORBA._TypeCode.BadKind ex_bk) {
            System.err.println("any_time: " + ex_bk);
        }
        catch(CORBA._TypeCode.Bounds ex_b) {
            System.err.println("any_time: " + ex_b);
        }
```

In the following code we check if the value of any_locality is of the expected kind, CORBA.TCKind.tk_string, and if so we query for its length. Note that the length refers to the type definition and not the current value. The method `length()` returns the maximum size of a bounded string, sequence, or array. If the type is unbounded it returns zero. We must again catch the exception `CORBA._TypeCode.BadKind`.

```
// get length any_locality.value
tc = any_locality.type();
try {
    if( tc.kind() == CORBA.TCKind.tk_string )
        System.out.println( "length of any_locality: "
            + tc.length() );
    else
        System.out.println(
            "any_locality does NOT contain a string.");
}
catch(CORBA._TypeCode.BadKind ex_bt) {
    System.err.println("any_locality: " + ex_bt);
}
```

When executing the client, the code above will produce the following result:

```
IfRepId of any_time: IDL:HelloWorldAny/Time:1.0

Type code of any_time: Time

        name: hour
        name: minute
length of any_locality: 0
```

1.3.3 Unpacking the Results

Now we proceed to the normal behavior of the client, that is, we obtain the results and print them. We can either print the Anys directly by using their predefined `toString()` method or we can obtain the contained values and can print them in a customized manner. We show both possibilities.

First we print the Anys `any_locality` and `any_time.value` in the default format. Then we obtain the string from `any_locality` by invoking the `to_string()` method. To get the time object from the Any `any_time.value` we call the constructor of the class `HelloWorldAny.Time`, which takes an Any as an argument. Once we have the values in the usual types we print the message in the same way as in the original example.

```
//print results to stdout
System.out.println("Print Anys:");
System.out.println("any_locality: ");
System.out.println( any_locality );
System.out.println("time:");
System.out.println( any_time.value );
```

```
    // get String from any_locality
    String locality = new
        String( any_locality.to_string() );

    // get struct from any_time
    HelloWorldAny.Time time = new
        HelloWorldAny.Time( any_time.value );

    // print results to stdout
    System.out.println("Hello World!");
    if( time.minute < 10 )
        System.out.println("The local time in " +
            locality +
            " is " + time.hour + ":0" +
            time.minute + "." );
    else
        System.out.println("The local time in " +
            locality +
            " is " + time.hour + ":" +
            time.minute + "." );
    }
    // catch CORBA system exceptions
    catch(CORBA.SystemException ex) {
        System.err.println(ex);
    }
  }
}
```

When invoking the client it prints the results in the following form:

```
Print Anys:

any_locality:
"Brisbane"

time:
struct Time{short hour=12; short minute=23;}

Hello World!
The local time in Brisbane is 12:23.
```

2 Interface Repository and Dynamic Invocation Interface

In this section we present a client that is capable of invoking operations on an object whose type was unknown to the client at compile time. So far, clients have used stub code generated by an IDL compiler to create a proxy object on which they have invoked methods corresponding to each operation.

The structure of the example is

◆ Initialize the ORB
◆ Browse the IR
◆ Unparse and print the type information obtained from the IR
◆ Create a Request object
◆ Invoke an operation using the DII
◆ Obtain and print the results

To make invocations on objects without having access to IDL-generated code we have to

◆ Obtain information about the interface type of the object
◆ Invoke a method without an IDL-generated client-side proxy class

The first task is carried out using the IR. The IR contains type information about interfaces. Typically the IR is populated by the IDL compiler. Our client will query the IR. It uses a standard method on the object reference, defined in CORBA::Object, to obtain a reference to an IR object. This IR object represents the target object's interface type. The interface type is stored as a type tree which the client can traverse.

The second task is carried out using the DII. It provides a *Request* object that can be used for the invocation of methods on arbitrary objects. The DII's interface Request is defined in the CORBA module using pseudo-IDL. It is the programmer's responsibility to initialize a Request pseudo-object with all the necessary information (a target object reference, an operation name, argument types, and values) in order to make an invocation.

Figure 10-2 illustrates the process by which interface information is obtained and used to invoke the object implementation. The IDL compiler creates the skeleton code for the server side as usual and populates the IR with the types specified in the IDL file. The client can then query the IR about the type of any object reference it obtains.

2.1 Initializing the ORB

The client obtains an object reference from, for example, a stringified object reference or from the Naming or Trading Service. For simplicity, we use stringified object references in our example. Note that we cannot narrow the object reference to its particular interface type since we do not know its type and do not have access to the narrow method, which is part of the code generated by the IDL compiler.

```
import java.io.*;
import CORBA.*;

public class DiiClient {
```

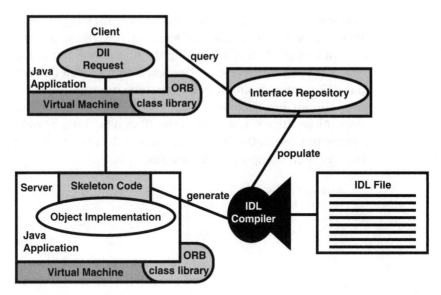

FIGURE 10-2. DII client.

```
public static void main(String args[]) {

    // get stringified IOR from command line
    String ior = new String( args[0] );

    try {
        // initialise the ORB
        CORBA.ORB orb = CORBA.ORB.init();

        // get object reference
        CORBA.Object obj = orb.string_to_object( ior );
```

We call the method _get_interface() on our new object reference. This is a standard method, provided by the class CORBA.Object, that returns an object of the type CORBA.InterfaceDef. The InterfaceDef interface is defined in the IR specification. The interfaces of the IR are explained in Chapter 2 and Appendix A.

```
// get interface definition from Interface Repository
    CORBA.InterfaceDef if_def = obj._get_interface();
```

2.2   Browsing the IR

The InterfaceDef interface has an operation, describe_interface(), which returns a structure FullInterfaceDescription. It contains a number of nested structures that represent the operations and attributes contained in the interface. One of the nested structures, OperationDescription, describing an operation, also contains nested structures describing the operation's parameters.

The structure FullInterfaceDescription represents a flattening of the objects in the IR to provide all the necessary type information in a single data structure without the need to make further calls to IR objects to query their types. Alternatively, traversal of the IR can be done by obtaining object references to OperationDef objects and AttributeDef objects that can be queried to discover their component definitions.

```
// using the Interface Repository
// get full interface description
CORBA.InterfaceDef_.FullInterfaceDescription full_if_desc =
    if_def.describe_interface();
```

In our client we store the interface description in a variable full_if_desc. The type is defined in the IDO as the following struct. We only show the type definitions we use in the example.

```
typedef string Identifier;
typedef sequence <OperationDescription> OpDescriptionSeq;

struct FullInterfaceDescription {
   Identifier       name;
   RepositoryId     id;
   RepositoryId     defined_in;
   VersionSpec      version;
   OpDescriptionSeq operations;
   AttrDescriptionSeq attributes;
   RepositoryIdSeq  base_interfaces;
   TypeCode    type;
}
```

We use the members name and operations, which are a sequence of OperationDescription structs:

```
typedef sequence <ParameterDescription> ParDescriptionSeq;
typedef sequence <ExceptionDescription> ExcDescriptionSeq;

struct OperationDescription {
   Identifier name;
   RepositoryId id;
   RepositoryId defined_in;
   VersionSpec version;
   TypeCode result;
   OperationMode mode;
   ContextIdSeq contexts;
   ParDescriptionSeq parameters;
```

```
  ExcDescriptionSeq exceptions;
};
```

In turn, parameters and exceptions that are part of an operation are described by structures.

2.3 A Simple Unparser

The following code traverses the nested structures and prints all operations of the interface in a simplified version in OMG IDL syntax. We go through all the operations defined in the interface, obtaining the result type in the form of a TypeCode, the operation name which is a string, and the parameters. The method `toString()` is available on TypeCode objects and prints them in IDL syntax.

```
int no_of_parameters;

// print various information
System.out.println("Querying the Interface Repository\n");
System.out.println("interface " + full_if_desc.name + " {\n" );

for( int i = 0; i < full_if_desc.operations.length; i++ ) {

    no_of_parameters =
        full_if_desc.operations[i].parameters.length;

    System.out.println("     " +

        // print the TypeCode of the operation's result
        full_if_desc.operations[i].result + " " +

        // print the name of the operation
        full_if_desc.operations[i].name + " ("
    );
```

The parameters are described by a sequence of structures of type ParamDescription:

```
enum ParameterMode { PARAM_IN, PARAM_OUT, PARAM_INOUT };

struct ParamDescription {
  Identifier    name;
  TypeCode    type;
  IDLType      type_def;
  ParameterMode mode;
};
```

The parameter's type member is of type TypeCode and its name is an Identifier, an alias of string. The parameter mode is an integer, and its values are defined in the enumerated type `CORBA.ParameterMode`. We have to convert the mode value into strings.

```
// define and initialize text representations
// for parameter modes
String mode, in, inout, out;
in = new String("in");
inout = new String("inout");
out = new String("out");

char last_char = ',';

// print parameters of the operations
for( int j = 0; j < no_of_parameters; j++ ) {

    // set the right text for the parameter mode
    switch (full_if_desc.operations[i].parameters[j].mode) {
        case CORBA.ParameterMode.PARAM_IN:
            mode = in; break;
        case CORBA.ParameterMode.PARAM_INOUT:
            mode = inout; break;
        case CORBA.ParameterMode.PARAM_OUT:
            mode = out; break;
        default:
            mode = new String("unknown mode");
    }

    // deal with separating commas
    if( j == no_of_parameters - 1 )
        last_char = ' ';

    // print mode, type and name of the parameter
    System.out.println("              " +
        mode + " " +
        full_if_desc.operations[i].parameters[j].type + " " +
        full_if_desc.operations[i].parameters[j].name + last_char
    );
  }
  System.out.println("   );\n};\n");
}
```

2.4   Initializing Requests

Now that we have discovered the type of the object, we want to invoke an operation on it. We will need the DII to do this. This requires the creation of a Request object as illustrated in Figure 10.3. A Request has three components:

- ◆ string. Carries the name of the operation to be invoked.
- ◆ NamedValue. Carries the type and value of the operation's result.
- ◆ NVList. Carries the mode, type, and value of the operation's parameters.

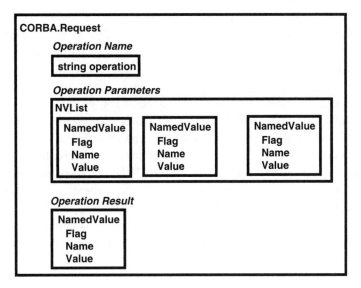

FIGURE 10-3. Request object.

2.5 Creating Supporting Objects

We now create and initialize the NamedValue for the result and the NVList containing the arguments to the operation. A NamedValue is a data type defined in pseudo-IDL in the module CORBA. It is a triple of

- ♦ A *name* of type string
- ♦ A *typed value* of type Any
- ♦ A *mode* of type Any

An NVList is an object containing a list of NamedValue objects. See Chapter 7 for details.

To initialize an operation result we need only set the type we expect by initializing the value with a dummy value of the right type. After the invocation the value will hold the result of the operation.

Unfortunately, there are no operations to create and manage NamedValue objects directly. Instead we create an NVList result_list of length one and insert a single element later using the method add_value(). This method has three parameters, one for each of the components of a NamedValue.

The tricky part is to create an Any that carries the type and the value of an argument. For out parameters we only need to put the type information into the Any. This seems to be straightforward since we have the TypeCode. However, there are no constructors for Anys that take TypeCodes as arguments. This means we have to traverse the type tree encoded in the TypeCode and construct the Any by hand. This is easy for predefined types such as short, char, and String, since we can use the Any constructors as shown in Chapter 6, for example, from_short, from_char, and from_string.

As also shown in Chapter 6, Anys can be constructed with an appropriate TypeCode initialized by using the method any() on Java objects, which correspond to IDL type definitions. However, the class definitions we need are generated by the IDL compiler, and so are not available without the stub code. There are no general mechanisms to create Anys defined in the language mapping, but particular ORB implementations provide such mechanisms in nonstandard ways. In fact, these mechanisms are used to implement the any() methods for user-defined types.

For example, the class Time which has been generated by the IDL compiler from the IDL file HelloWorldAny.idl contains the following code for the method any() for the IDL type struct Time.

```
public CORBA.Any any() throws CORBA.SystemException {
    pomoco.CORBA.Stream stream = new pomoco.CORBA.Stream();
    _write(stream);
    return new CORBA.Any(TypeCode(), stream.toByteArray());
}
```

For our example, we have implemented a class DiiAnySupport that hides the complexity of the Any generation. Its method TC2Any() creates an Any that is initialized according to a TypeCode argument. The implementation of the class is based on the methods shown above.

We must also provide values for in and inout parameters. The mechanism is the same, but we must provide the real values instead of dummy ones. The method TC2Any() does this job for us. When this method traverses the type tree it will query a user for appropriate values. The complete signature for TC2Any() is

```
Any TC2Any( TypeCode tc, int mode )
```

Depending on the value of mode, the user will be queried for values.

```
// using the DII to make an invocation
System.out.println("Make a DII call\n");

// create a support object
DiiAnySupport dii_any_support = new DiiAnySupport();

// create and initialize result
NVList result_list = orb.create_list( 0 );

result_list.add_value( "",
        dii_any_support.TC2Any(
```

Advanced Features ♦ 227

```
            full_if_desc.operations[0].result,
            CORBA.ParameterMode.PARAM_OUT ),
        0 );

// create and initialize arg_list
NVList arg_list = orb.create_list( 0 );

no_of_parameters =
        full_if_desc.operations[0].parameters.length;
for( int i = 0; i < no_of_parameters; i++ ) {

    arg_list.add_value(
        full_if_desc.operations[0].parameters[i].name,
        dii_any_support.TC2Any(
            full_if_desc.operations[0].parameters[i].type,
            full_if_desc.operations[0].parameters[i].mode ),
        full_if_desc.operations[0].parameters[i].mode + 1 );
}
```

2.6   Creating and Invoking a Request Object

Once we have initialized the result and the arguments, we can create and initialize a Request object by calling `_create_request()` on the object on which we want to invoke the operation. The method `_create_request()` has the following parameters:

- ♦ *Context*—which we do not use and hence initialize to a `null` object reference.
- ♦ *Operation name*—which we obtain from the interface description.
- ♦ *Arguments*—which we have created in NVList `arg_list`.
- ♦ *Result*—which is the first element of the NVList `result_list`.

Now we can call the method `invoke()` on the Request object, which results in the operation being invoked on the object implementation. Once the call is completed the Request object will place the result of the operation and the values for the inout and out parameters into the NVLists provided to its constructor.

```
// create request
CORBA.Request request = obj._create_request(
    null,                          // context - not used
    full_if_desc.operations[0].name, // operation name
    arg_list,                      // NVList with arguments
    result_list.item(0)            // NamedValue for result
);

// invoke request
request.invoke();
```

2.7 Getting Results

Next we print the value of the result and the values of the out parameters of the operation. We use the `toString()` method on the Any objects, which allows us to print Anys directly using `System.out.println()` as shown below.

```
// get result
System.out.println("result:\n  " + request.result().value() );

// get out parameters
CORBA.NVList nv_list = request.arguments();
for( int i = 0; i < no_of_parameters; i++ )
    System.out.println( nv_list.item( i ).name() +
        ":\n    " + nv_list.item( i ).value() );
}

// catch CORBA system exceptions
catch(CORBA.SystemException ex) {
    System.err.println(ex);
}
}
}
```

2.8 Executing the Client

When executing the DII client we can invoke operations on arbitrary objects. In our example we invoke the first operation defined in the interface. The following output is produced when the object reference used refers to an object supporting the Hello World interface introduced in Chapter 4.

```
.../DII/Visibroker > java DiiClient IOR:000000000000001b49444c3a48656c6c
6f576f726c642f476f6f644461793a312e30000000000001000000000000004c00010000
0000000e3133302e3130322e3137362e3900ae8e0000003000504d430000000000000014
48656c6c6f576f726c643a3a476f6f644461790000000000c476f6f644461794964706c6c00

Querying the Interface Repository

interface GoodDay {

    string hello (
        out short hour,
        out short minute
    );
};

Make a DII call

result:
    any[string=Brisbane, Queensland, Australia]
hour:
```

```
        any[short=13]
minute:
        any[short=47]
```

As another example, we use the DII client program to invoke the AnyHelloWorld server we implemented earlier. Again the client queries the IR and prints the interface specification in OMG IDL syntax. As in the previous section, the interface GoodDay again provides an operation hello(). However, this time the result and the only parameter are of type Any. The client creates the corresponding Request object and invokes it.

```
.../DII/Visibroker > java DiiClient IOR:000000000000001e49444c3a48656c6c
6f576f726c64416e792f476f6f644461793a312e3000000000000001000000000000000048
00010000000000e3133302e3130322e3137362e3900af650000002c00504d4300000001
0000001748656c6c6f576f726c64416e793a3a476f6f644461790000000000020a29b483

Querying the Interface Repository

interface GoodDay {

    any hello (
        out any any_time
    );
};

Make a DII call

result:
    any[any=any[string=Brisbane, Queensland, Australia]]
any_time:
    any[any=any[struct Time{short hour=14; short minute=28;}]]
```

There is a tool called *Universal CORBA Client,* which improves the client shown above by providing a good GUI for selecting operations and entering and displaying parameters. This tool was implemented by Gerald Vogt during the time he spent with the authors at DSTC in Brisbane, Australia, in 1996. The implementation uses Java and Visibroker for Java. The combination of portability provided by Java and interoperability through IIOP make the tool almost universally usable. Figure 10-4 shows the Universal CORBA Client at work.

3   *Tie Mechanism*

So far we have constructed object implementations by inheritance of skeleton classes generated by the IDL compiler. These skeletons implement the network management, marshaling and incoming request delegation of the

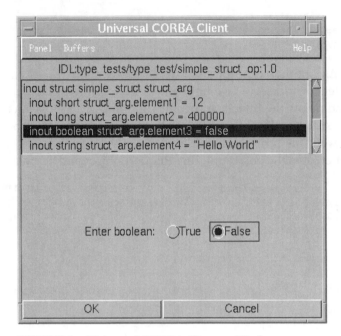

FIGURE 10-4. Universal CORBA Client at Work.

CORBA object. They are then extended to provide methods that support the operations in the IDL interface. This approach, however, has the following shortcomings.

- *Java single inheritance.* Since Java only supports single inheritance, an object implementation cannot extend any application-specific class since it already extends the skeleton class.
- *One implementation object for multiple interfaces.* There are occasions where it makes sense for one Java object to implement multiple IDL interfaces, for example, an application-specific interface and a general management interface. This cannot be achieved via Java extension because the implementation object needs to extend two or more skeletons.

A solution to these problems is to use *delegation* instead of *inheritance*. This is achieved by generating a *pseudo-implementation object* which inherits the skeleton. The pseudo-implementation object extends the skeleton with methods for the IDL operations. However, rather than implementing the operations, it calls methods on another object that actually implements the operations' semantics. Figure 10-5 compares the inheritance approach with the delegation approach. The delegation approach is also known as the *Tie* mechanism.

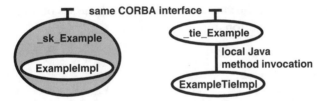

FIGURE 10-5. Inheritance versus delegation.

We use the Hello World example as introduced in Chapter 5 to demonstrate the Tie approach. We have to modify both the server class and the object implementation class, and introduce the pseudo-implementation class.

Let's start with the implementation class. The only difference to the inheritance approach is in the declaration of class GoodDayImpl.

```
class GoodDayImpl implements HelloWorld.GoodDayOperations {

    // implementation as before

}
```

While the implementation class extends the skeleton class in the inheritance approach, in the Tie approach it implements the interface HelloWorld. GoodDayOperations. The implementation class above could inherit another, application-specific, class.

The interface HelloWorld.GoodDayOperations is the same as the interface HelloWorld.GoodDay without the inherited functionality of CORBA.Object. It simply declares the signature of the methods corresponding to the IDL operations, and because this class is generated it ensures a type safe implementation class.

```
package HelloWorld;

public interface GoodDayOperations {
    public String hello(
        CORBA.short_var hour,
        CORBA.short_var minute )
        throws CORBA.SystemException;
};
```

We define a new class name for the server. We initialize the ORB and the BOA. Then we create the implementation object good_day_impl and supply it as a parameter to the constructor of the Tie object good_day_pseudo_impl. Finally, we notify the BOA that the object good_day_pseudo_impl is ready.

Figure 10-6 shows the various interfaces and classes of both approaches and illustrates their relationships.

```
public class HelloWorldTieServer {

    public static void main(String[] args) {
        try {
            //init orb
            CORBA.ORB orb = CORBA.ORB.init();

            //init basic object adapter
            CORBA.BOA boa = orb.BOA_init();

            // create an implementation object
            GoodDayImpl good_day_impl =
                new GoodDayImpl( args[0] );

            // create a Tie object
            HelloWorld._tie_GoodDay good_day_pseudo_impl =
                new HelloWorld._tie_GoodDay( good_day_impl );

            // notify BOA
            boa.obj_is_ready( good_day_pseudo_impl );
            System.out.println( orb.object_to_string(
                good_day_pseudo_impl ) );

            // wait for requests
            boa.impl_is_ready();
```

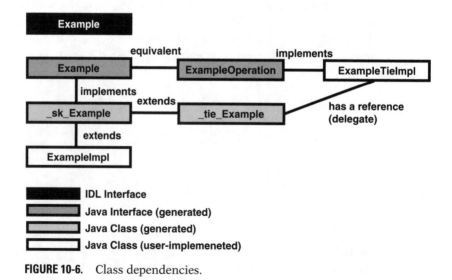

IDL Interface
Java Interface (generated)
Java Class (generated)
Java Class (user-implemeneted)

FIGURE 10-6. Class dependencies.

```
    }
    catch(CORBA.SystemException e) {
        System.err.println(e);
    }
  }
}
```

To understand what is happening behind the scenes, we will look at the class `HelloWorld._tie_GoodDay`. This is the Tie, or pseudo-implementation, class.

The Tie class extends the skeleton class, which connects it with the ORB run-time system and provides the marshaling and unmarshaling routines. The class has a private variable, an object reference of type `HelloWorld.GoodDayOperations`, called `delegate`. This variable will be initialized by each of the constructors. As we have already seen in the server class, the implementation class is provided as a parameter to the constructor. The second constructor uses the built-in name service to facilitate the bind mechanism as discussed in Chapter 8.

```
package HelloWorld;

public class _tie_GoodDay extends _sk_GoodDay {

    private GoodDayOperations delegate;

    public _tie_GoodDay( GoodDayOperations d ) {
        delegate = d;
    }

    public _tie_GoodDay( GoodDayOperations d, String name ) {
        super( name );
        delegate = d;
    }

    public String hello(
        CORBA.short_var hour,
        CORBA.short_var minute )
        throws CORBA.SystemException{

        return delegate.hello( hour, minute );
    };
};
```

Once a method is invoked by a client, the pseudo-implementation object calls the method `hello()` on the real implementation object `delegate` and returns the result from this invocation back to the client. Note that the out parameter is also set by the delegate.

4 Applet Server

So far we have only considered cases where applets invoke objects but do not provide object implementations of their own. In this section we will show using an example how object servers can be implemented as applets:

♦ Introduction of the application and interface specification
♦ Overview of implementation classes
♦ Object implementation
♦ Applet implementation

4.1 The Application

Since none of the examples introduced previously fit this case, we will use a fresh one, AppletTalk. It is based on two applets that can interact with each other by sending messages. Figure 10-7 illustrates this.

For simplicity we only consider two-party talk, although the implementation is easily extensible to support multiparty talks. The talking applets are instances of the same class. This class acts as a speaker, a client sending some text by invoking an operation offered by an object, as well as a listener, offering an object to receive messages.

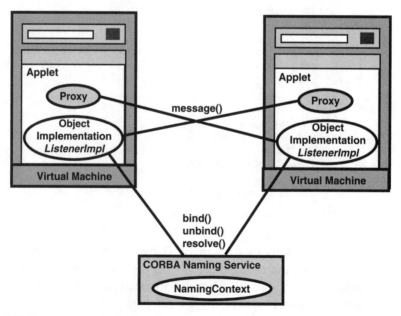

FIGURE 10-7. AppletTalk.

Applets register themselves with the CORBA Naming Services using the bind() operation. Interested parties can establish connections by resolving the name of the potential partner to an object reference. Once a party decides to quit the system it simply deregisters its name from the Naming Service using the unbind() method.

4.2 The Interface Specification

As we see in the IDL specification, a listener applet, which implements the interface Listener, provides an operation message. The operation has an in parameter which is a string. This is a message sent from the other party. The interface is defined inside a module, Talk.

```
module Talk {
    interface Listener {
        void message( in string msg );
    };
};
```

The IDL specification is rather simple; the complexity lies in the implementation. The main issue is that we have to handle two event loops: one for CORBA events, that is, incoming requests, and another one for events from the user.

4.3 Structure of the Implementation

Let's go through the implementation. We have the following implementation classes:

- `TalkAppletServer`–extends the java applet class. We override the following methods:
  - `init()`–initializes the GUI and the ORB. It also instantiates the implementation objects.
  - `action()`–handles user-initiated events. We override the implementation from the `applet` class to catch events caused when the user clicks buttons in the GUI.
  - `register()`–registers the object implementation with the Naming Service.
  - `connect()`–connects an applet (client) to another applet (server) by resolving a name into an object reference.
  - `display()`–displays a string in a particular text field. This method is used by the implementation object `ListenerImpl` to display the message received through a method invocation.
- `ListenerImpl`–the implementation of the IDL-defined interface.

4.4 Object Implementation

The implementation of the interface Listener follows the same pattern we have used before. We define a class ListenerImpl which extends the skeleton class Talk._sk_Listener. The constructor of the implementation class has a parameter of type TalkAppletServer, which is the class that implements the IDL operations. We store this reference in a private variable talk_applet.

```
class ListenerImpl extends Talk._sk_Listener {

    private TalkAppletServer talk_applet;

    // constructor
    ListenerImpl( TalkAppletServer _applet ) {
        talk_applet = _applet;
    }

    // method
    public void message( String msg ) throws CORBA.SystemException {

        talk_applet.display( msg );
        return;
    }
}
```

The implementation of the method message() is quite simple. We invoke the method display() on the applet talk_applet, which in turn displays the message in a text field of the applet.

4.5 Applet Implementation

The implementation of the applet TalkAppletServer has the typical applet structure. First we declare a number of private variables which determine the state of the applet. There are three variables for CORBA-related objects, orb, listener, and listener_impl, and two for convenience classes, easy_naming, and remote_ior_file. The others are for various GUI elements.

```
public class TalkAppletServer extends java.applet.Applet {
    private CORBA.ORB orb;
    private EasyNaming easy_naming;
    private RemoteIORFile remote_ior_file;
    private Talk.Listener listener;
    private ListenerImpl listener_impl;

    private Panel button_panel;
    private Panel text_panel;
    private Button register_button;
    private Button resolve_button;
```

```
private Button send_button;
private Button quit_button;
private TextField in_field;
private TextField out_field;
private String my_name;
```

The implementation of the `init()` method has two parts. The first part initializes the GUI components. The second part initializes the ORB and the BOA, and creates the object.

4.5.1 *Initializing the GUI*

In the first part we initialize the various GUI components. We create text fields for the incoming messages `in_field`, outgoing messages `out_field`, and a field to enter a stringified object reference `ior_field`. There are also two buttons: `connect_button`, to connect to an object specified in `ior_field`, and `send_button`, to send the message held in `out_field`.

```
public void init() {

    register_button = new Button("register");
    register_button.setFont(new Font("Helvetica", Font.BOLD, 20));
    resolve_button = new Button("resolve");
    resolve_button.setFont(new Font("Helvetica", Font.BOLD, 20));
    send_button = new Button("send");
    send_button.setFont(new Font("Helvetica", Font.BOLD, 20));
    quit_button = new Button("quit");
    quit_button.setFont(new Font("Helvetica", Font.BOLD, 20));
    in_field = new TextField();
    in_field.setFont(new Font("Helvetica", Font.BOLD, 14));
    out_field = new TextField();
    out_field.setEditable(false);
    out_field.setFont(new Font("Helvetica", Font.BOLD, 14));

button_panel = new Panel();
text_panel = new Panel();

button_panel.setLayout( new GridLayout(1,4));
button_panel.add( register_button );
button_panel.add( resolve_button );
button_panel.add( send_button );
button_panel.add( quit_button );

text_panel.setLayout( new GridLayout(2,1));
text_panel.add( in_field );
text_panel.add( out_field );

setLayout( new BorderLayout());
add( "Center", text_panel );
add( "South", button_panel );
```

We choose a layout for our GUI elements by using the layout manager class `BorderLayout` for the panels and `GridLayout` for the buttons and text fields. The effect is shown in the screen shots (Figures 10-8 and 10-9).

4.5.2 Initializing the ORB and Object Creation

In the second part of the implementation of the `init()` method we initialize the ORB and the BOA. Then we create the implementation object `listener_impl` by calling its constructor `ListenerImpl()` and passing to it a reference to the applet (`this`).

We also create an instance of the classes `RemoteIORFile` and `EasyNaming` for the use of the Naming Service as already explained in Chapters 8 and 9.

```
try {
    //init ORB
    // CORBA.ORB orb = CORBA.ORB.init();
    orb = CORBA.ORB.init( this );

    //init Basic Object Adapter
    CORBA.BOA boa = orb.BOA_init();

    // create a Listener object
    ListenerImpl listener_impl = new ListenerImpl( this );
```

We use the bootstrap support service `RemoteIORFile`, introduced in Chapter 9, which allows us to obtain a stringified object reference of a root naming context. We use an object of the class `EasyNaming` to query the Naming Service. The implementation of this class is shown in Chapter 8.

```
// proprietary bind to a remote IOR file server
        remote_ior_file =
            RemoteIORFile_var.bind("CosNaming.ior");
```

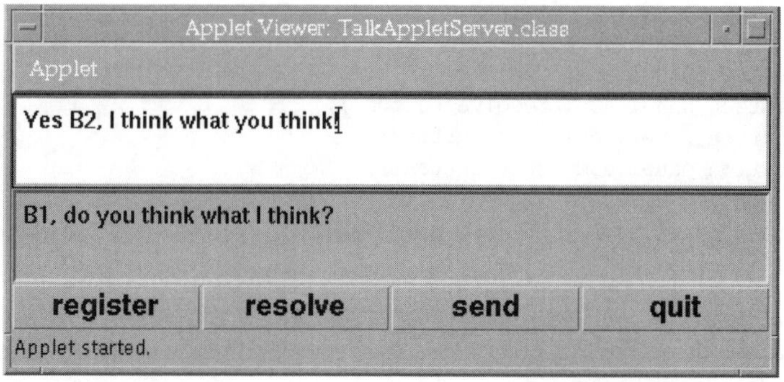

FIGURE 10-8. AppletTalk: B1.

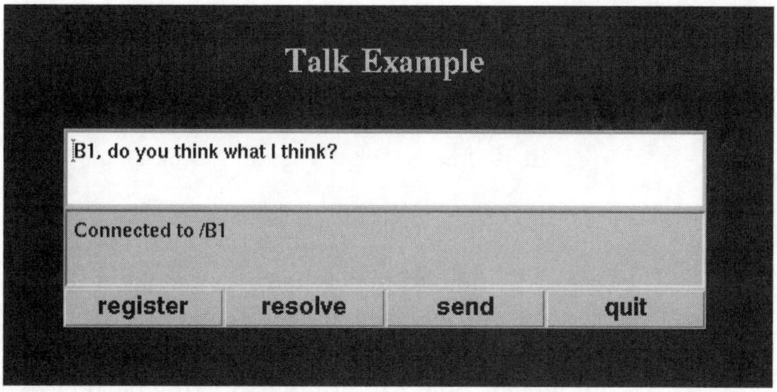

FIGURE 10-9. AppletTalk: B2.

```
easy_naming = new EasyNaming( orb,
    remote_ior_file.get_ior_string() );
```

Once the implementation object is created we notify the BOA by calling `obj_is_ready()` and display the stringified object reference in the `out_field`.

```
    // notify the BOA
    boa.obj_is_ready( listener_impl );
}
catch(CORBA.SystemException e) {
    System.err.println(e);
}
}
```

In the other examples we have seen so far, the last statement in a server's main routine was `impl_is_ready()`, which puts a server into an infinite loop, waiting for incoming requests.

Visibroker allows us to omit the call `impl_is_ready()`; the BOA is already aware of the existence of the implementation object due to our call to `obj_is_ready()`. There is, however, a need for a loop to avoid the termination of the program. In our case, the applet provides its own event loop.

Now we will look at the additional methods we have declared in the class. The method `register()` gets a name from the `in_field` and registers the object implementation `listener_impl` under this name with the Naming Service.

```
public void register() {

    try {
        my_name = new String( in_field.getText() );
        easy_naming.bind_from_string( my_name, listener_impl );
    }
```

```
    catch(CORBA.UserException ue) {
        out_field.setText( "register " + my_name + " failed: " + ue );
    }

    catch(CORBA.SystemException se) {
        out_field.setText( "CORBA System Exception: " + se );
    }
}
```

The connect() method plays the role of a client. It obtains a stringified object reference from the user interface, converts it into a live object reference, and narrows it to the type Talk.Listener. It then invokes the method message() on the new object to notify its talking partner that it is connected.

```
public void connect() {

    // invoke the operation
    try {
        //resolve name
        //and narrow it to Talk.Listener
        listener = Talk.Listener_var.narrow(
            easy_naming.resolve_from_string( in_field.getText() ) );

        // send initial message
        listener.message( "Connected to " + my_name );
    }

    // catch CORBA system exceptions
    catch(CORBA.UserException ue) {
        out_field.setText( "resolve failed: " + ue );
    }
    catch(CORBA.SystemException se) {
        out_field.setText( "CORBA System Exception: " + se );
    }
    return;
}
```

The display() method displays a string in the applet's text field out_field. It is used by the Listener implementation object to display incoming messages.

```
public void display( String msg ) {

    out_field.setText( msg );
    return;
}
```

The method quit() deregisters the chosen name from the Naming Service.

```
public void quit() {

    try {
        easy_naming.unbind_from_string( my_name );
    }
    catch(CORBA.UserException ue) {
            System.err.println(ue);
    }
    catch(CORBA.SystemException se) {
            System.err.println(se);
    }
}
```

Finally, we override the method action(). We watch for events caused by clicking one of the four buttons we have declared and created earlier. For each of the buttons we invoke an appropriate method.

```
public boolean action(Event ev, java.lang.Object arg) {

    // catch and process events
    if(ev.target == connect_button ) {

        // resolve name and connect to referenced object
        connect();
        return true;
    }

    if(ev.target == register_button ) {

        // register yourself
        register();
        return true;
    }

    if(ev.target == quit_button ) {

        // quit
        quit();
        return true;
    }

    if(ev.target == send_button ) {

        // invoke the operation
        try {
            listener.message( in_field.getText() );
        }

        // catch CORBA system exceptions
        catch(CORBA.SystemException ex) {
```

```
          System.err.println(ex);
    }
    return true;
  }
  return false;
 }
}
```

4.6 Executing the Application

Once the classes are compiled, we can start our AppletTalk example. We have two instances of the our class `TalkAppletServer`. One runs in a Web browser as shown in Figure 10-8. The other one runs in an Appletviewer on a different host (Figure 10-9). The two instances are registered under the names `/B1` and `/B2`, respectively.

The white text fields are the in fields, the gray ones the out fields. In the out field in Figure 10-8 we can still see the message that was sent from B2 after having resolved the name.

In Figure 10-9, the gray text field shows the message that has just been received from B1. The white text field shows the response from B1 which is yet to be sent.

OMG and CORBA Reference

This appendix contains detailed information, from a CORBA developer's perspective, about the OMG and the architecture documents and specifications it has produced.

First we present an overview of the history, goals, organizational structure, and processes of the OMG. Descriptions of all the committees, task forces, and special interest groups within the consortium are provided.

Second we give a detailed summary of the contents of the *Object Management Architecture Guide,* including the changes made to the Object Management Architecture (OMA) since the third revision in mid-1995. There are two main topics included here, the Core Object Model and the OMA Reference Architecture.

Third we summarize the CORBA2.0 specification. This section attempts to balance conciseness and detail, and covers all of the content of the July 1995 *Common Object Request Broker: Architecture and Specification* document that is relevant to ORB users, while briefly introducing the material relevant to ORB implementers. The major topics covered include

- The CORBA Object Model
- The Structure of the Object Request Broker
- OMG Interface Definition Language
- The interfaces to the ORB and CORBA Object
- The Basic Object Adapter
- A brief description of other language mappings
- The interoperability architecture
- The Dynamic Invocation and Dynamic Skeleton Interfaces
- The Interface Repository

1 The Object Management Group

The Object Management Group (OMG) is the world's largest computer industry consortium, with over 600 members in 1996. It is a nonprofit company that began in 1989 with eight members: 3Com Corporation, American Airlines, Canon, Data General, Hewlett-Packard, Philips Telecommunications N.V., Sun Microsystems, and Unisys Corporation. The organization remains fairly small and does not develop any technology or specifications itself. It provides a structure for its members to specify technology and then produce commercial implementations that comply with those specifications. The OMG's processes emphasize cooperation, compromise, and agreement rather than choosing one member's solution over another's.

1.1 OMG's Goals

The goals of the OMG are

- Promotion of the object-oriented approach to software engineering
- Development of a common architectural framework for writing distributed object-oriented applications, based on interface specifications for the objects in the application

1.2 The Organizational Structure of OMG

The OMG Board administers the organization and ratifies the activities of the other groups within the OMG. Most positions in the OMG are unpaid and are occupied by representatives of member companies.

The technical groupings of the OMG are overseen by the Architecture Board (AB), whose members are experienced system architects. The AB is elected by the OMG membership. It reviews all proposals for technology and specifications submitted for consistency and conformance to the OMA.

The structure of the committees, task forces, and other groups within the OMG reflect the structure of the OMA (see Figure A-1). Two committees oversee the technology adoption of a number of task forces and special interest groups (SIGs).

◆ Platform Technology Committee (PTC). This committee is concerned with infrastructure issues: the Object Request Broker (ORB), Common Facilities and Object Services, and the relationship of the OMA to object-oriented analysis and design.

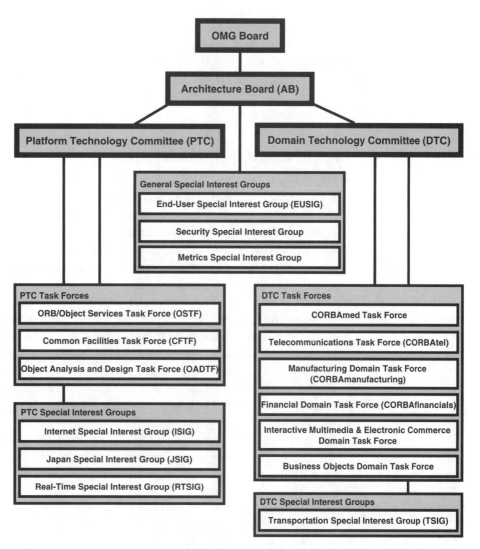

FIGURE A-1. Organization of the OMG.

◆ Domain Technology Committee (DTC). This committee is concerned with technologies that support application development in particular vertical markets, such as manufacturing, electronic commerce, or health care.

Task forces may issue Requests for Proposals (RFPs). These are detailed statements of a problem that needs to be solved. Responses are solicited in the form of IDL specifications with object semantics explained in English. Two rounds of submissions are taken, usually three months apart, and then the most suitable specification is selected by a vote of members and presented to the task force's controlling committee.

Special interest groups may not issue RFPs directly or adopt technology specifications, but may do so with the support of a task force. Usually SIGs discuss areas of common interest and report their findings to their controlling committee via documents and presentations. A number of SIGs do not belong to either the PTC or the DTC. Instead they report directly to the Architecture Board.

1.2.1   PTC Task Forces and SIGs

◆ ORB/Object Services Task Force (OSTF). This task force is responsible for specifying the ORB, which is published as the Common Object Request Broker Architecture and Specification (CORBA). The task force also specifies general purpose Object Services (published as CORBAservices). This is the area that supports the basic infrastructure of object interaction. This task force has adopted the largest number of specifications.

◆ Common Facilities Task Force (CFTF). This task force specifies technologies that provide services to applications at a high level. Its specifications are published as CORBAfacilities.

◆ Object Analysis and Design Task Force (OADTF). This task force is concerned with applying widely used object-oriented analysis and design methodologies to distributed object-oriented application development using CORBA. It is a new task force that has published some white papers but as yet no specifications.

◆ Internet Special Interest Group (ISIG). The ISIG is concerned with the convergence between distributed objects and the Internet, both as a distribution mechanism and as a growing area of commercial activity.

◆ Japan Special Interest Group (JSIG). The JSIG is a focus for Japanese developers of distributed objects. It is particularly concerned with internationalization issues across the OMG.

♦ Real-Time Special Interest Group (RTSIG). The RTSIG is concerned with issues of guaranteed performance of requests to distributed objects, embedded systems, and fault tolerance.

1.2.2   DTC Task Forces and SIGs

♦ CORBAmed Task Force (Healthcare). The CORBAmed task force is concerned with adopting specifications that meet the vertical domain requirements of the health care sector. It also promotes the use of object-oriented technology in the medical field.
♦ Telecommunications Task Force (CORBAtel). CORBAtel is working toward adoption of specifications that meet the needs of telecommunications providers. It also promotes the OMG and liaises with relevant telecommunications industry bodies.
♦ Manufacturing Domain Task Force (CORBAmanufacturing). CORBAmanufacturing promotes the use of CORBA technology in manufacturing industry computer systems and will adopt technology specifications tailored to that broad sector.
♦ Financial Domain Task Force (CORBAfinancials). CORBAfinancials promotes the use of financial services and accounting software based on OMG standards. They plan to adopt specifications for standard interfaces to this kind of software.
♦ Interactive Multimedia and Electronic Commerce Domain Task Force. This task force is interested in on-line commerce, including rights and royalties and electronic payment for media services.
♦ Business Objects Domain Task Force (BODTF). The area covered by the BODTF is broad: it includes any standard objects used in business processes. This covers such areas as workflow, document processing, task scheduling, etc. The first RFP issued by the BODTF was controversial in that it did not solicit a single well-focused specification, but rather invited submitters to specify anything that they consider to be a business object. It is unclear how the decision will be made about which specification(s) to adopt.
♦ Transportation Special Interest Group (TSIG). The TSIG examines the requirements of the transportation industry in the development of distributed object applications.

1.2.3   Architecture Board SIGs

♦ End User Special Interest Group (EUSIG). The EUSIG is becoming increasingly important as the OMG membership shifts from representing mainly technology vendors to including a large number of users of the technology. One example of the influence of this group is that all RFPs now include a section on responding to the concerns of the EUSIG. The EUSIG seeks to emphasize the usability of the specifications adopted throughout the OMG from the point of view of application builders in business, the military, and government.

◆ Security Special Interest Group. This SIG is similar to the EUSIG in that it feeds the security requirements of end users into the OMG-wide technology adoption process.

◆ Metrics Special Interest Group. This SIG investigates the measurement of performance of object technology and the measurement of the processes by which the technology is developed.

◆ Inactive SIGs. The following SIGs still exist, but are not meeting or developing documents currently:
  ◆ Database Special Interest Group
  ◆ Smalltalk Special Interest Group
  ◆ Parallel Object Systems Special Interest Group
  ◆ Class Libraries Special Interest Group

1.3   OMG Technology Adoption Process

The process, in brief, is as follows:

◆ A task force issues a Request for Information (RFI) on a particular technology area.

◆ RFI submissions are considered in the process of drawing up a Request for Proposals (RFP) which solicits submissions addressing its proposal from contributing members of the OMG.

◆ Any member company that wishes to respond to an RFP must submit a letter of intent (LOI) stating that they will be willing to release a commercial implementation of their submitted specification within one year of its adoption, should it be chosen.

◆ A voting list is established from OMG members who express an interest in selecting from the submissions.

◆ A first submission takes place, usually about three months after the issue of the RFP. Typically there are three to six submissions.

◆ Questions are asked and feedback provided on the initial submissions at the TF session at one of the six annual OMG meetings.

◆ The submitters consider each other's specifications, and frequently some or all of them decide to produce a consensus merger of specifications that align fairly closely.

◆ Second (final) submissions are made, usually after another three months, and if there is more than one submission the choice of which to adopt is put to a vote.

- The adopted specification is then presented to a Technical Committee plenary session, and a yes/no vote to adopt the chosen submission is put to the entire OMG membership. This usually passes without problem.
- The Architecture Board then considers the broader implications of the new specification on the whole OMA. They may approve the specification unequivocally, suggest revisions, or simply reject the specification and issue a new RFP. Reissue of RFPs does not usually occur.
- Once the Architecture Board is happy with the specification, it is ratified by the OMG Board based on a further vote by the members.

The form of submissions to the OMG's task forces and technical committees is usually a specification detailing the problem area that is being solved and proposing a number of interface definitions (in OMG IDL). The IDL is accompanied by English text describing the semantics of the objects and the roles and relationships to other objects in the specification and outside of it. The interfaces are described in terms of the actions of their operations, and not in terms of a particular underlying implementation.

2   *The Object Management Architecture*

This section introduces the OMA and provides a summary of the technical parts of the third edition of the OMG publication, the *Object Management Architecture Guide,* which consists of two main parts: the Core Object Model and the Reference Model.

2.1   Overview of the OMA

The OMA is the framework within which all OMG-adopted technology fits. It provides two fundamental models on which CORBA and the other standard interfaces are based: the Core Object Model and the Reference Model.

The Core Object Model defines the concepts that allow distributed application development to be facilitated by an Object Request Broker (ORB). The Core Object Model is restricted to abstract definitions that do not constrain the syntax of object interfaces or the implementations of objects or ORBs. It then defines a framework for refining the model to a more concrete form. The model provides the basis for CORBA, but is more relevant to ORB designers and implementers than to distributed object application developers.

The Reference Model places the ORB at the center of groupings of objects with standardized interfaces that provide support for application object developers. The groups identified are: Object Services, which provide infrastructure; Domain Interfaces, which provide special support to applications from various industry domains; Common Facilities, which provide application-level services across domains; and Application Interfaces, which is the set of all other objects developed for specific applications. The Reference Model is directly relevant to CORBA programmers because it provides the big picture from which components and frameworks can be drawn to support developers of distributed applications.

The Reference Model also provides the framework for the OMG's technology adoption process. It does this by identifying logical groupings of interface specifications that are provided by organizational groups (task forces and SIGs) which specify and adopt them.

2.2   Core Object Model

This section provides a detailed explanation of the theoretical underpinnings of CORBA. These specifics will not be of interest to everyone. We have tried to provide a readable summary of the contents of the OMG's *Object Management Architecture Guide*. This section will mostly be of interest to readers with a background in object-oriented theory, but it starts from first principles, and so is readable by anyone with a somewhat broader interest than simply using CORBA as an application development platform. The remaining sections of this appendix do not rely on the material provided here.

2.2.1   Scope of the Core Object Model

The main goals of the Core Object Model are portability and interoperability. The most important aspect of portability considered is *design portability*. This means knowledge of an object's interface and the ability to create applications whose components do not rely on the existence or location of a particular object implementation. The Core does not define the syntax of interface descriptions, but does describe the semantics of types and their relationships to one another.

Interoperability means being able to invoke operations on objects regardless of where they are located, which platform they execute on, or what programming language they are implemented in. This is achieved by the ORB, which relies on the semantics of objects and operations described in the Core Object Model. The ORB also requires some extensions to the Core that provide specifications for specific communication protocols, an interface definition syntax, and basic services to object implementations. CORBA provides these extensions.

The Core Object Model is not a meta-model. This means that it cannot have more than one possible concrete instance of the basic concepts. It consists of an abstract set of concepts that allow understanding of objects and their interfaces. However, these concepts cannot be redefined or replaced, only extended and made more concrete. The Core Model is specialized using *Components* and *Profiles* to provide a concrete architecture for an ORB.

2.2.2 Components and Profiles

A Component is an extension to the abstract Core Object Model that provides more concrete specialization of the concepts defined in the Core. The Core, together with one or more Components, produces what is called a *Profile*. CORBA is a Profile that extends the Core with several Components which provide specializations such as a syntax for object interfaces, and a protocol for interoperation between objects implemented using different ORBs.

Figure A-2 shows how Components and Profiles are used to add to the Core Object Model.

2.2.3 Concept Definitions

The Core Object Model is a classical object model. This means that actions in the system are performed by sending request messages to objects. The request will identify an operation and its parameters. The object will then interpret the message and perform some actions, and then possibly send a return message to the caller containing any resulting values.

The concepts defined in the Core Object Model are

- ♦ Objects
- ♦ Operations, including their signatures, parameters, and return values
- ♦ Non-object Types
- ♦ Interfaces
- ♦ Substitutability

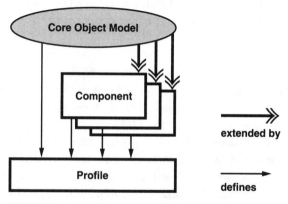

FIGURE A-2. Components and Profiles.

Objects   Objects are defined simply as models of entities or concepts. For example, an object can model a document, a date, an employee, a subatomic particle, or a compiler. The important characteristic of an object is its identity, which is fixed for the life of the object and is independent of the object's properties or behavior. This identity is represented by an *object reference.*

Operations, Signatures, Parameters, and Return Values   An operation is an action offered by an object which is known to the outside world by its signature. The notion of sending a request to an object is equivalent to the notion of invoking an operation on an object. An operation's signature has the following components:

- ♦ A name
- ♦ A set of parameters
- ♦ A set of result types

Operation names are unique within a particular object. No syntax for describing operations and their types is provided.

When a request is sent to an object, it nominates an operation and provides arguments matching the parameters in that operation's signature. The operation then performs some action on those arguments and will return zero or more results. It is important to note that object references may be returned as part of the result of an operation.

Operations may cause some side effects, usually manifested as changes in the encapsulated state of the object. When an object cannot process a request it will typically return an exception message, but exceptions are defined in a separate component that is part of CORBA, not in the core object model.

The Core Object Model does not specify whether or not requests are accepted by an object in parallel, or what the consequences of parallel execution would be if they were. An implementation of objects could choose to provide atomic operations or a sequence of operations for transaction management.

Non-object Types   Unlike the object models of Smalltalk and Eiffel, there are types in the OMA Core that are not objects. These are usually called data types. The set of objects and non-object types makes up the whole of the denotable values in the OMA.

While the Core Object Model does not specify a set of non-object types, another component of CORBA does. Even though the OMA Core is designed to be extensible into several Profiles via different sets of Components, the likelihood of an alternative profile to CORBA being specified in the OMA is almost nonexistent. This design decision has been made so that new components can be added to CORBA in a consistent manner, and so that new versions of CORBA can be defined in terms of the makeup of its components and their versions.

2.2.4 *Interfaces and Substitutability*

An *interface* is a collection of operation signatures. Typically the interface to an object is the set of operations offered by that object, but this is left, once again, to CORBA to specify. Interfaces are related to one another by substitutability relationships. This means that an object offering an interface can be used in place of an object offering a "similar" interface. The Core Object Model simply defines substitutability as being able to use one interface in place of another without "interaction error." However, it is useful to examine a more concrete definition.

The simplest form of substitutability is when two interfaces offer exactly the same operations. Generally, if an interface A offers a superset of the operations offered by another interface B, then A is substitutable for B. Substitutability is not symmetrical, except in the simple case where A and B offer the same operations. However, it is transitive. That is, if A is substitutable for B and B is substitutable for a third interface C, then A is also substitutable for C.

2.2.5 *Inheritance*

Since interfaces may offer operations with the same signatures that have different purposes and semantics it is useful to have an assertion of compatibility between them. In order to ensure a semantic relationship, the model introduces inheritance. If interface A inherits from interface B, then A offers all of the operations of B, and may also offer some additional operations. The set of operations of A is therefore a superset of the operations of B, and hence A is substitutable for B. However, because the relationship between A and B is explicit, we can be certain that the operations they have in common serve the same purpose, and A and B don't merely coincidentally share signatures. Figure A-3 shows this example in a graphical form.

The Core Object Model defines *subtyping* as a form of substitutability dependent on inheritance of interfaces. That is, an interface A that inherits from an interface B is a subtype of B. We can also say that B is a supertype of A. In the Core Object Model, subtyping is the only acceptable form of substitutability.

The supertype of all objects in the Core Object Model is an abstract type *Object* that has an empty set of operations. The inheritance hierarchy places Object at the root and all other objects as its subtypes and is also called the type graph.

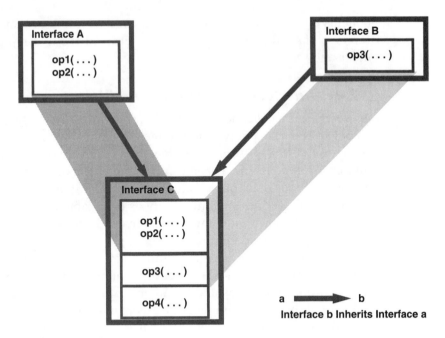

FIGURE A-3. Inheritance.

2.3 The Reference Model

The OMA Reference Model is an architectural framework for the standard-ization of interfaces to infrastructure and services that applications can use. The object-oriented paradigm emphasizes reusability of components that perform small, well-defined parts of an application's functionality. The Reference Model allows users of components to understand what support they can expect in what areas from ORB vendors and third-party compo-nent providers.

2.3.1 Overview

The Reference Model is shown in Figure A-4, which identifies five main components of the OMA:

- ♦ Object Request Broker
- ♦ Object Services
- ♦ Common Facilities
- ♦ Domain Interfaces
- ♦ Application Interfaces

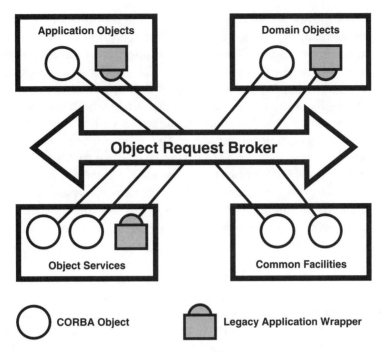

FIGURE A-4. The OMA Reference Model.

Only the last of these is not intended to have interfaces specified through OMG processes. Application objects are the project specific part of an integrated application.

2.3.2   *Object Request Broker*

The ORB is defined in the CORBA specification document. CORBA builds on the OMA Core Object Model and provides

- ♦ An extended CORBA Core including a syntax and semantics for an Interface Definition Language (IDL).
- ♦ A framework for interoperability, including two specific protocol definitions.
- ♦ A set of language mappings from IDL to implementation languages (C, C++, Smalltalk, Ada'95).

The ORB is situated at the conceptual (and graphical) center of the Reference Model. It acts as a message bus between objects that may be located on any machine in a network, implemented in any programming language, and executed on any hardware or operating system platform. The caller only needs an object reference and well-formed arguments in the language mapping of choice to invoke an operation as if it were a local function and receive results. This is called location and access transparency.

At the heart of CORBA is the IDL, which is covered in detail later in this appendix. It provides a way of defining the interfaces of objects independently of the programming language in which they are implemented. It is a strongly typed declarative language with a rich set of data types for describing complex parameters. An IDL interface acts as a contract between developers of objects and the eventual users of their interfaces. It also allows the user of CORBA objects to compile the interface definitions into hidden code for the transmission of invocation requests across networks and machine architectures without knowledge of the network protocol, the target machine architecture, or even the location of the object being invoked.

2.3.3   Object Services

This set of interface specifications provides fundamental services that application developers may need in order to find and manage their objects and data, and to coordinate the execution of complex operations. Object Services are the building blocks from which other components of the OMA can be constructed and which application objects may require. The OMG brand name for these services is CORBAservices. The published services include

- Naming
- Events
- Life Cycle
- Persistent Object
- Relationships
- Externalization
- Transactions
- Concurrency Control
- Licensing
- Query
- Properties
- Security
- Time
- Collections
- Trading

Some of these are simply framework interfaces that will be inherited by application or other objects, for example, the Life Cycle Service. Others represent low-level components on which higher level application-oriented components can be built, for example, Transaction Service. Yet others provide basic services used at all levels of applications, such as the Naming and Trading Services. These last two services provide a means of locating objects by name, or by type and properties, for late binding in an application. See Chapter 8 for a detailed description of these services.

2.3.4 *Common Facilities*

Common Facilities are those end-user-oriented interfaces which provide facilities across application domains. The first such specification adopted, published by the OMG as *CORBAfacilities*, is the Distributed Document Component Facility, based on OpenDoc. Work is being completed on Internationalization and Time Facilities, Data Interchange and Mobile Agent Facilities, a well as a Printing facility. New work to introduce a Meta-Object facility (a repository for IDL and non-IDL types) and a Systems Management facility are under way.

2.3.5 *Domain Interfaces*

The OMG contains a large number of SIGs and Domain Task Forces that focus on particular application domains such as Telecommunications, the Internet, business objects, manufacturing, and health care. In early 1996 this area of standardization was separated from the Common Facilities where it was called Vertical Facilities. Several RFIs and RFPs are in progress in the Domain Task Forces. Some examples are the Common Business Object Facility, Product Data Management Enablers, and Control and Management of Audio/Visual Streams.

2.3.6 *Specification Adoption in the OMG*

Technology adoption in the OMG emphasizes the use of existing technologies and rapid market availability. To this end, submitters of specifications must vouch that an implementation of the specification exists and that, should their submission be adopted, they will make an implementation commercially available within one year of adoption. The adoption process was detailed earlier.

3 *Common Object Request Broker Architecture*

This section provides a summary of the *Common Object Request Broker: Architecture and Specification*, version 2.0, including

♦ An overview of CORBA
♦ The CORBA object model
♦ The structure of the Object Request Broker
♦ OMG Interface Definition Language
♦ The interfaces to the ORB and CORBA Object
♦ The Basic Object Adapter
♦ A brief description of other language mappings
♦ The interoperability architecture
♦ The Dynamic Invocation and Dynamic Skeleton Interfaces
♦ The Interface Repository

3.1 Overview

CORBA is the specification of the functionality of the Object Request Broker, the crucial message bus that conveys operation invocation requests and their results to CORBA objects resident anywhere, however they are implemented. The CORBA specification provides certain interfaces to components of the ORB, but leaves the interfaces to other components up to the ORB implementer.

The notion of transparency is at the center of CORBA. *Location transparency* is the ability to access and invoke operations on a CORBA object without needing to know where the object resides. The idea is that it should be equally easy to invoke an operation on an object residing on a remote machine as it is to invoke a method on an object in the same address space.

Programming language transparency provides the freedom to implement the functionality encapsulated in an object using the most appropriate language, whether because of the skills of the programmers, the appropriateness of the language to the task, or the choice of a third-party developer who provides off-the-shelf component objects. The key to this freedom is an implementation-neutral interface definition language, OMG IDL, which provides separation of interface and implementation.

IDL interface definitions inform clients of an object offering an interface, exactly what operations an object supports, the types of their parameters, and what return types to expect. A client programmer needs only the IDL to write client code that is ready to invoke operations on a remote object. The client uses the data types defined in IDL through a *language mapping*. This mapping defines the programming language constructs (data types, classes, etc.) that will be generated by the IDL compiler supplied by an ORB vendor.

The IDL compiler also generates *stub code* that the client links to, and this translates, or *marshals*, the programming language data types into a wire format for transmission as a request message to an object implementation. The implementation of the object has linked to it similar marshaling code, called a *skeleton*, that *unmarshals* the request into programming language data types, perhaps using a different IDL compiler with a different language mapping. In this way the object's method implementation can be invoked and the results returned by the same means. Figure A-5 illustrates the use of stub, skeleton, and ORB to make a remote invocation.

IDL and IDL compilers allow programs providing and using object interfaces to agree on the form of their exchanges, even though they may have been developed completely independently, in different languages, or using different ORB technologies. This means that objects offering the same interfaces are substitutable, and that clients can decide which object to use at run time with the assurance that there will be no interaction mismatches. Because the implementation of a particular object offering an interface is hidden, there may be Quality of Service differences, or even differences in the semantics of operations. However, the Trading Service allows clients to find the most appropriate object that matches their particular performance, location, cost, or other criteria.

The interfaces to components of the ORB are all specified in IDL. This provides a language-neutral representation of the computational interface of the ORB. However, certain parts of these definitions are designated as pseudo-IDL (PIDL), which means that their implementations are not necessarily CORBA objects and data types. Any interface definition that is commented as "pseudo-IDL" may be implemented as a *pseudo-object*. This usually means that it is a library that is linked into the application using it. Although operations on pseudo-objects are invoked in the same way as operations on real CORBA objects, their references and pseudo-IDL data types cannot be passed as parameters to real CORBA objects.

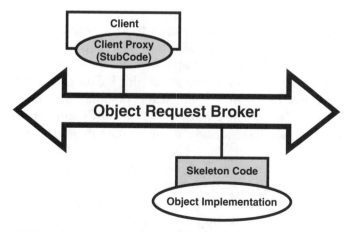

FIGURE A-5. Stub, ORB, and skeleton.

3.2 Object Model

The OMA Core Object Model provides some fundamental definitions of concepts that are extended by the CORBA specification. CORBA uses the same concepts as the OMA Core, but makes them more specific and concrete. The definitions below refer to the way in which these concepts are declared, but do not provide syntax for declarations. The syntax is all provided by the IDL.

3.2.1 Object Implementations and Object References

It is necessary to distinguish between object implementations and object references. The former is the code that implements the operations defined by an IDL interface definition, and the latter is the object's identity, which is used by clients to invoke its operations.

An object implementation is the part of a CORBA object that is provided by an application developer. It usually includes some internal state, and will often cause side effects on things that are not objects, such as a database, or a screen display, or a telecommunications network element. The methods of this implementation may be accessed by any mechanism, but in practice most object implementations will be invoked via the skeleton code generated by an IDL compiler.

Object references are handles to objects. A given object reference will always denote a single object, but several distinct object references may denote the same object. Object references can be passed to clients of objects, either as an operation's output parameter or result, where the IDL for an operation nominates an interface type, or they can be passed as strings which can be turned into live object references that can have operations invoked on them.

Object references are opaque to their users. That is, they contain enough information for the ORB to send a request to the correct object implementation, but this information is inaccessible to their users. Object references contain information about the location and type of the object denoted, but do so in a sophisticated manner so that if the object has migrated or is not active at the time, the ORB can perform the necessary tasks to redirect the request to a new location or activate an object to receive the request.

Unless an object has been explicitly destroyed, or the underlying network and operating system infrastructure is malfunctioning, the ORB should be able to convey an operation invocation to its target and return results. The ORB also supports operations that interpret the object reference and provide the client with some of the information it contains.

3.2.2   *Types*

Types are defined using predicate logic in the CORBA specification. Object types are related in an inheritance hierarchy, with the type *Object* at the root. An object type derived from another can be substituted for it. Object types may be specified as parameters and return types for operations, and may be used as components in structured data types. A set of non-object types are defined with specific properties in CORBA. These are represented by constructs in OMG IDL. The usual kind of basic numeric, string, and boolean types are defined. A type called *Any* is also given as a basic type. It can store any legitimate value of a CORBA type in a self-describing manner. See Chapter 6 for detailed descriptions of Anys.

The basic types can be used as components for a rich set of structured types, including structures, arrays, variable length sequences, and discriminated unions. The syntax and specification of CORBA types are given in the OMG IDL description.

3.2.3   *Interfaces*

An *interface* is a description of the operations that are offered by an object, and can also contain structured type definitions used as parameters to those operations. Interfaces are specified in OMG IDL and are related in an inheritance hierarchy. In CORBA, interface types and object types have a one-to-one mapping. This is a restriction of the OMA Core Object Model, which implies that objects have single interfaces but does not state that this must be the case. The term *principal interface* is used to indicate the most specific (most derived) interface type that an object supports. The Multiple Interfaces RFP is currently soliciting submissions in the OMG, and a model for objects with multiple interfaces will probably be introduced in a revised CORBA specification.

3.2.4   *Operation Semantics*

There are two kinds of operation execution semantics defined for static (stub code) invocations:

♦ *At-Most-Once.* An operation is a named action that a client can request an invocation of. The invocation of an operation results in the ORB conveying the arguments to the object implementation and returning the results (if any) to the requester, which is blocked and waiting for a successful termination or an exception. The semantics of the invocation are "at-most-once". That is, the operation will execute exactly once if a successful completion takes place, or if an exception is raised it will have executed no more than once.

♦ *Best-Effort*. If an operation is declared using the oneway keyword then the requester does not wait for the operation to complete and the semantics is "best-effort".

Both these kinds of requests can be made using the generated stubs or using the Dynamic Invocation Interface (DII), but the DII also offers a third type of execution semantics, namely, *deferred-synchronous*. This allows the requester to send the request without blocking and at some later time to poll for the results.

3.2.5 Operation Signatures

Each operation has a signature, expressed in IDL, that contains the following mandatory components:

♦ An operation identifier (also called an operation name).
♦ The type of the value returned by the operation.
♦ A (possibly empty) list of parameters, each with a name, type, and direction indication. The direction will be one of in, out, or inout, stating that the parameter is being transmitted from the client to the object, is being returned as a result from the operation, or is client data to be modified by the operation, respectively.

An operation signature may also have the following optional components:

♦ A raises clause that lists user-defined exceptions that the operation may raise. Any operation may raise system exceptions.
♦ A oneway keyword that indicates "best-effort" semantics. The signature must have a void return type and may not contain any out or inout parameters or a raises clause.
♦ A context clause that lists the names of operating system, user, or client program environment values that must be transmitted with the request. Contexts are transmitted as sets of string pairs and are not type safe. We recommend that client applications look up appropriate context parameters and pass them as actual arguments to operations.

3.2.6 Attributes

An interface may contain *attributes*. These are declared as named types, with a possible readonly modifier. They are logically equivalent to a pair of operations. The first, an *accessor operation*, retrieves a value of the specified type. The second, a *modifier operation*, takes an argument of the specified type and sets that value. Readonly attributes will only have an accessor. Attributes cannot raise user-defined exceptions.

The execution semantics for attributes are the same as for operations. Attributes do not necessarily represent a state variable in an object, and executing the modifier operation with a particular argument does not guarantee that the same value will be returned by the next accessor execution. Section 3.4.6 contains a full syntax for operation and attribute declarations.

3.2.7 *Exceptions*

An exception is a specialized non-object type in CORBA. It contains optional fields of named data types which provide further information about what caused an abnormal termination of an operation.

3.3   ORB Structure

As we have mentioned, OMG IDL provides the basis of agreement about what can be requested of an object implementation via the ORB. The IDL is not just a guide to clients of objects. IDL compilers use the interface definitions to create the means by which a client can invoke a local function, and an invocation then happens, as if by magic, on an object on another machine. The code generated for the client to use is known as *stub code*, and the code generated for the object implementation is called *skeleton code*. Figure A-6 shows the ORB Core, stub and skeleton code, and the interfaces to the ORB described below.

Stub and skeleton codes interface with the ORB run-time system to convey requests and results for static invocations. Static means that the IDL is statically defined at compile time, and only operations on known interface types can be invoked.

The CORBA standard also defines an interface to allow requests to be built dynamically for any operation by a client. This is known as the Dynamic Invocation Interface (DII). A symmetric interface called the Dynamic Skeleton Interface (DSI), is defined for responding to arbitrary requests.

CORBA defines an interface for communicating with the ORB from either client or server. This interface deals mainly with ORB initialization and object reference manipulation.

Finally, object implementations need extra facilities for managing their interactions with the ORB. A component called an *Object Adapter* fills this role. It is responsible for operating systems process management for implementations on behalf of the ORB. It also informs the ORB when implementations are ready to receive requests.

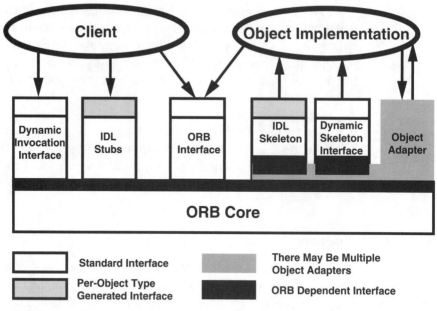

FIGURE A-6. ORB interfaces.

3.3.1 Client Stubs

When a client wishes to invoke an IDL-defined operation on an object reference as if it were a local method or function, it must link in stubs for the method that convey invocations to the target object. In object-oriented implementation languages the stubs are methods on a local *proxy object* that delegates invocations on those methods to the remote implementation object. The stubs are generated from an IDL compiler for the language and ORB environment that the client is using.

3.3.2 Dynamic Invocation Interface

A *Request* is a notional message that is sent to an object denoted by an object reference to request the invocation of a particular operation with particular arguments. The DII defines the form of such a message so that clients which know of an object by reference and can determine its interface type, can thereby build Requests without requiring an IDL compiler to generate stub code. A Request interface is defined in pseudo-IDL. It provides operations to set the target object for the invocation, name the operation to be invoked, and add arguments to send to it. It also provides operations to invoke the operation and retrieve any resulting values. As noted earlier, the implementation of pseudo-IDL is provided as a library and the operations map to local methods on a non-CORBA object.

The DII defines various types of execution semantics for operations invoked using Request pseudo-objects. The usual synchronous at-most-once semantics are available, as well as a *deferred-synchronous* option. The latter sends the request and immediately returns to the client code to allow further processing while waiting for a response. Details of this functionality are given later in this appendix and a programming example is provided in Chapter 10.

3.3.3 Implementation Skeleton

Once a Request reaches a server that supports one or more objects, there must be a way for it to invoke the right method on the right implementation object. The translation from a wire format to in-memory data structures (unmarshaling) uses the language mapping to the implementation language. This is achieved by the skeleton code generated by an IDL compiler.

3.3.4 Dynamic Skeleton Interface

Implementation code may be written that deals with requests in a generic manner by looking at the requested operation and its arguments and interpreting the semantics dynamically. This is called the Dynamic Skeleton Interface (DSI) and is realized by allowing the implementer access to the request in the form of a ServerRequest pseudo-object, which is the same as the DII Request, except for the invocation operations.

An example use of the DSI is a minimal wrapper around some legacy command processing code which accepts each request it receives with a single string argument. It then parses the string for a numeric value and sets this in a register before passing the operation name to an interpreter. It then checks the contents of the register and, unless an error bit is set, encodes the rest of the register as a numeric string and passes it back as the result. Clients can then write IDL that matches the expected pattern and use the generated stubs in a type-safe way to invoke the server, which was implemented before the IDL was written.

3.3.5 Object Adapters

An Object Adapter is a component that an object implementation uses to get access to an ORB and that the ORB uses to manage the run-time environment of the object implementations. An adapter is used, rather than extending the interface to the ORB, so that different Object Adapters suitable for different implementations can be used for greater efficiency.

Object Adapters are not provided with complete interface descriptions in the standard because of the large variety of platforms and environments in which objects execute. For example, an object that manages a data stream for audio/video may need its adapter to exert some flow control or Quality of Service management over operating systems and network resources.

Currently CORBA defines only one such interface, the Basic Object Adapter (BOA). Its purpose is to generate and interpret object references and to activate and deactivate object implementations. The interface to the BOA is described in detail later in this appendix.

3.4   OMG Interface Definition Language

OMG IDL is a declarative language for defining the interfaces of CORBA objects. It is a language-independent way in which implementers and users of objects can be assured of type-safe invocation of operations, even though the only other information that needs to pass between them is an object reference. IDL is used by ORB-specific IDL compilers to generate stub and/or skeleton code that converts in-memory data structures in one programming language into network streams. It then unpacks them on another machine into equivalent data structures in another (or the same) language, making a method call and then transmitting the results in the opposite direction.

The syntax of IDL is drawn from C++, but it contains different and unambiguous keywords. There are no programming statements, since its only purpose is to define interface signatures. To do this a number of constructs are supported:

- *Constants* to assist with type declarations
- *Data type declarations* to use for parameter typing
- *Attributes* which get and set a value of a particular type
- *Operations* which take parameters and return values
- *Interfaces* which group data type, attribute, and operation declarations
- *Modules* for name space separation

3.4.1   Lexical Analysis
OMG IDL uses the ISO Latin-1 character set.

Identifiers   Identifiers must start with a letter and may be followed by zero or more letters, numbers, and underscores. The only strange feature of the lexical analysis of IDL is that identifiers are case sensitive, but cannot coexist with other identifiers that differ only in case. To put it another way, to identify the same entity the identifier must use the same case in each instance, but another identifier with the same spelling and different case may not coexist with it. For example, short DisplayTerminal and interface displayTerminal denote different entities, but may not both be declared in the same IDL. The reason for this is that language mappings to case-insensitive languages would not cope with both identifiers.

Preprocessing The standard C++ preprocessing macros are the first thing to be dealt with in lexical analysis. They include #include, #define, #ifdef, and #pragma. The fewer preprocessing directives placed in IDL files the clearer the style.

Keywords Keywords are all in lowercase, and other identifiers may not differ only in case.

Comments Both styles of C++ comments are used in IDL. The "/*" characters open a comment and "*/" closes it. These comments cannot be nested. The characters "//" indicate that the rest of a line is a comment.

Punctuation The curly brace is used to enclose naming scopes, and closing braces are always followed by a semicolon. Declarations are always followed by a semicolon. Lists of parameters are surrounded by parentheses with the parameters separated by commas.

3.4.2 Modules and Interfaces

The purpose of IDL is to define interfaces and their operations. To avoid name clashes when using several IDL declarations together, the *module* is used as a naming scope. Modules can contain any well-formed IDL, including nested modules.

Interfaces also open a new naming scope, and can contain constants, data type declarations, attributes, and operations.

```
// RoomBooking.idl
module RoomBooking {
    interface Room{};
};
```

Any interface name in the same scope can be used as a type name, but interfaces in other name scopes can be referred to by giving a scoped name that is separated in C++ style by double colons. For example, Room Booking::Room is the name of the empty interface declared above. This name can also be written ::RoomBooking::Room to explicitly show that it is relative to the global scope.

Modules may be nested inside other modules, and their contents may be named relative to the current naming scope. For example,

```
module outer {
   module inner { // nested module
      interface inside {};
   };

   interface outside { // can refer to inner as a local name
      inner::inside get_inside();
   };
};
```

The get_inside() operation returns an object reference of type ::outer::inner:inside, but may use the relative form of the name due to its position in the same scope as the inner module.

Interfaces may be mutually referential. That is, declarations in each interface may use the name of the other as an object type. To avoid compilation errors, an interface type must be forward-declared before it is used. That is,

```
interface A; // forward declaration

interface B { // B can use forward-declared interfaces as type names
   A get_an_A();
};

interface A {
   B get_a_B();
};
```

The example above declares the existence of an interface with name A, before defining interface B, which has an operation returning an object reference to an A. It then defines A, which has an operation returning reference to an object of type B. Forward declaration of interfaces is often used for formatting and readability rather than mutual recursion.

When a declaration in a module needs some mutual reference to a declaration in another module, this is achieved by closing the first module and reopening it after some other declarations. This is shown in the following declaration:

```
module X {
   // forward declaration of A
   interface A;
}; // close the module to allow interfaces A needs to be declared

module Y {
   interface B {// B can use X::A as a type name
      X::A get_an_A();
   };
}
```

```
module X {// re-open module to define A

    interface C {// C can use A unqualified as it is in the same scope
      A get_an_A();
    };

    interface A {// A can use Y::B as a type name
      Y::B get_a_B();
    };
};
```

Reopening modules is a recent addition to OMG IDL, and as yet most IDL compilers do not accept it as valid syntax.

3.4.3 *Inheritance*

The set of operations offered by an interface can be extended by declaring a new interface which inherits from the existing one. The existing interface is called a *base interface* and the new interface is called a *derived interface*. Inheritance is declared by using a colon after the new interface name, followed by a base interface name, as the following example shows:

```
module InheritanceExample {

    interface A {
      typedef unsigned short ushort;
        ushort op1();
    };

    interface B : A {
      boolean op2(ushort num);
    };
};
```

In the example above, interface B extends interface A and offers operations op1() and op2(). The data type declarations are also inherited, allowing the use of ushort as a parameter type in op2(). All interfaces implicitly inherit from CORBA::Object. This becomes clear when looking at the language mapping. In Java, for example, interface A will map to a Java interface A, which extends a Java interface called CORBA.Object provided by the ORB. In the same manner interface B will map to a Java interface B which extends A.

OMG IDL allows any non-object types declared in an interface to be redefined in a derived interface. We consider this to be an oversight, and it is not recommended that this feature ever be used. The beauty of inheritance is that it is a clean mechanism for determining subtyping and substitutability of interfaces. An object implementing interface B above would be able to be used where an object of type A was required, as B is a subtype of A. For example, changing the type declaration of the identifier ushort in interface B would change the semantics of operation op1() and compromise B's substitutability for A.

3.4.4 *Multiple Inheritance*

An interface may inherit from several other interfaces. The syntax is the same as single inheritance, and the base interfaces are separated by commas. For example,

```
interface C : A, B, VendorY::componentX {
   ...
};
```

The names of the operations in each of the inherited interfaces (including the operations they inherit from other interfaces) must be unique and may not be redeclared in the derived interface. The exception to this rule is when the operations are inherited into two or more classes from the same base class. This is known as *diamond inheritance* (the inheritance graph is in the shape of a diamond). For example,

```
module DiamondInheritanceExample {

   interface Base {
      string BaseOp();
   };

   interface Left:Base {
      short LeftOp(in string LeftParam);
   };

   interface Right:Base {
      any RightOp(in long RightParam);
   };

   interface Derived:Left,Right {
      octet DerivedOp(in float DerivedInParam,
         out unsigned long DerivedOutParam);
   };
};
```

Figure A-7 shows the IDL in graphical form. Both interfaces Left and Right contain the operation BaseOp(), but they can both be inherited by Derived because BaseOp() comes from the same base interface.

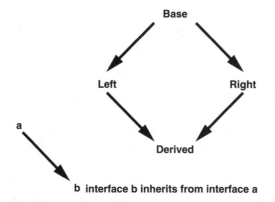

b interface b inherits from interface a

FIGURE A-7. Diamond inheritance.

3.4.5 *Types and Constants*

The name of any interface declared in IDL becomes an object type name that can be used as the type of any operation parameter or return value, or as a component in a structured type declaration; for example, to declare the length of an array. The basic types are able to represent numerics, strings, characters, and booleans. The definitions of these are very precise to allow unambiguous marshaling. The structured types available in IDL are structures, discriminated unions, arrays, and sequences. Exceptions can be considered to be a special case of structures that are only used in raises clauses of operations.

Basic Types The set of basic types provided by IDL and their required characteristics are as follows:

Type Keyword	*Description*
(unsigned) short	Signed [unsigned] 16-bit 2s complement Integer
(unsigned) long	Signed [unsigned] 32-bit 2s complement Integer
float	16-bit IEEE floating point number
double	32-bit IEEE floating point number
char	ISO Latin-1 character
boolean	Boolean type taking values TRUE and FALSE
string	Variable-length string of characters whose length is available at run time

octet	8-bit uninterpreted type
enum	Enumerated type with named integer values
any	A value from any possible IDL type, basic or constructed, object or non-object

The keyword typedef allows aliases to be created for any legal type declaration. In the case of template types (types that require a parameter to determine their length or contents) a typedef is required before the type can be used in an operation or attribute declaration. See the string example below.

Strings may be bounded or unbounded. Bounded strings are a template type. That is, their declaration contains a maximum length parameter in angle brackets. For example,

```
interface StringProcessor {
    typedef octstring string <8>;
    typedef centastring string <100>;

  //...
    octstring MiddleEight(in string str);
    centastring PadOctString(in octstring ostr, char pad_char);
};
```

Enumerated types are declared with a name, which can be used as a valid type thereafter, and a comma-separated list of identifiers. The identifiers used in an enum declaration must be unique within a name space. For example,

```
enum glass_color {gc_clear, gc_red, gc_blue, gc_green};
```

Any   The Any type has an API defined in pseudo-IDL that describes how values are inserted and extracted from it, and how the type of its contained value may be discovered. This is addressed in Chapter 6.

Structures   Structures are declared with the keyword struct, which must be followed by a name. This name is usable as a valid type name thereafter. This is followed by a semicolon-separated list of named type fields, as in C and C++. For example,

```
interface HardwareStore {
  struct window_spec {
      glass_color color;
    height      float;
    width       float;
  };
```

Discriminated Unions Discriminated unions are declared with the keyword union, which must be followed by a name. The name, once again, becomes a valid type name for use in subsequent declarations. The keyword switch follows the type name and it is parameterized by a scalar type (integer, char, boolean, or enum) which will act as the discriminator. The body of the union is enclosed in braces and contains a number of case statements followed by named type declarations. For example,

```
enum fitting_kind {door_k, window_k, shelf_k, cupboard_k};
```

```
union fitting switch (fitting_kind) {
    case door_k:    door_spec        door;
    case window_k : window_spec win;
    default:          float       width;
};
```

The default case is optional but may not appear more than once. In each language mapping there is a means of accessing the discriminator value by name in order to determine which of the fields of the union contains a value. The value of a union consists of the value of the discriminator and the value of the element that it nominates. If the discriminator is set to a value not mentioned in a case label, and there is no default case, then that part of the union's value is undefined.

Sequences Sequences are template types. That means that their declarations nominate other types which will be contained within the sequence. A sequence is an ordered collection of items that can grow at run time. Its elements are accessed by index. Sequences may be bounded or unbounded. All sequences have two characteristics at run time, a maximum and a current length. The maximum length of bounded sequences is set at compile time. The advantage of sequences is that only the current number of elements is transmitted to a remote object when a sequence argument is passed.

Sequence declarations must be given a typedef alias in order to be used as types in operation parameters or return types. Here are some example sequences of hardware fittings used to convey orders to a hardware store:

```
// union type "fitting" declared above.
```

```
typedef sequence <fitting> HardwareOrderSeq;
typedef sequence <fitting, 10> LimitedHWOrderSeq;

typedef sequence <sequence <fitting>, 3> ThreeStoreHWOrderSeq;
typedef sequence <sequence <fitting> > ManyStoreHWOrderSeq;
```

Sequence is the only unaliased complex type that may be used in angle brackets. All other types must be typedefed before sequences of them can be declared. Note that there is a space between the two closing angle brackets in the final declaration above. If these were put side by side they would be parsed as the operator >>, which can be used when declaring integer constants. A better style would be to declare ThreeStoreHWOrderSeq as a sequence of HardwareOrderSeq.

Arrays   Arrays are usually declared within a typedef because they must be named before using them as an operation parameter or return type. However, they may be declared as an element type of a union or member type of a struct.

Arrays at run time will have a fixed length. The entire array (regardless of useful content) will be marshaled and transmitted in a request if used in a parameter or return type. In contrast, sequences passed as arguments or returned as results will only be transmitted up to their length at the time of the invocation.

Arrays are declared by adding one or more square-bracketed dimensions containing an integer constant. For example,

```
typedef window(10)        WindowVec10;
typedef fitting(3)(10)    FittingGrid;

struct bathroom {
    float        width;
    float        length;
    float        height;
    boolean      has_toilet;
    fitting(6)   fittings;
};
```

Exceptions   Exceptions are declared in exactly the same manner as structures, using the keyword exception in place of struct.

The CORBA module contains declarations of twenty-six Standard Exceptions to address network, ORB, and operating system errors. These exceptions may be raised by any operation, either implicitly by the ORB or explicitly in the operation implementation. Each Standard Exception, also known as a System Exception, has two pieces of data associated with it.

◆ A completion status, an enumerated type with three possible values, COMPLETED_YES, COMPLETED_NO, and COMPLETED_MAYBE, indicating that the operation implementation was either executed in full, not at all, or that this cannot be determined.

◆ A long integer minor code that can be set to some ORB-dependent value for more information.

Further user-defined exceptions may be declared in IDL and associated with operations in the raises clause of their signatures. An operation may only raise user exceptions that appear in its signature.

Here are some examples of user-defined exceptions:

```
exception OrderTooLarge {
    long max_items;
    long num_items_submitted;
};

exception ColorMismatch {
    sequence <color> other_window_colors;
    color   color_submitted;
};
```

It is good style to include values of arguments that are relevant to the cause of a failure in an exception. That way exception handling can be done by a generic handler that does not know what arguments were given that may have caused the exception. The handler can determine the context of the operation that raised the exception from the values in the exception.

Constants Constant values can be declared at global scope or within modules and interfaces. The declaration begins with the keyword const, followed by a type name, an identifier, and then an equals sign and a value. The type name must be an alias for a boolean, numeric, character, or string type. Numerical values can be declared as expressions, with the full range of C++ bitwise, integer, and floating point mathematical operators available. For example,

```
const short max_storage_bays = 200;
const short windows_per_bay = 45;
const long max_windows =   max_storage_bays * windows_per_bay;
const string initial_quote = "fox in socks on knox on blocks";
const HardwareStore::CashAmount balance = (max_storage_bays - 3) / 1.45
```

3.4.6   *Operations and Attributes*

Operation declarations are similar to C++ function prototypes. They contain an operation name, a return type (or void to indicate that no value is expected), and a parameter list, which may be empty. In addition, an operation may have a raises clause which specifies what user exceptions the operation may raise, and it may have a context clause which gives a list of names of string properties from the caller's environment that need to be supplied to the operation implementation.

Lists of parameters to operations are surrounded by parentheses, and the parameters are separated by commas. Each parameter must have a directional indicator so that it is clear which direction the data travels in. These are in, out, and inout and indicate, respectively, client to object, return parameter, and client value modified by object and returned. These points are shown in the IDL below.

```
// interface HardwareStore cont..
    typedef float CashAmount;
    typedef sequence <window_spec> WindowSeq;

    CashAmount OrderFittings(in HardwareOrderSeq order)
        raises (OrderTooLarge);

    void OrderWindows(

            in WindowSeq        order,
            in CashAmount       willing_to_pay,
            out CashAmount      total_price,
            out short           order_number)
    raises (OrderTooLarge, ColorMismatch)
    context ("LOCAL_CURRENCY");
```

Operations can be declared oneway if the caller is to send some noncritical message to an object. Oneway operation invocations will use best-effort semantics. The caller will get an immediate return and will not know for certain if the request has been invoked. For obvious reasons there can be no out or inout parameters declared on oneway operations. There must be no raises clause and the operation must have a void return type. The following declaration illustrates this.

```
// interface HardwareStore cont...

oneway void requestAccountStatement(in short customer_id);
```

An attribute is logically equivalent to a pair of accessor functions, one to access the value, the other to modify it. Read-only attributes require only an accessor function.

Attributes are simpler to declare than operations. They consist of the keyword attribute followed by the type of the attribute(s) and then an attribute name list. The optional keyword readonly may precede the attribute declaration.

```
// interface HardwareStore cont...

    readonly attribute CashAmount min_order, max_order;
    readonly attribute FittingSeq         new_fittings;
        attribute string          quote_of_the_day;
```

The attributes above could be replaced by the following IDL:

```
CashAmount min_order();
CashAmount max_order();
FittingSeq new_fittings();
string get_quote_of_the_day();
void set_quote_of_the_day(in string quote);
```

As declared, the operations and attributes are equivalent. The actual names chosen for the methods in the object implementation are determined by the language mapping. Attributes and operations can both raise standard exceptions. However, operations can be given raises clauses, which allows better handling of error conditions.

3.4.7   Contexts

Contexts provide a way of passing string-to-string mappings from the computing environment of the client to the object implementation. The specification does not define the way in which an ORB populates contexts to pass to objects. Some ORBs treat contexts as equivalent to UNIX or DOS environment variables. Others require users to build context objects explicitly. The string literals within a context clause must start with a letter and may end with "*", the wild card matching character. The matching character will cause the ORB to find all context items with the leading characters in common. Some ORB implementations with name spaces in the user or operating system context will use the "." character as a scope delimiter.

In general, contexts are a hole in an otherwise type-safe interface definition language. The use of wild-card pattern matching is especially dangerous since the IDL author has no way at specification time of knowing what names will be defined in the context of all callers. A broad pattern match may cause many kilobytes of strings to be transmitted unnecessarily for an otherwise lightweight operation invocation. It is much better for the client to use the local system libraries to read the context, place a particular value into an IDL-specified data type variable, and convey that information as an argument to the operation.

3.5   ORB and Object Interfaces

The ORB interface is available directly to clients and object implementations for a few object management reasons. These include creating string representations of object references and transforming them back again, copying and deleting object references, and comparing object references against the empty, or nil, object reference.

As mentioned above, there are a number of interfaces defined within the CORBA standard that use the IDL syntax for programming-language-neutral API definitions. They are interfaces to ORB components that are implemented as libraries, or in whatever way ORB implementers see fit. The IDL is commented as Pseudo-IDL, or PIDL.

3.5.1 Stringified Object References

Since object references are opaque, the only way to correctly make an object reference persistent is to stringify it. A stringified object reference can be passed by means such as e-mail, Web sites, or pen and paper, and when supplied as an argument to the string_to_object() operation, it will produce a valid object reference that can be invoked. In order to use generated stubs to do this, the returned object reference must be passed to the *narrow()* method of the appropriate interface stub to cast the object reference into a reference to a more specific interface than Object.

```
module CORBA { //PIDL

  interface ORB {
    string object_to_string( in Object obj );
    Object string_to_object( in string obj );

    // several other operations are defined here but used in
    // other contexts, such as the ORB initialization and the DII
  };
};
```

The object_to_string() operation takes an object and produces a string. This string may be passed to the converse operation, string_to_object(), to generate a new object reference that can be invoked and will send its requests to the same object passed to object_to_string().

3.5.2 Managing Object References

This subsection addresses the Pseudo-IDL for the CORBA::Object interface. This is the base interface for all CORBA objects, and its operations can be invoked on any object reference. However, the functionality is implemented in the libraries provided by the ORB and results are not obtained by sending a request to the object implementation.

Object references, although opaque to their users, always contain certain information that can be extracted by using the correct operations. The main components in an object reference are

♦ Abstract information about the name and location of the object implementation

♦ The interface type of the object
♦ Reference data, that is, a unique key that differentiates this object from other objects in the same implementation (server)

The get_implementation() and get_interface() operations described below provide access to the first two components, and the get_id() operation on the BOA interface provides access to the third. Many ORBs provide this information in other forms by additional operations not required by the standard.

```
module CORBA {

    interface Object { // PIDL
        ImplementationDef      get_implementation();
        InterfaceDef           get_interface();
        boolean                is_nil();
        Object                 duplicate();
        void                   release();
        boolean                is_a(in string logical_type_id);
        boolean                non_existent();
        boolean                is_equivalent(in Object other_object);
        unsigned long          hash(in unsigned long maximum);

        // the create_request operation used by the DII is defined here
    };
};
```

The get_implementation() operation returns an ORB-dependent interface called ImplementationDef, which the standard does not specify. This interface should provide information about how the BOA launches implementations of objects. Usually the BOA does this by starting a new process or task running from a particular executable file with certain arguments.

The get_interface() operation returns a standard interface from the Interface Repository. This allows a client to investigate the IDL definition of an interface via calls to objects that represent the IDL in the Interface Repository. This approach can be used to discover the operations available on an object reference when its type is unknown at compile time. The DII can then be used to invoke these operations.

The is_nil() operation returns TRUE if this object reference denotes no object. Object implementations that return object references as output parameters or return values may choose to return a nil object reference rather than raise an exception. Different language bindings implement object references differently and an invocation on a nil object reference may result in a fatal error.

The duplicate() and release() operations are very important in programming languages where programmers do explicit memory management (such as C and C++). Luckily in Java this is done for us automatically. These operations ensure correct management of copies of an object reference. When an object reference is to be passed to another object or thread of control, the opaque type that implements the object reference *must not* be copied by using features of the implementation language. The duplicate() operation must be used instead. The reason is that when a remote client uses an object reference, a proxy object is created locally on which the client can invoke operations directly. The proxy, in concert with the ORB, then creates the request that ends up at the object implementation.

A proxy object keeps a counter of all object references that refer to it. This is called a *reference count*. If a copy of a reference to that proxy is created without the knowledge of the proxy, then it cannot increase its reference count. Then when the counted references are released the proxy assumes that no other references to it exist and it will deallocate its resources and delete itself. Now the copied reference refers to a deleted proxy and invocations made on it will incur a run-time error. This is illustrated in Figure A-8.

When duplicate() is called to obtain a new copy of the object reference, the proxy will increase its reference count and wait for all references to call release() before cleaning up and going away. This makes the importance of using release() equally clear. If the last reference to a proxy is deleted without calling release() the proxy will continue to consume memory, and probably network resources, until the process or task in which it executes dies. Figure A-9 illustrates this case.

Figure A-10 shows the correct use of duplicate() and release() where the reference count in the proxy reflects the actual number of references to it.

Figure A-11 shows what occurs when an object reference is duplicated to be passed across machine boundaries. The figure does not show the temporary increase in the reference count on Proxy Object B before the skeleton code does a release() when passing the reference back to the client.

The is_a() operation returns TRUE if the Interface Repository identifier passed to it refers to a type of which this object is a subtype. It is mainly used in dynamically typed languages that cannot support a *narrow()* method. We recommend the use of narrow, which can be attempted for various object types and will return a valid object reference if it is of a compatible type, or raise an exception if not.

The non_existent() operation returns TRUE if the object implementation denoted by this reference has been destroyed. The ORB will return FALSE if the object exists or if it cannot determine the answer definitively.

The is_equivalent() operation is the *only* way within CORBA to determine whether two object references denote the same object. All references that are created by calling duplicate() on a single object reference will be equiva-

Client **Server**

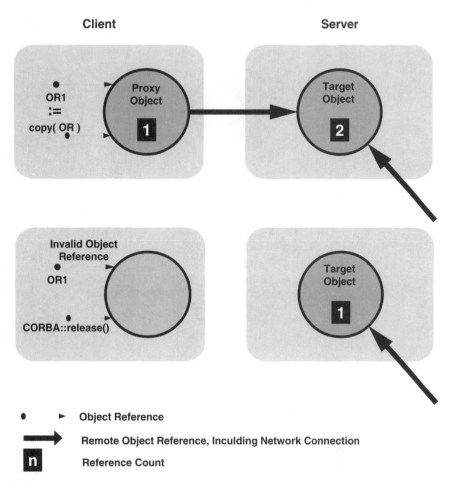

- ► Object Reference

→ Remote Object Reference, Inculding Network Connection

n Reference Count

FIGURE A-8. Invalid object reference copy.

lent to the original reference, and with each other. Even so, it is possible that two references that actually denote the same object may return a FALSE result from this operation. That is, a TRUE result guarantees that the object denoted is the same, but a FALSE result does not guarantee that two references denote different objects. String representations obtained from object_to_string() are ORB dependent, and can be different each time they are generated. Hence they do not offer a means of comparing references.

The hash() operation provides a way of selecting a small number of possibly identical references in a chained hash table, which can be compared pairwise for a match. This is more efficient than comparing a reference against every object reference in a list. Most CORBA application programmers will never need to use is_equivalent() or hash().

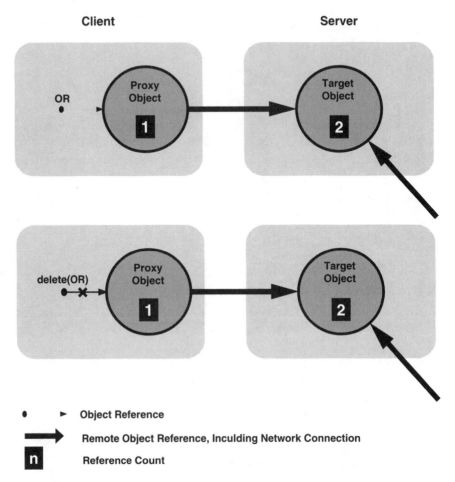

- ● ► Object Reference

——► Remote Object Reference, Including Network Connection

n Reference Count

FIGURE A-9. Invalid object reference deletion.

3.5.3 *Initialization*

The CORBA module contains a pseudo-IDL operation ORB_init() for boot-strapping the ORB.

```
module CORBA {  // PIDL
    typedef string ORBid;
    typedef sequence <string> arg_list;
    ORB ORB_init(inout arg_list argv, in ORBid orb_identifier);
};
```

ORB_init() is provided to obtain a reference to an ORB pseudo-object. Ordinarily, operations must be associated with an interface, but ORB_init() is

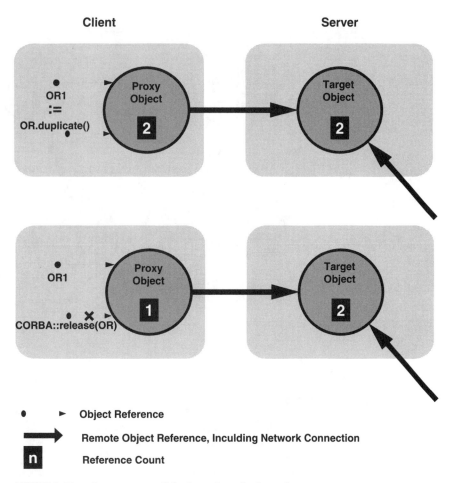

Client   **Server**

• Object Reference

Remote Object Reference, Inculding Network Connection

n Reference Count

FIGURE A-10.   Correct use of duplicate() and release().

freestanding. ORB_init() takes the command-line arguments from a UNIX shell style process launch and removes any that are intended for the ORB. It also takes the name of the ORB to be initialized in the form of a string.

The ORB interface supports some further operations to allow any ORB user to get access to fundamental Object Services and/or Facilities by name. The most important of these for object implementations is a BOA. Remember that the BOA is used to inform the ORB that objects are ready for use and that a server (the process or task that implements a collection of objects) is ready to accept requests on its objects. The following IDL shows the signature of BOA_init(), which is the way to obtain a reference to a BOA pseudo-object.

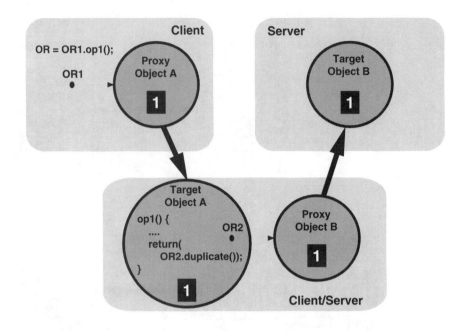

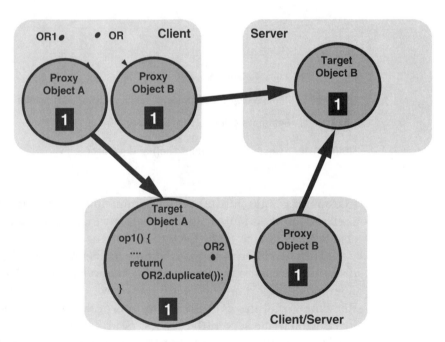

FIGURE A-11. Proxy creation when passing object references.

```
module CORBA {
    interface ORB { // PIDL
        typedef string OAid;
        typedef sequence <string> arg_list;

        BOA BOA_init(inout arg_list argv,
                in OAid boa_identifier);
```

As with the ORB initialization, the argument list may be scanned for BOA-specific arguments and it will be returned with these removed. The Object Adapter identifier parameter, boa_identifier, must be passed a string specified by the particular ORB vendor.

The declarations below allow the ORB user to find out which basic services and facilities the ORB supports and obtain references to their objects. The list_initial_services() operation provides a list of the strings that identify the services and facilities, and the resolve_initial_references() operation takes any of these strings as an argument and returns an object reference.

```
// interface ORB cont …
    typedef string  ObjectId;
    typedef sequence <ObjectId> ObjectIdList;

    exception InvalidName {};

    ObjectIdList list_initial_services();

    Object resolve_initial_references (in ObjectId identifier)
        raises (InvalidName);

    }; // interface ORB
}; // module CORBA
```

The resolve_initial_references() operation is a bootstrap to get object references to CORBAservices, such as the Naming Service, Interface Repository and Trading Service. The argument is a string specified in each CORBA Service specification, for example, "NameService" for the Naming Service and "TradingService" for the Trading Service.

The type of interface expected as a return type is well known, and the object reference returned can be narrowed to the correct object type:

- ◆ CosNaming::NamingContext for the Naming Service.
- ◆ CosTrading::Lookup for the Trading Service.

See Chapter 8 for a full explanation of how to obtain these references using the Java language binding and how to use them to obtain references to application objects.

3.6 Basic Object Adapter

For the object implementer, the BOA is the interface used to inform the ORB when objects come into existence and when running processes or tasks are ready to accept incoming requests on those objects. However, for the client, the BOA is the component of the ORB that ensures that an invocation on an object reference always reaches a running object that can respond to it. That is, the BOA is capable of launching processes, waiting for them to initialize, and then dispatching requests to them. To do this it needs access to the Implementation Repository, a component proprietary to each ORB that stores information about where the executable code that implements objects resides and how to run it correctly.

The CORBA specification lists the creation, destruction, and look-up of information relating to object references as one of the BOA's primary functions. It provides Pseudo-IDL descriptions of interfaces to do this. These will be described below for completeness. However, in effect, creation and destruction of object references is managed by code that is generated by IDL compilers as part of the implementation skeleton. When implementation objects are created their object references are usually created with them.

3.6.1 Registration, Activation, and Deactivation of Implementations

Let's look at what a program that implements some objects needs to do to allow the skeletons for those objects to be called and cause the methods of the objects to be invoked.

```
module CORBA {   // PIDL

    interface BOA {
        void impl_is_ready  (in ImplementationDef impl);
        void deactivate_impl  (in ImplementationDef impl);
        void obj_is_ready  (in Object obj, in ImplementationDef impl);
        void deactivate_obj  (in Object obj);

        // continued ....
    };
};
```

The program implementing an object may have been started by some external means or by the BOA using the information in the Implementation Repository. The BOA should use policy information in the Implementation Repository to determine how to start the program (or *server process*) and what registration calls to expect. Four policies are explained in the CORBA specification:

◆ *Shared server activation policy.* According to CORBA, each object should register itself with an obj_is_ready() operation if the process it runs in supports many objects. This is called the shared server activation policy. The obj_is_ready() operation is invoked to associate a running object implementation with an entity in the Implementation Repository. When an object can no longer respond to requests it should inform the BOA using the deactivate_obj() operation. Most ORBs provide automatic deregistration of objects in the destructor of the generated skeleton code.

◆ *Unshared server activation policy.* In the unshared server activation policy the process encapsulates an application that supports only one object interface. In this case, when all the other initialization has been completed, the impl_is_ready() operation should be invoked. This associates the single object with an entity in the Implementation Repository. The deactivate_impl() operation informs the BOA that the server can no longer service requests.

◆ *Server-per-method activation policy.* In the server-per-method policy a new process is started for each request received by the BOA. The standard says that no registration call is needed in this case, but ORBs that support this policy often require an impl_is_ready() call to notify the ORB that requests can be served.

◆ *Persistent server policy.* A persistent server is a process that is started by some means other than BOA activation. Typically, an operating system script or user command starts the server. In this case the impl_is_ready() operation should be used to register the server with the BOA.

Some ORB BOAs support only impl_is_ready(), and don't allow objects to be activated individually, while others support both approaches, even in programs that use the shared activation policy. Some offer the above activation policies explicitly, but not necessarily using the registration operations specified. Others support complementary policies that consider the caller's identity. Most ORBs implement impl_is_ready() as a dispatch loop that doesn't return while the server is accepting requests and which calls deactivate_impl() if interrupted.

In short, BOA implementations vary a great deal, and object implementers should not only be aware of their responsibilities when initializing implementations, but also of the peculiarities of their ORB. See Chapter 7 for details of what Java ORBs require.

3.6.2 BOA Implementation

The BOA is a logical component of the ORB, but its implementation is usually divided between the ORB run-time system and the generated code from the IDL compiler. As one would expect, the ORB run-time system will take responsibility for launching processes and the skeleton code will provide the interface that is invoked to register the objects. Two common strategies are used by ORBs for object-oriented languages when incorporating the BOA and skeleton code into the object implementation.

The first is to inherit the generated BOA class into each implementation of an interface described in the IDL file. The BOA base class is then responsible for supporting interactions between the ORB and the implementation methods.

The second approach is to generate a freestanding class that implements the same functionality, but is not inherited by the class that implements the object's application semantics. When a logical CORBA object is instantiated the application implementer must actually instantiate two objects, a BOA object and an implementation object. The BOA object must then be given a reference to the implementation object so that it can delegate incoming requests there. This is called the *Tie* approach, since the application developer must "tie" the BOA and implementation objects together when they are created.

In the programming chapters of this book we use the inheritance approach, but Tie is covered in Chapter 10.

3.6.3 *Other Functions*

The BOA interface description provided in the CORBA module contains several additional operations that are seldom used by any ORB implementation. The generation of object references is usually done implicitly when a programming language reference to an implementation object is passed as a parameter. The handling of authentication and access control is done by a higher-level service. The reference data in an object reference may be used for many purposes, among them retrieval of persistent state. The following IDL support object reference creation for non-object-oriented languages and retrieval of information from object references:

```
// interface CORBA::BOA PIDL cont ...

interface Principal;
    typedef sequence <octet, 1024> ReferenceData;

Object create(
            in ReferenceData      id,
            in InterfaceDef       intf,
            in ImplementationDef impl);

void dispose(in Object obj);
ReferenceData get_id(in Object obj);
```

```
void change_implementation (
        in Object              obj,
        in ImplementationDef impl);

Principal get_principal(
        in Object              obj,
        in Environment ev);

}; // interface BOA
}; // module CORBA
```

Generation of Object References   As explained earlier, an object reference has three main components:

- ♦ A unique key within the server implementation.
- ♦ The object's interface type.
- ♦ A way of locating its implementation.

Not surprisingly, these are the parameters that the create() operation needs to create a new object reference. It is unlikely that this operation will actually be offered in most ORB implementations, as object references are created implicitly from implementation objects by the ORB. The way to safely delete an object reference is by passing it to the dispose() operation.

The change_implementation() operation associates a new object implementation with a particular object reference. This must be done with care, making sure to deactivate the object before switching its implementation. There are security problems with providing access to a new object implementation using an existing object reference. Most objects will be associated with a single implementation for the duration of their life span.

Access Control   The get_principal() operation is used to determine the identity of a client that caused the activation of an object. It will generally be used by a higher-level security service.

Persistence   The get_id() operation will return the reference data of an object reference which is guaranteed to be unique within the server that implements the object. Activation and deactivation of servers requires that object state information is stored persistently, for example, in a database. The reference data can be used as a database key to retrieve this information when a server is reactivated.

3.7 Language Mappings

The OMG has standardized four language bindings and has RFPs issued to standardize several more. The current list of adopted specifications is as follows:

- C
- C++
- Smalltalk
- Ada

The languages undergoing standardization are

- COBOL
- Java

3.7.1 C

The C mapping was published along with the CORBA1.1 specification. It provides an example of how to implement CORBA clients and servers in a non-object-oriented language. Operation and interface names are concatenated to provide function names, and object references are passed explicitly as parameters.

3.7.2 C++

The C++ language mapping is the most widely supported language mapping at the moment. Its syntactic resemblance to IDL provides class definitions that mirror IDL interface definitions very closely. The generated stub code can be incorporated by inheritance into object implementation classes or can delegate to them. The major drawback of this mapping is that implementers of clients and servers must pay very close attention to memory management responsibilities. The rules for allocation and deallocation of data memory are just as complex as old-style remote procedure call (RPC) programming. Some helper classes are defined that can deallocate memory when they go out of scope, but these must be declared and used with care since they might deallocate memory that is still being used by another object.

3.7.3 Smalltalk

Smalltalk is a dynamically typed, single-inheritance, object-oriented language in which all types are first-class objects. The data type mappings use existing Smalltalk classes, and operations map to methods on classes. The way in which IDL interfaces map to Smalltalk objects is unconstrained. Explicit protocol mappings are made for some IDL types, such as unions and Anys which provide a standard way of accessing their discriminators and TypeCodes, respectively. However, implicit mappings may be used by programmers.

3.8   Interoperability

The CORBA2.0 specification has a section called "Interoperability." It specifies an architecture for interoperability, as well as an *out-of-the-box interoperability protocol*, running over TCP/IP, and a second protocol that uses the DCE RPC transport.

The specification contains a lot of technical detail about the protocols specified and about bridging between proprietary protocols. Here we will give an overview of the framework within which the two specified protocols exist and of the mandatory Internet Inter-ORB Protocol (IIOP). The rest of the standard applies to ORB implementers and will not be covered.

3.8.1   *The ORB Interoperability Architecture*

The architecture contains definitions of ORB domains, bridges, and Interoperable Object References (IORs). It defines domains as islands within which objects are accessible because they use the same communication protocols, the same security, and the same way of identifying objects. In order to establish interoperability between domains, one of these elements must be replaced with a common element, or a bridge must be set up to facilitate translation of the protocol, identity, authority, etc., between domains.

The approach of the architecture is to identify the things that can be used as common representations (canonical forms) between domains and then suggest ways in which ORB domains can create half-bridges which communicate using the common representation. The first step, a common object reference format, is defined as part of the architecture. The IOR contains the same information as a single domain object reference, but adds a list of protocol profiles indicating which communication protocols the domain of origin can accept requests in. The protocol interoperability problem is addressed in a separate component called the General Inter-ORB Protocol (GIOP). Security interoperability is not yet addressed in CORBA. However, an RFP for a secure IIOP has been issued. Allowance is also made for the introduction of third-party protocols called Environment-Specific Inter-ORB Protocols (ESIOPs) within this framework. Figure A-12 illustrates the relationships between these protocols.

3.8.2   *General Inter-ORB Protocol*

The GIOP defines a linear format for the transmission of CORBA requests and replies without requiring a particular network transport protocol.

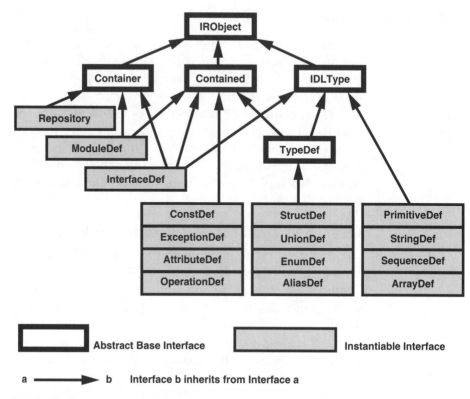

FIGURE A-12. ORB protocols.

3.8.3 Internet Inter-ORB Protocol

The IIOP is a specialization of the GIOP that specifies the use of TCP/IP (the Internet protocol). It defines some primitives to assist in the establishment of TCP connections. This protocol is required for compliance with CORBA2 Interoperable, and is intended to provide a base-level interoperability between all ORB vendors' products, even though most vendors will continue to support proprietary protocols. Java ORBs are all associated with C++ ORB products which have adopted IIOP, and so even though a particular product may support legacy protocols, the availability of IIOP can be assumed.

3.8.4 Other Approaches

As can be seen in Figure A-12, the interoperability architecture allows for the specification of ESIOPs which provide "islands of interoperability," but which should be able to be bridged to other ORBs using IIOP. The first adopted ESIOP is the DCE Common Inter-ORB Protocol (DCE-CIOP), which was already used by a number of ORBs before the introduction of GIOP/IIOP.

Before the CORBA2.0 specification was introduced, each ORB vendor had to choose or invent a protocol for the transmission of invocation requests and responses. Most vendors have a customer base with extant objects that use a certain protocol, and so it is in their interest to continue to support old protocols alongside IIOP. The best of these products allow object implementations to "plug in" protocols at will and to respond to requests delivered in several protocols.

3.9 Dynamic Interfaces

This section describes the interfaces to the symmetrical pair of ORB components, the DII on the client side and the DSI on the server side. The DII enables a client to invoke operations on an interface for which it has no compiled stub code. It also allows a client to invoke an operation in *deferred synchronous mode;* that is, it can send the request, do some further processing, and then check for a response. This is useful regardless of whether or not the interface type is known at compile time, since it is not available via a static, or stub-based, invocation.

The DSI is used to accept a request for any operation, regardless of whether it has been defined in IDL or not. The mechanism allows servers to implement a class of generic operations of which it knows the form but not the exact syntax. It helps in writing client code that uses compiled IDL stubs based on an abstract IDL template. The client can then invoke operations on a compiled proxy stub in a type-safe manner.

3.9.1 Requests (DII)

The heart of the DII is the Request interface. A Request has an object reference and a target operation name associated with it, as well as operations to add arguments. Once the request has the correct arguments it is invoked using the invoke() operation. Like a stub invocation this operation blocks until the response (or an exception) is returned.

3.9.2 Deferred Synchronous Invocation

The send() operation provides the means for a deferred synchronous invocation. This returns to the caller immediately and allows the client to perform some processing while the request is being transmitted and executed. The get_response() operation, when called in this situation, will either block until the request has returned its response or, if a flag is set, it will return a status value indicating whether or not the request has completed. Operations are also provided, but not specified in Pseudo-IDL, for sending the requests to multiple objects and getting the responses from these invocations.

The Pseudo-IDL in the CORBA document does not specify the types of all the parameters and return values of the operations on a Request, and so we provide the details of these operations in Chapter 7. The use of the DII in Java is demonstrated in Chapter 10.

3.9.3   ServerRequests (DSI)

In a particular BOA implementation, an object reference is usually associated with an object implementation of the equivalent type in a particular language binding. However, an implementation that can deal with requests of several object types, called a *Dynamic Implementation Routine* (DIR), could be associated with an object reference instead. In this case, the BOA does not look up a particular method and make an up-call by passing it the arguments in a request. Instead it creates a ServerRequest pseudo-object and passes this to the DIR. This is the definition of the ServerRequest interface:

```
module CORBA {

    pseudo interface ServerRequest {
        Identifier   op_name();
        Context      ctx();
        void         params(inout NVList params);
        Any          result();
    };
};
```

The DIR can check the interface on which the request was made and look up its details using the Interface Repository. It could also be expecting requests of a known form and not require any IDL details. It can use the interface above to check the operation name, unpack the arguments, and find a location in which to place the result.

The Java language binding is much closer to the Pseudo-IDL for ServerRequest than for request. See the language mapping of the DSI in Chapter 7 for details.

3.9.4   Named Value Lists and Contexts

The Pseudo-IDL for the Request and ServerRequest interfaces uses the Pseudo-IDL type NVList to represent the values in an argument list. It is a type that is defined in each individual language mapping for the best implementation. However, it is logically equivalent to the following Pseudo-IDL definition:

```
struct NamedValue {
   Identifier      name;
   any             argument;
   long            len;  // length/count of argument value
   Flags           arg_modes;  // in, out, or inout
};
```

```
typedef sequence <NamedValue> NVList;
```

The other type that is used in Requests is the Context. This is another construct that is more concretely defined in particular language bindings. Its Pseudo-IDL may not be directly translated using the language mapping. The Pseudo-IDL is not given here, but is explained in full in Chapter 7. Contexts are used to pass string name to string value mappings, specified in an operation's context clause, from caller to object. We consider contexts to be an undesirable mechanism for passing information around, as do most ORB vendors.

3.10 Interface Repository

The Interface Repository (IR) is a fundamental service in CORBA that provides information about the interface types of objects supported in a particular ORB installation. It can be thought of as a set of objects that encapsulate the IDL definitions of all CORBA types available in a particular domain.

The IR specification defines a set of interfaces that correspond to each construct in IDL: module, interface, operation, sequence, constant, etc. It also uses the idea of a containment hierarchy to relate objects of these types to one another. The Container interface is inherited by all IDL construct description interfaces that contain other constructs, and the Contained interface is inherited by all the interfaces that describe IDL constructs contained in others. For example, an interface can be contained in a module and can contain an attribute.

The term *abstract interface* is used below to indicate that an interface is only meant to be inherited into other interfaces. No objects of an abstract interface type will ever be instantiated. The term *concrete interface* is used to mean that objects of this interface type will be instantiated.

All of the interfaces shown here are defined in the CORBA module. There are two mechanisms for finding out the properties of virtually all IDL constructs:

♦ The interfaces named idl-constructDef provide attributes and operations that explain the construct's properties and relationship to other IDL constructs. For example, SequenceDef is an interface definition with an attribute, bound, that gives the upper bound of a bounded sequence, or zero for an unbounded sequence. It has another attribute to return the type of the elements of the sequence it is describing.

◆ The Contained interface has a describe() operation that returns an enum value to identify the kind of IDL construct, and a value of type Any that contains a structure dependent on that kind. The CORBA module defines a structure corresponding to each IDL construct named IdlconstructDescription. The structure contains the name, repository identifier, the container where this construct is defined, its version, and some other members, depending on the kind. For example, InterfaceDescription contains a list of base interfaces of the interface it describes.

This design has received a good deal of criticism. Some of the problems that have been observed with the current specification are

◆ It contains a large amount of redundancy.
◆ Often operations return RepositoryIds, which then need to be resolved at the Repository interface, rather than object references to the idlconstructDef objects denoted by the Ids.
◆ Values are returned in a generic manner by base interfaces (e.g., in an Any) and then need to be interpreted based on an enum type. This functionality should have been pushed down to well-typed operations in the derived interfaces.

A significant revision by the OMG is under way that will correct some of these problems.

We recommend that you use Figure A-13 as a basis for understanding the relationships between interfaces since the IR specification can get rather confusing.

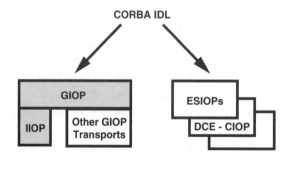

FIGURE A-13. Structure of the interface repository.

3.10.1   The Abstract Base Interfaces

The interfaces to various syntactic constructs in IDL share common properties inherited from a number of abstract base interfaces.

- The IRObject interface provides an attribute returning a value from an enumerated type that distinguishes between all IDL syntactic constructs. This attribute is available on all object references in the IR and allows the user to determine what kind of IDL construct description object they have a reference to.
- The Contained interface is inherited by all interfaces representing user-defined IDL constructs and offers attributes to discover the name of the construct and to obtain a structure that describes it.
- The Container interface is inherited by the Repository, ModuleDef, and InterfaceDef interfaces of the IR and contains operations to look up and describe the contents of these containers. It also contains operations to create all the objects that inherit from Contained. These creation operations establish a containment relationship between the Container and the object that its operations create.
- The IDLType interface is inherited by all the interfaces that represent data types, including all the basic type interfaces and user-defined data type interfaces. It is also inherited by InterfaceDef because interface types can be used wherever data types are used in IDL. IDLType offers a single attribute that returns the TypeCode of the construct it describes.
- The TypedefDef interface is inherited by all the user-defined type interfaces that are given a type name: structs, unions, enums, and typedef aliases. It offers a single operation that describes the type.

3.10.2   Data Type Interfaces

There is an IDL interface for each IDL construct representing a data type:

- ConstantDef.
- StructDef.
- UnionDef.
- EnumDef.
- AliasDef. Typedefs that rename a defined type.
- PrimitiveDef. CORBA-defined types than cannot be changed by users.
- StringDef.
- SequenceDef.
- ArrayDef.

3.10.3   Non-data-type Interfaces

There is an IDL interface for each IDL construct that is not a data type:

♦ Repository. Top-level naming scope. Can contain constants, typedefs, exceptions, interface definitions, and modules.

♦ ModuleDef. A logical grouping of interfaces. Can contain constants, type-defs, exceptions, interface definitions, and other modules.

♦ InterfaceDef. Can contain constants, typedefs, exceptions, operations, and attributes.

♦ AttributeDef.

♦ OperationDef. Consists of a list of parameters and raised exceptions.

♦ ExceptionDef.

3.10.4   IDL Definitions of the IR Interfaces

The IDL for the IR separates the functionality of the operations and attributes into *read* and *write* sections. The implementations of the IR that we have seen implement only the read part of the specification. The repository is usually populated by the IDL compiler using proprietary means. The purpose of this section is to allow users to investigate the functionality of an interface at run time, so we will ignore the write interface.

The IRObject Interface

```
enum DefinitionKind {
   dk_none, dk_all,
   dk_Attribute, dk_Constant, dk_Exception, dk_interface,
   dk_Module, dk_Operation, dk_Typedef,
   dk_Alias, dk_Struct, dk_Union, dk_Enum,
   dk_Primitive, dk_String, dk_Sequence, dk_Array,
   dk_Repository
};

interface IRObject {
   readonly attribute DefinitionKind def_kind;
};
```

This base interface offers only a read-only attribute that indicates what kind of IDL object we have.

The Contained Interface

```
typedef string VersionSpec;

interface Contained: IRObject {

   attribute RepositoryId id;
   attribute Identifier name;
   attribute VersionSpec version;
```

The read/write attributes are

♦ A global id
♦ A simple name
♦ A version (default set to 1.0)

```
readonly attribute Container defined_in;
readonly attribute ScopedName absolute_name;
readonly attribute Repository containing_repository;
```

The read-only attributes are

♦ The module, interface, or repository where the text of this construct is defined
♦ The scoped name of this instance of the construct
♦ The repository object where this construct definition object is kept

```
struct Description {
    DefinitionKind kind;
    any value;
};
Description describe ();
```

The describe() operation returns a Description structure containing a kind and a value. The value returned depends on the kind. We will see what values correspond to each kind when we reach the concrete interfaces. The type name for the value will be of the form idl-constructDescription, for example, InterfaceDescription for interfaces.

The Container Interface

```
typedef sequence <Contained> ContainedSeq;

interface Container: IRObject {
    Contained lookup (in ScopedName search_name);
```

The lookup() operation finds an object with a scoped name relative to this container. If the scoped name begins with "::" then the name is found from the enclosing repository.

```
ContainedSeq contents (
    in DefinitionKind limit_type
    in boolean exclude_inherited
);
```

The contents() operation returns a sequence of the objects in this container. The list may be limited to a certain type and may exclude inherited objects.

```
ContainedSeq lookup_name (
    in Identifier search_name
    in long levels_to_search
    in DefinitionKind limit_type
    in boolean exclude_inherited
);
```

The lookup_name() operation performs a recursive search down the containment hierarchy for a simple name. Restrictions can be placed on the number of levels to search, the types searched for, and whether or not to look at inherited objects.

The IDLType Interface

```
interface IDLType: IRObject {
    readonly attribute TypeCode type;
};
```

This interface is inherited by built-in types, like sequences and arrays, and offers only the TypeCode of the object.

The TypedefDef Interface

```
interface TypedefDef: Contained, IDLType {};
```

```
struct TypeDescription {
    Identifier name;
    RepositoryId id;
    RepositoryId defined_in;
    VersionSpec version;
    TypeCode type;
};
```

This interface combines the functions of the Contained and IDLType interfaces. Since it is the base class for all user-defined data type description objects and a derived interface of Contained, it has a description structure that is returned by the describe() operation, which it inherits. The TypeDescription structure has a similar form to the other idl-constructDescription structures. It serves for all interfaces derived from TypedefDef, since its type member can describe any CORBA type.

The Repository Interface   This interface is the outer shell of the containment hierarchy, and it is where all the definitions for the base, or primitive types, are contained. It is also the starting point for browsing, and allows users to find definitions using their RepositoryIds.

```
enum PrimitiveKind {
   pk_null, pk_void, pk_short, pk_long, pk_ushort, pk_ulong,
   pk_float, pk_double, pk_boolean, pk_char, pk_octet,
   pk_any, pk_TypeCode, pk_Principal, pk_string, pk_objref
};
```

```
interface Repository: Container {
   Contained lookup_id (in RepositoryId search_id);
   PrimitiveDef get_primitive (in PrimitiveKind kind);
};
```

The lookup_id() operation finds an object with a certain identifier in this repository. The get_primitive() operation returns a primitive definition object contained in this repository.

3.10.5   The Multiply Derived Interfaces

Figure A-13 shows that ModuleDef and InterfaceDef are the only concrete interfaces in this specification that inherit directly from more than one abstract interface.

The ModuleDef Interface

```
interface ModuleDef: Container, Contained {};
```

```
struct ModuleDescription {
   Identifier name;
   RepositoryId Id;
   RepositoryId defined_In;
   VersionSpec version;
};
```

ModuleDef offers the operations from Container and Contained and a structure that allows them to be described in terms of name, id, and version. This will be the value in the Any returned from Contained::describe() for modules.

The InterfaceDef Interface   The InterfaceDef interface inherits operations from all three of the second-level base interfaces.

```
interface InterfaceDef: Container, Contained, IDLType {
   attribute InterfaceDefSeq base_interfaces;
   boolean Is_a (in RepositoryId interface_id);
```

base_interfaces allows us to find all the interfaces that this interface directly inherits. Is_a() returns TRUE if this interface has the identifier passed as an argument, FALSE otherwise.

```
                struct FullInterfaceDescription {
                    Identifier name;
                    RepositoryId Id;
                    RepositoryId defined_in;
                    VersionSpec version;
                    OpDescriptionSeq operations;
                    AttrDescriptionSeq attributes;
                    RepositoryIdSeq base_interfaces;
                    TypeCode type;
                };

};//InterfaceDef

FullInterfaceDescription describe_interface();

struct InterfaceDescription {
    Identifier name;
    RepositoryId Id;
    RepositoryId defined_in;
    VersionSpec version;
    RepositoryIdSeq base_interfaces;
};
```

The describe_interface() operation returns a FullInterfaceDescription structure that contains all the information about an interface's contents in a number of sequences that contain other Idl-constructDescription structures. A FullInterfaceDescription contains all the information needed to construct a request to invoke an operation on an object of this interface type using the DII. See the DII section in Chapter 10 for an example of its use.

InterfaceDescription is the structure contained in the Any returned by the describe() operation inherited from Contained.

3.10.6 Interfaces Derived from TypedefDef

The TypedefDef abstract interface is derived from Contained and IDLType. TypedefDef adds a TypeCode attribute. All the interfaces derived from it are structured types that must be user-defined.

StructDef

```
struct StructMember {
    Identifier name;
    TypeCode type;
    IDLType type_def;
};

typedef sequence <StructMember> StructMemberSeq;
```

```
interface StructDef: TypedefDef {
    attribute StructMemberSeq members;
};
```

A StructDef describes its members by name and type, giving both a TypeCode and a reference to the object that describes that type.

UnionDef

```
struct UnionMember {
    Identifier name;
    any label;
    TypeCode type;
    IDLType type_def;
};

typedef sequence <UnionMember> UnionMemberSeq;

interface UnionDef: TypedefDef {
    readonly attribute TypeCode discriminator_type;
    attribute IDLType discriminator_type_def;
    attribute UnionMemberSeq members;
};
```

A UnionDef describes its discriminator type by TypeCode and by reference to the object describing that type with discriminator_type and discriminator_type_def, respectively. Its members are accessed in a similar manner to those of a structure but contain a label value in addition to the name and type.

EnumDef

```
typedef sequence <identifier> EnumMemberSeq;

interface EnumDef: TypedefDef {
    attribute EnumMemberSeq members;
};
```

The only information an enumerated type definition requires over that inherited from TypedefDef is the list of names used for its values.

AliasDef

```
interface AliasDef: TypedefDef {
    attribute IDLType original_type_def;
};
```

Aliases are typedefs that simply equate two type names. The AliasDef interface has an attribute that refers to the object that describes the original type.

3.10.7 Interfaces Derived from IDLType

These objects represent the primitives and system-defined types.

PrimitiveDef

```
interface PrimitiveDef: IDLType {
    readonly attribute PrimitiveKind kind;
};
```

The kind attribute returns an enumerated value identifying the basic type that this object represents.

StringDef

```
interface StringDef: IDLType {
    attribute unsigned long bound;
};
```

A bound value of 0 means that the string is unbounded.

SequenceDef

```
interface SequenceDef: IDLType {
    attribute unsigned long bound;
    readonly attribute TypeCode element_type;
    attribute IDLType element_type_def;
};
```

A bound of 0 means that the sequence is unbounded. The other two attributes identify the type contained in the sequence by TypeCode and object reference.

ArrayDef

```
interface ArrayDef: IDLType {
    attribute unsigned long length;
    readonly attribute TypeCode element_type;
    attribute IDLType element_type_def;
};
```

Multidimensional arrays are created by having another array as the element, described by element_type and identified by element_type_def.

3.10.8   *Interfaces Derived Directly from Contained*

ConstantDef

```
interface ConstantDef: Contained {
    readonly attribute TypeCode type;
    attribute IDLType type_def;
    attribute any value;
};
```

```
struct ConstantDescription {
    Identifier name;
    RepositoryId id;
    RepositoryId defined_in;
    VersionSpec version;
    TypeCode type;
    any value;
};
```

A constant has a type, described by type and referenced as another IR object in type_def. It also has a value. The ConstantDescription structure is returned as the value of the Any returned by the describe() operation inherited from Contained.

ExceptionDef

```
interface ExceptionDef: Contained {
    readonly attribute TypeCode type;
    attribute StructMemberSeq members;
};
```

```
struct ExceptionDescription {
    Identifier name;
    RepositoryId id;
    RepositoryId defined_in;
    VersionSpec version;
    TypeCode type;
};
```

An exception, like a structure, has a list of members that return more specific information about the exception. The inherited describe() operation returns an ExceptionDescription structure in an Any.

AttributeDef

```
enum AttributeMode {ATTR_NORMAL, ATTR_READONLY};
```

```
interface AttributeDef: Contained {
    readonly attribute TypeCode type;
```

```
    attribute IDLType type_def;
    attribute AttributeMode mode;
};

struct AttributeDescription {
    Identifier name;
    RepositoryId id;
    RepositoryId defined_in;
    VersionSpec version;
    TypeCode type;
    AttributeMode mode;
};
```

AttributeDef supplies information about an attribute's type, as well as a reference to the object in which that type is defined. The mode attribute indicates whether this is a read-only attribute or not. The inherited describe() operation returns an AttributeDescription structure in an Any.

OperationDef   Operations are perhaps the most complex entities that the IR describes. They contain parameters and return types and may also raise exceptions and carry context. Parameters are represented by structures, whereas definitions of exceptions are objects.

Here are the types required for the OperationDef interface and the OperationDescription structure:

```
enum OperationMode {OP_NORMAL, OP_ONEWAY};

enum ParameterMode {PARAM_IN, PARAM_OUT, PARAM_INOUT};

struct ParameterDescription {
    Identifier name;
    TypeCode type;
    IDLType type_def;
    ParameterMode mode;
};
typedef sequence <ParameterDescription> ParDescriptionSeq;

typedef Identifier ContextIdentifier;
typedef sequence <ContextIdentifier> ContextIdSeq;

typedef sequence <ExceptionDef> ExceptionDefSeq;
typedef sequence <ExceptionDescription> ExcDescriptionSeq;
```

This is the IDL for the interface that describes operations and the structure returned by the describe() operation inherited from Contained.

```
interface OperationDef: Contained {
    readonly attribute TypeCode result;
    attribute IDLType result_def;
```

```
    attribute ParDescriptionSeq params;
    attribute OperationMode mode;
    attribute ContextIdSeq contexts;
    attribute ExceptionDefSeq exceptions;
};

struct OperationDescription {
    Identifier name;
    RepositoryId id;
    RepositoryId defined_in;
    VersionSpec version;
    TypeCode result;
    OperationMode mode;
    ContextIdSeq contexts;
    ParDescriptionSeq parameters;
    ExcDescriptionSeq exceptions;
};
```

The params attribute of OperationDef is a list of ParameterDescription structures. The contexts attribute gives a list of scoped names of context objects that apply to the operation.

3.10.9 *RepositoryIds*

There are three forms of repository identifiers:

- ♦ IDL format. The string starts with "IDL:" and then uses the scoped name followed by a major and minor version number to globally identify an object. Objects with the same major number are assumed to be derived from one another. The identifier with the larger minor number is assumed to be a subtype of the one with the smaller minor number.
- ♦ DCE UUID format. The string starts with "DCE:" and is followed by a UUID, a colon, and then a minor version number.
- ♦ LOCAL format. The string starts with "LOCAL:" and is followed by an arbitrary string. This format is for use with a single repository that does not communicate with ORBs outside its naming domain.

A P P E N D I X $\quad$ B

Useful Tables

This appendix summarizes a number of Java mappings for predefined IDL types. First we show methods to insert values into Any objects and to obtain values from Any objects. Second is a summary of the definition of TCKind in each mapping. Third we give the definitions of TypeCodes for predefined IDL types. Finally, the definitions of container classes for predefined IDL types are given. Each section has a separate subsection for each of the three Java ORBs: Visibroker, OrbixWeb, and Joe.

1 $\;$ *Any for Predefined IDL Types*

The IDL type any is mapped to a Java class. For predefined IDL types, these classes provide methods to insert a value into an Any object and to retrieve values from an Any object.

1.1 $\;$ **Visibroker**

Visibroker for Java defines the following methods in the class CORBA.Any.

1.1.1   Short

```
public short to_short() throws SystemException
public Any from_short(short value) throws SystemException
```

1.1.2   Long

```
public int to_long() throws SystemException
public Any from_long(int value) throws SystemException
```

1.1.3   UnsignedShort

```
public short to_ushort() throws SystemException
public Any from_ushort(short value) throws SystemException
```

1.1.4   UnsignedLong

```
public int to_ulong() throws SystemException
public Any from_ulong(int value) throws SystemException
```

1.1.5   Float

```
public float to_float() throws SystemException
public Any from_float(float value) throws SystemException
```

1.1.6   Double

```
public double to_double() throws SystemException
public Any from_double(double value) throws SystemException
```

1.1.7   Boolean

```
public boolean to_boolean() throws SystemException
public Any from_boolean(boolean value) throws SystemException
```

1.1.8   Char

```
public char to_char() throws SystemException
public Any from_char(char value) throws SystemException
```

1.1.9   Octet

```
public byte to_octet() throws SystemException
public Any from_octet(byte value) throws SystemException
```

1.1.10   Enum

```
public int to_enum(TypeCode typeCode) throws SystemException
public Any from_enum(int value,
               TypeCode typeCode) throws SystemException
```

1.1.11 Any

```
public Any to_any() throws SystemException
public Any from_any(Any value) throws SystemException
```

1.1.12 TypeCode

```
public TypeCode to_TypeCode() throws SystemException
public Any from_TypeCode(TypeCode value) throws SystemException
```

1.1.13 Principal

```
public byte[] to_Principal() throws SystemException
public Any from_Principal(byte value[]) throws SystemException
```

1.1.14 Object

```
public Object to_Object() throws SystemException
public Any from_Object(Object value) throws SystemException
```

1.1.15 String

```
public String to_string() throws SystemException
public Any from_string(String value) throws SystemException
```

1.2 OrbixWeb

OrbixWeb defines the class IE.Iona.Orbix2.CORBA.Any which provides the following methods.

1.2.1 Short

```
public void insertShort(short s) throws SystemException;
public short extractShort() throws SystemException;
```

1.2.2 Long

```
public void insertLong(int 1) throws SystemException;
public int extractLong() throws SystemException;
```

1.2.3 UnsignedShort

```
public void insertUShort(short s) throws SystemException;
public short extractUShort() throws SystemException;
```

1.2.4 UnsignedLong

```
public void insertULong(int 1) throws SystemException;
public int extractULong() throws SystemException;
```

1.2.5 Float

```
public void insertFloat(float f) throws SystemException;
public float extractFloat() throws SystemException;
```

1.2.6 Double

```
public void insertDouble(double d) throws SystemException;
public double extractDouble() throws SystemException;
```

1.2.7 Char

```
public void insertChar(char c) throws SystemException;
public char extractChar() throws SystemException;
```

1.2.8 Octet

```
public void insertOctet(byte b) throws SystemException;
public byte extractOctet() throws SystemException;
```

1.2.9 String

```
public void insertString(String s) throws SystemException;
public void insertString(String s, int length) throws SystemException;
public String extractString() throws SystemException;
```

1.2.10 Boolean

```
public void insertBoolean(boolean b) throws SystemException;
public boolean extractBoolean() throws SystemException;
```

1.2.11 Any

```
public void insertAny(Any a) throws SystemException;
public Any extractAny() throws SystemException;
```

1.2.12 TypeCode

```
public void insertTypeCode(TypeCode tc) throws SystemException;
public TypeCode extractTypeCode() throws SystemException;
```

1.2.13 Object

```
public void insertObject( IE.Iona.Orbix2.CORBA.Object.Ref oref)
                    throws SystemException;
public IE.Iona.Orbix2.CORBA.Object.Ref extractObject()
                    throws SystemException;
```

1.3   Joe

Joe provides a class sunw.corba.Any which has the following methods.

1.3.1 Octet

```
public static synchronized byte getOctetFromAny(Any a)
    throws SystemException
public static Any createAnyFromOctet(byte x)
    throws SystemException
```

1.3.2 Char

```
public static synchronized char getCharFromAny(Any a)
    throws SystemException
public static Any createAnyFromChar(char x)
    throws SystemException
```

1.3.3 Boolean

```
public static synchronized boolean getBooleanFromAny(Any a)
    throws SystemException
public static Any createBooleanFromAny(boolean x)
    throws SystemException
```

1.3.4 Short

```
public static synchronized short getShortFromAny(Any a)
    throws SystemException
public static Any createAnyFromShort(short x)
    throws SystemException
```

1.3.5 UnsignedShort

```
public static synchronized short getUnsignedShortFromAny(Any a)
    throws SystemException
public static Any createAnyFromUnsignedShort(short x)
    throws SystemException
```

1.3.6 Long

```
public static synchronized int getLongFromAny(Any a)
    throws SystemException
public static Any createAnyFromLong(int x)
    throws SystemException
```

1.3.7 AnyFromUnsignedLong

```
public static synchronized int getAnyFromUnsignedLong(Any a)
    throws SystemException
public static Any createAnyFromUnsignedLong(int x)
    throws SystemException
```

1.3.8 Float

```
public static synchronized float getFloatFromAny(Any a)
    throws SystemException
```

```
public static Any createAnyFromFloat(float x)
   throws SystemException
```

1.3.9   Double

```
public static synchronized double getDoubleFromAny(Any a)
   throws SystemException
public static Any createAnyFromDouble(double x)
   throws SystemException
```

1.3.10   String

```
public static synchronized String getStringFromAny(Any a)
   throws SystemException
public static Any createAnyFromString(String x)
   throws SystemException
```

1.3.11   Object

```
public static synchronized ObjectRef getObjectFromAny(Any a)
   throws SystemException
public static Any createAnyFromObject(ObjectRef x)
   throws SystemException
```

2   TCKind

All three ORBs provide the same definition for TCKind, the kind of TypeCodes. However, they are defined in different classes:

♦ Visibroker defines them in the class CORBA.TCKind.
♦ OrbixWeb defines them in the class IE.Iona.Orbix2.CORBA.TCKind.
♦ Joe defines them in the class sunw.corba.TCKind.

```
public final static int tk_null;

public final static int tk_void;

public final static int tk_short;

public final static int tk_long;

public final static int tk_ushort;

public final static int tk_ulong;

public final static int tk_float;

public final static int tk_double;
```

```
public final static int tk_boolean;

public final static int tk_char;

public final static int tk_octet;

public final static int tk_any;

public final static int tk_TypeCode;

public final static int tk_Principal;

public final static int tk_objref;

public final static int tk_struct;

public final static int tk_union;

public final static int tk_enum;

public final static int tk_string;

public final static int tk_sequence;

public final static int tk_array;

public final static int tk_alias;

public final static int tk_except;
```

3   *TypeCodes for Predefined IDL Types*

TypeCodes are mapped to a Java class. TypeCodes for predefined IDL types
are mapped to variables (or constants) of the class TypeCode.

3.1   Visibroker

Visibroker for Java defines a class CORBA.TCKind that defines the following
variables for TypeCodes of predefined IDL types.

```
public static TypeCode tc_null;
public static TypeCode tc_void;
public static TypeCode tc_short;
public static TypeCode tc_long;
public static TypeCode tc_ushort;
public static TypeCode tc_ulong;
public static TypeCode tc_float;
```

```
public static TypeCode tc_double;
public static TypeCode tc_boolean;
public static TypeCode tc_char;
public static TypeCode tc_octet;
public static TypeCode tc_any;
public static TypeCode tc_TypeCode;
public static TypeCode tc_Principal;
public static TypeCode tc_Object;
public static TypeCode tc_string;
```

3.2 OrbixWeb

OrbixWeb defines the following constants in the class `IE.Iona.Orbix2._CORBA`.

```
public static final TypeCode _tc_null;
public static final TypeCode _tc_void;
public static final TypeCode _tc_short;
public static final TypeCode _tc_long;
public static final TypeCode _tc_ushort;
public static final TypeCode _tc_ulong;
public static final TypeCode _tc_float;
public static final TypeCode _tc_double;
public static final TypeCode _tc_boolean;
public static final TypeCode _tc_char;
public static final TypeCode _tc_octet;
public static final TypeCode _tc_any;
public static final TypeCode _tc_TypeCode;
public static final TypeCode _tc_Principal;
public static final TypeCode _tc_Object;
public static final TypeCode _tc_struct;
public static final TypeCode _tc_union;
public static final TypeCode _tc_enum;
public static final TypeCode _tc_string;
public static final TypeCode _tc_NamedValue;
```

3.3 Joe

Joe defines the following variables in the class `sunw.corba.TypeCodeStub`.

```
public static TypeCodeRef tcNull;
public static TypeCodeRef tcOctet;
public static TypeCodeRef tcChar;
public static TypeCodeRef tcFloat;
public static TypeCodeRef tcDouble;
public static TypeCodeRef tcShort;
public static TypeCodeRef tcUnsignedShort;
public static TypeCodeRef tcLong;
public static TypeCodeRef tcUnsignedLong;
public static TypeCodeRef tcString;
```

```
public static TypeCodeRef tcBoolean;
public static TypeCodeRef tcObject;
```

4 Container Classes for Predefined IDL Types

Container classes have been introduced to overcome the mismatch of the parameter-passing semantics between OMG IDL and CORBA.

4.1 Visibroker

Visibroker for Java defines the following container classes for predefined IDL types in the package CORBA.

4.1.1 Boolean

```
public final class boolean_var extends Object

    public boolean value
    public boolean_var(boolean newValue)
    public boolean_var()
```

4.1.2 Byte

```
public final class byte_var extends Object

    public byte value
    public byte_var(byte newValue)
    public byte_var()
```

4.1.3 Char

```
public final class char_var extends Object

    public char value
    public char_var(char newValue)
    public char_var()
```

4.1.4 Double

```
public final class double_var extends Object

    public double value
    public double_var(double newValue)
    public double_var()
```

4.1.5 Float

```
public final class float_var extends Object

    public float value
    public float_var(float newValue)
    public float_var()
```

4.1.6 Int

```
public final class int_var extends Object

    public int value
    public int_var(int newValue)
    public int_var()
```

4.1.7 Short

```
public final class short_var extends Object

    public short value
    public short_var(short newValue)
    public short_var()
```

4.1.8 String

```
public final class String_var extends Object

    public String value
    public String_var(String newValue)
    public String_var()
```

4.1.9 TypeCode

```
public final class TypeCode_var extends Object

    public TypeCode value
    public TypeCode_var(TypeCode newValue)
    public TypeCode_var()
```

4.1.10 Object

```
public final class Object_var extends Object

    public Object value
    public Object_var(Object newValue)
    public Object_var()
```

4.1.11 Any

```
public final class Any_var extends Any
```

```
public Any value
public Any_var()
```

4.2   OrbixWeb

OrbixWeb defines the following container classes for predefined IDL types in the package IE.Iona.Orbix2.CORBA.

4.2.1   Boolean
```
public class BooleanHolder

    public boolean value
    public boolean_var(boolean _value)
```

4.2.2   Byte
```
public class ByteHolder

    public byte value
    public byte_var(byte _value)
```

4.2.3   Char
```
public class CharHolder

    public char value
    public char_var(char _value)
```

4.2.4   Double
```
public class DoubleHolder

    public double value
    public double_var(double _value)
```

4.2.5   Float
```
public class FloatHolder

    public float value
    public float_var(float _value)
```

4.2.6   Int
```
public class IntHolder

    public int value
    public int_var(int _value)
```

4.2.7 Short

```
public class ShortHolder

    public short value
    public short_var(short _value)
```

4.3 Joe

Joe defines the following container classes for predefined IDL types in the package sunw.corba.

4.3.1 Boolean

```
public class BooleanHolder extends Object

    public boolean value
    public booleanHolder(boolean initial)
    public booleanHolder()
```

4.3.2 Byte

```
public class ByteHolder extends Object

    public byte value
    public byteHolder(byte initial)
    public byteHolder()
```

4.3.3 Char

```
public class CharHolder extends Object

    public char value
    public charHolder(char initial)
    public charHolder()
```

4.3.4 Double

```
public class DoubleHolder extends Object

    public double value
    public doubleHolder(double initial)
    public doubleHolder()
```

4.3.5 Float

```
public class FloatHolder extends Object
```

```
public float value
public floatHolder(float initial)
public floatHolder()
```

4.3.6   Int

`public class IntHolder extends Object`

```
public int value
public intHolder(int initial)
public intHolder()
```

4.3.7   Short

`public class ShortHolder extends Object`

```
public short value
public shortHolder(short initial)
public shortHolder()
```

4.3.8   String

`public class StringHolder extends Object`

```
public String value
public StringHolder(String initial)
public StringHolder()
```

4.3.9   TypeCode

`public class TypeCodeHolder extends Object`

```
public TypeCodeRef value
public TypeCodeHolder(TypeCodeRef initial)
public TypeCodeHolder()
```

4.3.10   Object

`public class ObjectHolder extends Object`

```
public ObjectRef value
public ObjectHolder(ObjectRef initial)
public ObjectHolder()
```

4.3.11   Any

`public class AnyHolder extends Object`

```
public Any value
public AnyHolder()
public AnyHolder(Any initial)
```

4.3.12 Principal

public class PrincipalHolder extends Object

```
public PrincipalRef value
public PrincipalHolder()
public PrincipalHolder(Principal initial)
```

4.3.13 Long

public class LongHolder extends Object

```
public Long value
public LongHolder()
public LongHolder(Long initial)
```

4.3.14 LongLong

public class LongLongHolder extends Object

```
public LongLong value
public LongLongHolder()
public LongLongHolder(LongLong initial)
```

4.3.15 UnsignedLong

public class UnsignedLongHolder extends Object

```
public UnsignedLong value
public UnsignedLongHolder()
public UnsignedLongHolder(UnsignedLong initial)
```

4.3.16 UnsignedLongLong

public class UnsignedLongLongHolder extends Object

```
public UnsignedLongLong value
public UnsignedLongLongHolder()
public UnsignedLongLongHolder(UnsignedLongLong initial)
```

Listing of all Example Code

This appendix contains complete listings of all example code introduced throughout the book. The sections of this appendix correspond to the chapters of the book in sequence but not in number, as some chapters do not contain examples. There are separate subsections for IDL specifications and the Java code from each of the ORBs we have used for the particular example. Note that this code is also available on-line from Wiley's Web site http://www.wiley.com/compbooks/.

1   *Java*

1.1   **SimpleHelloWorld**

1.1.1   GoodDay.java

```
interface GoodDay {

    // method
    public String hello();
}
```

1.1.2   GoodDayImpl.java

```
class GoodDayImpl implements GoodDay {

    private String locality;

    // constructor
    GoodDayImpl( String m_locality ) {
        locality = new String( m_locality );
    }

    // method
    public String hello() {
        return "Hello World, from " + locality;
    }
}
```

1.1.3   SimpleHelloWorldApplet.java

```
import java.awt.*;

public class SimpleHelloWorldApplet extends java.applet.Applet {

    private GoodDayImpl good_day;
    private Button hello_world_button;
    private TextField text_field;

    public void init() {

        hello_world_button = new Button("Invoke local method");
        hello_world_button.setFont(new Font("Helvetica",
            Font.BOLD, 20));
        text_field = new TextField();
        text_field.setEditable(false);
        text_field.setFont(new Font("Helvetica", Font.BOLD, 14));

        setLayout( new GridLayout(2,1));
        add( hello_world_button );
        add( text_field );

        // create object of class GoodDay
        good_day = new GoodDayImpl( "Brisbane" );

    }

    public boolean action(Event ev, java.lang.Object arg) {

        // catch and process events
        if(ev.target == hello_world_button ) {

            // invoke the operation and display result
            text_field.setText( good_day.hello() );
```

```
        return true;
    }
    return false;
  }
}
```

1.1.4   SimpleHelloWorldApplication.java

```java
import java.io.*;

public class SimpleHelloWorldApplication {

    public static void main(String args[]) {
        // create object of class GoodDayImpl
        GoodDayImpl good_day = new GoodDayImpl( "Brisbane" );

        // invoke method hello() and print result
        System.out.println( good_day.hello() );
    }
}
```

1.1.5   SimpleHelloWorldApplet.html

```html
<html>
<header>
<! -- SimpleHelloWorldApplet.html -->
<title>
Simple Hello World Example
</title>
<BODY BGCOLOR=15085A TEXT=FFD700 LINK==FFFFFF VLINK=FFFFFF ALINK=FFFFFF>
<center>
<pre>

</pre>
<h1>
Simple Hello World Example
</h1>
</center>
<pre>

</pre>
<center>
<applet code=SimpleHelloWorldApplet.class width=400 height=80>
</applet>
</center>

</body>
</html>
```

2   First Java ORB Applications

2.1   SimpleHelloWorld

2.1.1   Interface Specification

SimpleHelloWorld.idl

```
module SimpleHelloWorld {
   interface GoodDay {
     string hello();
   };
};
```

2.1.2   Visibroker

SimpleGoodDayImpl.java

```java
import CORBA.*;

class SimpleGoodDayImpl extends SimpleHelloWorld._sk_GoodDay {

    private String locality;

    // constructor
    SimpleGoodDayImpl( String m_locality ) {

        // calling the constructor of the super class
        super( "SimpleGoodDayImplV1.0" );

        // initialize locality
        locality = new String( m_locality );
    }

    // method
    public String hello() throws CORBA.SystemException {

        return "Hello World, from " + locality;
    }
}
```

SimpleHelloWorldApplet.java

```java
import java.awt.*;

public class SimpleHelloWorldApplet extends java.applet.Applet {

    private SimpleHelloWorld.GoodDay good_day;
    private Button hello_world_button;
    private TextField text_field;

    public void init() {
        hello_world_button = new Button("Invoke remote method");
```

```
      hello_world_button.setFont(new Font("Helvetica",
          Font.BOLD, 20));
      text_field = new TextField();
      text_field.setEditable(false);
      text_field.setFont(new Font("Helvetica", Font.BOLD, 14));

      setLayout( new GridLayout(2,1));
      add( hello_world_button );
      add( text_field );

   try {
      //initialize the ORB (using this applet)
      CORBA.ORB orb = CORBA.ORB.init( this );

      // bind to object
      good_day = SimpleHelloWorld.GoodDay_var.bind();

   }
   // catch CORBA system exceptions
   catch(CORBA.SystemException ex) {
       System.err.println(ex);
   }
 }

   public boolean action(Event ev, java.lang.Object arg) {

      // catch and process events
      if(ev.target == hello_world_button ) {

         // invoke the operation
         try {
            text_field.setText( good_day.hello() );
         }

         // catch CORBA system exceptions
         catch(CORBA.SystemException ex) {
             System.err.println(ex);
         }

         return true;
      }

      return false;
   }
}
```

SimpleHelloWorldAppletServer.java

```
import CORBA.*;

public class SimpleHelloWorldAppletServer extends java.applet.Applet {

   public void init() {
```

```
        try {
            //init ORB
            CORBA.ORB orb = CORBA.ORB.init();

            //init Basic Object Adapter
            CORBA.BOA boa = orb.BOA_init();

            // create a SimpleGoodDay object
            SimpleGoodDayImpl simple_good_day_impl =
                new SimpleGoodDayImpl( "Berlin" );

            // export the object reference
            boa.obj_is_ready( simple_good_day_impl );

            // print stringified object reference
            System.out.println(
                orb.object_to_string( simple_good_day_impl ) );

            // wait for requests
            boa.impl_is_ready();
        }
        catch(CORBA.SystemException e) {
            System.err.println(e);
        }
    }
}
```

SimpleHelloWorldClient.java

```
import java.io.*;

public class SimpleHelloWorldClient {

    public static void main(String args[]) {

        try {
            // initialize the ORB.
            CORBA.ORB orb = CORBA.ORB.init();

            // get object reference from command-line argument
            CORBA.Object obj = orb.string_to_object( args[0] );

            // and narrowed it to SimpleHelloWorld.GoodDay
            SimpleHelloWorld.GoodDay good_day =
                SimpleHelloWorld.GoodDay_var.narrow( obj );

            // invoke the operation and print the result
            System.out.println( good_day.hello() );
        }

        // catch CORBA system exceptions
```

```
        catch(CORBA.SystemException ex) {
            System.err.println(ex);
        }
    }
}
```

SimpleHelloWorldServer.java

```java
import CORBA.*;

public class SimpleHelloWorldServer {

    public static void main(String[] args) {

        if( args.length != 1 ) {
            System.out.println(
                "Usage: java SimpleHelloWorldServer <location>");
            System.exit( 1 );
        }

        try {
            //init ORB
            CORBA.ORB orb = CORBA.ORB.init();

            //init Basic Object Adapter
            CORBA.BOA boa = orb.BOA_init();

            // create a SimpleGoodDay object
            SimpleGoodDayImpl simple_good_day_impl =
                new SimpleGoodDayImpl( args[0] );

            // export the object reference
            boa.obj_is_ready( simple_good_day_impl );

            // print stringified object reference
            System.out.println(
                orb.object_to_string( simple_good_day_impl ) );

            // wait for requests
            boa.impl_is_ready();
        }
        catch(CORBA.SystemException e) {
            System.err.println(e);
        }
    }
}
```

2.1.3 SimpleHelloWorldApplet.html

```html
<html>
<header>
```

```
<! -- SimpleHelloWorldApplet.html -->
<title>
Simple Hello World Example
</title>
<BODY BGCOLOR=15085A TEXT=FFD700 LINK==FFFFFF VLINK=FFFFFF ALINK=FFFFFF>
<center>
<pre>

</pre>

<h1>
Simple Hello World Example
</h1>
</center>
<pre>

</pre>
<center>
<applet code=SimpleHelloWorldApplet.class width=400 height=80>
</applet>
</center>

</body>
</html>
```

2.1.4   *SimpleHelloWorldAppletServer.html*

```
<html>
<header>
<! -- SimpleHelloWorldAppletServer.html -->
<title>
Simple Hello World Server Example
</title>
<BODY BGCOLOR=15085A TEXT=FFD700 LINK==FFFFFF VLINK=FFFFFF ALINK=FFFFFF>
<center>
<pre>

</pre>
<h1>
Simple Hello World Example
</h1>
</center>
<pre>

</pre>
<center>
<applet code=SimpleHelloWorldAppletServer.class width=400 height=80>
</applet>
</center>

</body>
</html>
```

2.1.5 OrbixWeb
SimpleHelloWorldApplet.java

```java
import java.awt.*;
import IE.Iona.Orbix2._CORBA;
import IE.Iona.Orbix2.CORBA.SystemException;

public class SimpleHelloWorldApplet extends java.applet.Applet {

    private SimpleHelloWorld.GoodDay.Ref good_day;
    private Button hello_world_button;
    private TextField text_field;

    public void init() {

        hello_world_button = new Button("Invoke remote method");
        hello_world_button.setFont(new Font("Helvetica",
            Font.BOLD, 20));
        text_field = new TextField();
        text_field.setEditable(false);
        text_field.setFont(new Font("Helvetica", Font.BOLD, 14));

        setLayout( new GridLayout(2,1));
        add( hello_world_button );
        add( text_field );

        try {
            // bind to object
            good_day = SimpleHelloWorld.GoodDay._bind();

        }
        // catch CORBA system exceptions
        catch(SystemException ex) {
            System.err.println(ex);
        }
    }

    public boolean action(Event ev, java.lang.Object arg) {

        // catch and process events
        if(ev.target == hello_world_button ) {

            // invoke the operation
            try {
                text_field.setText( good_day.hello() );
            }

            // catch CORBA system exceptions
            catch(SystemException ex) {
                System.err.println(ex);
            }
```

```
        return true;
    }

    return false;
  }
}
```

SimpleHelloWorldClient.java

```java
import java.io.*;
import IE.Iona.Orbix2._CORBA;
import IE.Iona.Orbix2.CORBA.SystemException;

public class SimpleHelloWorldClient {

    public static void main(String args[]) {

        // SimpleHelloWorld.GoodDay.Ref good_day = null;
        // SimpleHelloWorld.GoodDay.Ref good_day;

        try {

            System.out.println( "string_to_object" );
            IE.Iona.Orbix2.CORBA.Object.Ref obj =
                _CORBA.Orbix.string_to_object ( args[0] );

            System.out.println( "narrow" );
            SimpleHelloWorld.GoodDay.Ref good_day = SimpleHelloWorld.GoodDay
(obj);

            // invoke the operation and print the result
            System.out.println( "invoke" );
            System.out.println( good_day.hello() );
        }

        // catch CORBA system exceptions
        catch( SystemException ex ) {
            System.err.println(ex);
        }
    }
}
```

2.1.6   Joe
SimpleHelloWorldApplet.java

```java
// SimpleHelloWorldApplet.java
import java.awt.*;
import sunw.joe.*;
import sunw.corba.*;

public class SimpleHelloWorldApplet extends JoeApplet {
```

```
private SimpleHelloWorld.GoodDayRef good_day;
private Button hello_world_button;
private TextField text_field;

public void init() {

   hello_world_button = new Button("Invoke remote method");
   hello_world_button.setFont(new Font("Helvetica",
      Font.BOLD, 20));
   text_field = new TextField();
   text_field.setEditable(false);
   text_field.setFont(new Font("Helvetica", Font.BOLD, 14));

   setLayout( new GridLayout(2,1));
   add( hello_world_button );
   add( text_field );

try {
   ObjectRef obj;

   // find object
   obj = find( "MyGoodDay" );
   good_day = SimpleHelloWorld.GoodDayStub.narrow( obj );

}
// catch CORBA user exceptions
catch(UserException ex) {
   System.err.println(ex);
}
// catch CORBA system exceptions
catch(SystemException ex) {
   System.err.println(ex);
}
}

public boolean action(Event ev, java.lang.Object arg) {

   // catch and process events
   if(ev.target == hello_world_button ) {

      // invoke the operation
      try {
         text_field.setText( good_day.hello() );
      }

      // catch CORBA system exceptions
      catch(SystemException ex) {
         System.err.println(ex);
      }

      return true;
   }

   return false;
```

```
        }
    }
```

SimpleHelloWorldClient.java

```java
import sunw.corba.*;
import sunw.joe.*;

class SimpleHelloWorldClient {
    public static void main(String args[]) {
        Joe joe = null;
        try {
            joe = new Joe("");

            // get object reference from command-line argument
            sunw.corba.ObjectRef obj =
                joe.stringToObject( args[0] );

            // and narrow it to SimpleHelloWorld.GoodDay
            SimpleHelloWorld.GoodDayRef good_day =
                SimpleHelloWorld.GoodDayStub.narrow( obj );

            // invoke the operation and print the result
            System.out.println( good_day.hello() );
        }

            // catch CORBA system exceptions
            catch(SystemException ex) {
                System.err.println( ex );
            }
        }
    }
```

2.2   HelloWorld

2.2.1   Interface Specification
HelloWorld.idl

```
module HelloWorld{
    interface GoodDay {
        string hello(
            out short hour,
            out short minute );
    };
};
```

2.2.2   Visibroker
GoodDay.java

```java
import java.util.Date;

class GoodDayImpl extends HelloWorld._sk_GoodDay {
```

```
    private String locality;

    // constructor
    GoodDay( String m_locality ) {
        locality = new String( m_locality );
    }

    // method
    public String hello(
            CORBA.short_var hour,
            CORBA.short_var minute
        ) throws CORBA.SystemException {

        // get local time of the server
        Date date = new Date();
        hour.value = (short) date.getHours();
        minute.value = (short) date.getMinutes();

        return locality;
    }
}
```

GoodDayImpl.java

```
import java.util.Date;

class GoodDayImpl extends HelloWorld._sk_GoodDay {

    private String locality;

    // constructor
    GoodDayImpl( String m_locality ) {
        super( "GoodDayImpl" );
        locality = new String( m_locality );
    }

    // method
    public String hello(
            CORBA.short_var hour,
            CORBA.short_var minute
        ) throws CORBA.SystemException {

        // get local time of the server
        Date date = new Date();
        hour.value = (short) date.getHours();
        minute.value = (short) date.getMinutes();

        return locality;
    }
}
```

HelloWorldApplet.java

```
import java.awt.*;
import HelloWorld.*;
```

```
import CORBA.*;

public class HelloWorldApplet extends java.applet.Applet {

    private CORBA.short_var minute;
    private CORBA.short_var hour;

    private HelloWorld.GoodDay good_day;
    private String text;
    private String locality;
    private Button hello_world_button;
    private TextField text_field;

    public void init() {

        minute = new CORBA.short_var();
        hour = new CORBA.short_var();

        hello_world_button = new Button("Invoke remote method");
        hello_world_button.setFont(new Font("Helvetica",
            Font.BOLD, 20));
        text_field = new TextField();
        text_field.setEditable(false);
        text_field.setFont(new Font("Helvetica", Font.BOLD, 14));

        setLayout( new GridLayout(2,1));
        add( hello_world_button );
        add( text_field );

        try {
            // initialize the ORB (using this applet)
            CORBA.ORB orb = CORBA.ORB.init( this );

            // bind to "HelloWorld.GoodDay"
            good_day = HelloWorld.GoodDay_var.bind();
        }

        // catch CORBA system exceptions
        catch(CORBA.SystemException ex) {
            System.err.println(ex);
        }
    }

    public boolean action(Event ev, java.lang.Object arg) {
        // catch and process events
        if(ev.target == hello_world_button ) {
            // invoke the operation
            try {
                locality = new String( good_day.hello( hour, minute ) );
            }
```

```
        // catch CORBA system exceptions
        catch(CORBA.SystemException ex) {
            System.err.println(ex);
        }

        if( minute.value < 10 )
            text = new String("The local time in " + locality +
                " is " + hour.value + ":0" + minute.value + "." );
        else
           text = new String("The local time in " + locality +
                " is " + hour.value + ":" + minute.value + "." );
        text_field.setText( text );
        return true;
      }
     return false;
   }
}
```

HelloWorldClient.java

```
import java.io.*;

public class HelloWorldClient {

    public static void main(String args[]) {

        // create _var objects for out parameters
            CORBA.short_var minute = new CORBA.short_var();
            CORBA.short_var hour = new CORBA.short_var();

            try {
             // initialize the ORB
             CORBA.ORB orb = CORBA.ORB.init();

             // get object reference from command-line argument
             CORBA.Object obj = orb.string_to_object( args[0] );

             // and narrowed it to HelloWorld.GoodDay
             HelloWorld.GoodDay good_day =
                 HelloWorld.GoodDay_var.narrow( obj );

             // invoke the operation
             String locality = new String(
                 good_day.hello( hour, minute ) );

             // print results to stdout
             System.out.println("Hello World!");
             if( minute.value < 10 )
                 System.out.println("The local time in " + locality +
                     " is " + hour.value + ":0" + minute.value + "." );
```

```
                 else
                     System.out.println("The local time in " + locality +
                         " is " + hour.value + ":" + minute.value + "." );
        }

      // catch CORBA system exceptions
      catch(CORBA.SystemException ex) {
          System.err.println(ex);
      }
    }
}
```

HelloWorldServer.java

```
public class HelloWorldServer {

    public static void main(String[] args) {
        try {
            //init orb
            CORBA.ORB orb = CORBA.ORB.init();

            //init basic object adapter
            CORBA.BOA boa = orb.BOA_init();

            // create a GoodDay object
            GoodDayImpl good_day_impl = new GoodDayImpl( args[0] );

            // export the object reference
            boa.obj_is_ready( good_day_impl );
            System.out.println( orb.object_to_string( good_day_impl ) );

            // wait for requests
            boa.impl_is_ready();
        }
        catch(CORBA.SystemException e) {
            System.err.println(e);
        }
    }
}
```

2.2.3   HelloWorldApplet.html

```
<html>
<header>
<! -- HelloWorldApplet.html -->
<title>
Hello World Example
</title>
<BODY BGCOLOR=15085A TEXT=FFD700 LINK==FFFFFF VLINK=FFFFFF ALINK=FFFFFF>
<center>
<pre>
```

```
</pre>

<h1>
Hello World Example
</h1>
</center>
<pre>

</pre>
<center>
<applet code=HelloWorldApplet.class width=400 height=80>
</applet>
</center>

</body>
</html>
```

2.2.4   OrbixWeb
HelloWorldClient.java

```
import java.io.*;
import IE.Iona.Orbix2._CORBA;
import IE.Iona.Orbix2.CORBA.SystemException;
import IE.Iona.Orbix2.CORBA.ShortHolder;

public class HelloWorldClient {

    public static void main(String args[]) {

        // create Holder objects for out parameters
        ShortHolder minute = new ShortHolder();
        ShortHolder hour = new ShortHolder();

        try {

          IE.Iona.Orbix2.CORBA.Object.Ref iRef =
              _CORBA.Orbix.string_to_object ( args[0] );
          HelloWorld.GoodDay.Ref good_day_ref =
              HelloWorld.GoodDay._narrow (iRef);

          // invoke the operation
          String locality = new String(
              good_day_ref.hello( hour, minute ) );

          // print results to stdout
          System.out.println("Hello World!");
          if( minute.value < 10 )
              System.out.println("The local time in " + locality +
              " is " + hour.value + ":0" + minute.value + "." );
```

```
            else
        System.out.println("The local time in " + locality +
            " is " + hour.value + ":" + minute.value + "." );
    }

  // catch CORBA system exceptions
  catch( SystemException ex ) {
      System.err.println(ex);
  }
 }
}
```

2.2.5   Joe

HelloWorldApplet.java

```
// HelloWorldApplet.java
import java.awt.*;
import sunw.joe.*;
import sunw.corba.*;

public class HelloWorldApplet extends JoeApplet {

    private ShortHolder minute;
    private ShortHolder hour;

    private HelloWorld.GoodDayRef good_day;
    private String text;
    private String locality;
    private Button hello_world_button;
    private TextField text_field;

    public void init() {

        minute = new ShortHolder();
        hour = new ShortHolder();

        hello_world_button = new Button("Invoke remote method");
        hello_world_button.setFont(new Font("Helvetica",
            Font.BOLD, 20));
        text_field = new TextField();
        text_field.setEditable(false);
        text_field.setFont(new Font("Helvetica", Font.BOLD, 14));

        setLayout( new GridLayout(2,1));
        add( hello_world_button );
        add( text_field );

        try {
         ObjectRef obj;
```

```
     // find object
     obj = find( "MyOtherGoodDay" );
     good_day = HelloWorld.GoodDayStub.narrow( obj );
    }
    // catch user exceptions
    catch(UserException ex) {
        System.err.println(ex);
    }
    // catch system exceptions
    catch(SystemException ex) {
        System.err.println(ex);
    }
}

public boolean action(Event ev, java.lang.Object arg) {
    // catch and process events
    if(ev.target == hello_world_button ) {
      // invoke the operation
      try {
          locality = new String( good_day.hello( hour, minute ) );
      }
      // catch system exceptions
      catch(SystemException ex) {
          System.err.println(ex);
      }
      if( minute.value < 10 )
          text = new String("The local time in " + locality +
              " is " + hour.value + ":0" + minute.value + "." );
      else
         text = new String("The local time in " + locality +
              " is " + hour.value + ":" + minute.value + "." );
      text_field.setText( text );
      return true;
    }
    return false;
  }
}
```

HelloWorldClient.java

```
import java.io.*;
import sunw.corba.*;
import sunw.joe.*;

public class HelloWorldClient {

    public static void main(String args[]) {

        // create Holder objects for out parameters
        ShortHolder minute = new ShortHolder();
        ShortHolder hour = new ShortHolder();
```

```
                Joe joe = null;
                try {
                    joe = new Joe("");

                    // get object reference from command-line argument
                    sunw.corba.ObjectRef obj =
                        joe.stringToObject( args[0] );

                    // and narrow it to HelloWorld.GoodDay
                    HelloWorld.GoodDayRef good_day =
                        HelloWorld.GoodDayStub.narrow( obj );

                    // invoke the operation
                    String locality = new String(
                        good_day.hello( hour, minute ) );

                    // print results to stdout
                    System.out.println("Hello World!");
                    if( minute.value < 10 )
                        System.out.println("The local time in " + locality +
                            " is " + hour.value + ":0" + minute.value + "." );
                    else
                        System.out.println("The local time in " + locality +
                            " is " + hour.value + ":" + minute.value + "." );
                }

                // catch CORBA system exceptions
                catch(SystemException ex) {
                    System.err.println(ex);
                }
            }
        }
```

3 Locating Services

3.1 Naming

3.1.1 Interface Specification
CosNaming.idl

```
module CosNaming
{
    typedef string Istring;

    struct NameComponent {
      Istring id;
      Istring kind;
    };
```

```
typedef sequence <NameComponent> Name;

enum BindingType { nobject, ncontext };

struct Binding {
  Name binding_name;
  BindingType binding_type;
};

typedef sequence <Binding> BindingList;

interface BindingIterator;

interface NamingContext {

  enum NotFoundReason { missing_node, not_context, not_object };

  exception NotFound {
    NotFoundReason why;
    Name rest_of_name;
  };

  exception CannotProceed {
    NamingContext cxt;
    Name rest_of_name;
  };

  exception InvalidName {};
  exception AlreadyBound {};
  exception NotEmpty {};

  void bind(in Name n, in Object obj)
    raises( NotFound, CannotProceed, InvalidName, AlreadyBound );

  void rebind(in Name n, in Object obj)
    raises( NotFound, CannotProceed, InvalidName );

  void bind_context(in Name n, in NamingContext nc)
    raises( NotFound, CannotProceed, InvalidName, AlreadyBound );

  void rebind_context(in Name n, in NamingContext nc)
    raises( NotFound, CannotProceed, InvalidName );

  Object resolve(in Name n)
    raises( NotFound, CannotProceed, InvalidName );

  void unbind(in Name n)
    raises( NotFound, CannotProceed, InvalidName );

  NamingContext new_context();

  NamingContext bind_new_context(in Name n)
    raises( NotFound, AlreadyBound, CannotProceed, InvalidName );
```

```
    void destroy()
      raises( NotEmpty );

    void list(in unsigned long how_many,
          out BindingList bl, out BindingIterator bi
    );
  };

  interface BindingIterator {

    boolean next_one(out Binding b);

    boolean next_n(in unsigned long how_many,
          out BindingList bl);

    void destroy();
  };
};
```

3.1.2   Visibroker
Bind.java

```java
public class Bind {

    public static void main(String args[]) {

        try {
            //init
            CORBA.ORB orb = CORBA.ORB.init();
            CORBA.BOA boa = orb.BOA_init();

            IORFile ior_file = new IORFile( args[0] );

            System.out.println( "create Easy Naming");
            EasyNaming easy_naming = new EasyNaming( orb,
                ior_file.get_ior_string() );

            // test str2name
            easy_naming.bind_from_string(args[1],
                            easy_naming.get_root_context());
        }

        catch(CORBA.SystemException e) {
            System.out.println(e);
        }
        catch(CORBA.UserException naming_exception) {
        System.err.println( naming_exception );
        }
        System.out.println("Bind OK");
    }
}
```

EasyNaming.java

```
public class EasyNaming {

    private CosNaming.NamingContext root_context;

    EasyNaming( CORBA.ORB orb, String ior_string ) {

        try {
            CORBA.Object obj = orb.string_to_object( ior_string );
            root_context = CosNaming.NamingContext_var.narrow( obj );
            System.out.println("Root context:");
            System.out.println( orb.object_to_string( root_context ));
            System.out.println("");
        }
        catch(CORBA.SystemException corba_exception) {
            System.err.println(corba_exception);
        }


    }

    public void bind_from_string( String str, CORBA.Object obj )
        throws
        CosNaming._NamingContext.InvalidName,
        CosNaming._NamingContext.AlreadyBound,
        CosNaming._NamingContext.CannotProceed,
        CosNaming._NamingContext.NotFound, CORBA.SystemException {

        CosNaming.NameComponent[] name = str2name( str );
        CosNaming.NamingContext context = root_context;
        CosNaming.NameComponent[] _name = new CosNaming.NameComponent[1];

        try {
            root_context.bind( name, obj );
        }
        catch( CosNaming._NamingContext.NotFound not_found ) {
            // bind step by step

            // create and bind all non-existent contexts in the path
            for( int i = 0; i < name.length - 1; i++ ) {
                _name[0] = name[i];
                try {
                    // see if the context exists
                    context = CosNaming.NamingContext_var.narrow(
                        context.resolve( _name ) );
                    System.out.println("Resolved " + _name[0].id);
                }
                catch( CosNaming._NamingContext.NotFound nf ) {
                    System.out.println("Creating " + _name[0].id);
                    // if not then create a new context
                    context = context.bind_new_context( _name );
```

```
        }
        // let other exceptions propagate to caller
    }

            // bind last component to the obj argument
            _name[0] = name[ name.length - 1 ];
            context.bind( _name, obj );
        }
        // let other exceptions propagate to caller
    }

    public void rebind_from_string( String str, CORBA.Object obj )
        throws
        CosNaming._NamingContext.InvalidName,
        CosNaming._NamingContext.AlreadyBound,
        CosNaming._NamingContext.CannotProceed,
        CosNaming._NamingContext.NotFound, CORBA.SystemException {

        CosNaming.NameComponent[] name = str2name( str );
        CosNaming.NamingContext context = root_context;
        CosNaming.NameComponent[] _name = new CosNaming.NameComponent[1];

        try {
            root_context.rebind( name, obj );
        }
        catch( CosNaming._NamingContext.NotFound not_found ) {
            // bind step by step

        // create and bind all non-existent contexts in the path
        for( int i = 0; i < name.length - 1; i++ ) {
            _name[0] = name[i];
            try {
                // see if the context exists
                context = CosNaming.NamingContext_var.narrow(
                    context.resolve( _name ) );
                System.out.println("Resolved " + _name[0].id);
            }
            catch( CosNaming._NamingContext.NotFound nf ) {
                System.out.println("Creating " + _name[0].id);
                // if not then create a new context
                context = context.bind_new_context( _name );
            }
            // let other exceptions propagate to caller
        }

            // bind last component to the obj argument
            _name[0] = name[ name.length - 1 ];
            context.bind( _name, obj );
        }
        // let other exceptions propagate to caller
    }
```

```
public void unbind_from_string( String str )
   throws
   CosNaming._NamingContext.InvalidName,
   CosNaming._NamingContext.NotFound,
   CosNaming._NamingContext.CannotProceed, CORBA.SystemException {

   root_context.unbind( str2name( str ) );
}

public CORBA.Object resolve_from_string( String str )
   throws
   CosNaming._NamingContext.InvalidName,
   CosNaming._NamingContext.NotFound,
   CosNaming._NamingContext.CannotProceed,
   CosNaming._NamingContext.InvalidName, CORBA.SystemException {

   return root_context.resolve( str2name( str ) );
}

public CosNaming.NamingContext get_root_context() {
   return root_context;
}

public CosNaming.NameComponent[] str2name( String str )
   throws CosNaming._NamingContext.InvalidName {

   int i, j, c, components, name_length;
   CosNaming.NameComponent[] name;

   char[] char_str = str.toCharArray();

   // count name components (separated by '/')
   for( i = 0, components = 0; i < char_str.length; i++ ) {
      if( char_str[i] == '/' )
          components++;
   }

   name = new CosNaming.NameComponent[components];
   char[][] id = new char[components][];
   String s[] = new String[components];

   if( char_str[0] != '/' ) {
      System.out.println(
          "str2name: invalid name, must start with '/'" );
      throw new CosNaming._NamingContext.InvalidName();
   }

   for( i = 0, c = 0; i < char_str.length; c++ ) {

      // skip separator
      if( char_str[i] == '/' )
          i++;
```

```
            // get length of a name component
            for( j = i, name_length = 0;
                  (j > char_str.length ) && ( char_str[j] != '/' ); j++ ) {
                 name_length++;
            }
            id[c] = new char[ name_length ];
            for( j = 0; j < name_length; j++ ) {
                id[c][j] = char_str[i+j];
            }
            i = j + i + 1;
            System.out.println( "str2name: name_component[" + c + "] = " +
                 id[c] );
            // create name component
            s[c] = new String( id[c] );
            name[c] = new CosNaming.NameComponent( s[c], "" );
        }
        return name;
    }
}
```

IORFile.java

```java
import java.io.RandomAccessFile;

public class IORFile {

    private String ior_string;

    // constructor
    public IORFile( String file_name ) {

        try {
            RandomAccessFile file = new RandomAccessFile( file_name, "r");
            ior_string = new String( file.readLine() );
        }
        catch ( java.io.IOException io_exception )
                { System.out.println( io_exception ); }
    }

    // methods

    public String get_ior_string() {
        return ior_string;
    }
}
```

Resolve.java

```java
public class Resolve {

    public static void main(String args[]) {
```

```
        try {
            //init
            CORBA.ORB orb = CORBA.ORB.init();
            CORBA.BOA boa = orb.BOA_init();

            IORFile ior_file = new IORFile( args[0] );

            System.out.println( "create Easy Naming");
            EasyNaming easy_naming = new EasyNaming( orb,
                ior_file.get_ior_string() );

            // test str2name
            System.out.println(
                orb.object_to_string(
                    easy_naming.resolve_from_string( args[1] ) ));
        }

        catch(CORBA.SystemException e) {
            System.out.println(e);
        }
        catch(CORBA.UserException naming_exception) {
        System.err.println( naming_exception );
        }
    }
}
```

3.2   Trading

3.2.1   *Interface Specification*
CosTrading.idl

```
module CosTrading {
    // forward references to our interfaces
    interface Lookup;
    interface Register;
    interface Link;
    interface Proxy;
    interface Admin;
    interface OfferIterator;
    interface OfferIdIterator;

    // type definitions used in more than one interface

    typedef string Istring;
    typedef Object TypeRepository;

    typedef Istring PropertyName;
    typedef sequence<PropertyName> PropertyNameSeq;
    typedef any PropertyValue;
```

```
struct Property {
    PropertyName name;
    PropertyValue value;
};

typedef sequence<Property> PropertySeq;

struct Offer {
    Object reference;
    PropertySeq properties;
};
typedef sequence<Offer> OfferSeq;

typedef string OfferId;
typedef sequence<OfferId> OfferIdSeq;

typedef Istring ServiceTypeName; // similar structure to IR::Identifier

typedef Istring Constraint;

enum FollowOption {
    local_only,
    if_no_local,
    always
};

typedef Istring LinkName;
typedef sequence<LinkName> LinkNameSeq;
typedef LinkNameSeq TraderName;

typedef string PolicyName; // policy names restricted to Latin1
typedef sequence<PolicyName> PolicyNameSeq;
typedef any PolicyValue;
struct Policy {
    PolicyName name;
    PolicyValue value;
};

typedef sequence<Policy> PolicySeq;

// exceptions used in more than one interface

exception UnknownMaxLeft {};

exception NotImplemented {};

exception IllegalServiceType {
    ServiceTypeName type;
};
```

```
exception UnknownServiceType {
   ServiceTypeName type;
};

exception IllegalPropertyName {
   PropertyName name;
};

exception DuplicatePropertyName {
   PropertyName name;
};

exception PropertyTypeMismatch {
   ServiceTypeName type;
   Property prop;
};

exception MissingMandatoryProperty {
   ServiceTypeName type;
   PropertyName name;
};

exception ReadonlyDynamicProperty {
   ServiceTypeName type;
   PropertyName name;
};

exception IllegalConstraint {
   Constraint constr;
};

exception InvalidLookupRef {
   Lookup target;
};

exception IllegalOfferId {
   OfferId id;
};

exception UnknownOfferId {
   OfferId id;
};

exception DuplicatePolicyName {
   PolicyName name;
};

// the interfaces

interface TraderComponents {
   readonly attribute Lookup lookup_if;
```

```
        readonly attribute Register register_if;
        readonly attribute Link link_if;
        readonly attribute Proxy proxy_if;
        readonly attribute Admin admin_if;
    };

    interface SupportAttributes {
        readonly attribute boolean supports_modifiable_properties;
        readonly attribute boolean supports_dynamic_properties;
        readonly attribute boolean supports_proxy_offers;
        readonly attribute TypeRepository type_repos;
    };

    interface ImportAttributes {
        readonly attribute unsigned long def_search_card;
        readonly attribute unsigned long max_search_card;
        readonly attribute unsigned long def_match_card;
        readonly attribute unsigned long max_match_card;
        readonly attribute unsigned long def_return_card;
        readonly attribute unsigned long max_return_card;
        readonly attribute unsigned long max_list;
        readonly attribute unsigned long def_hop_count;

        readonly attribute unsigned long max_hop_count;
        readonly attribute FollowOption def_follow_policy;
        readonly attribute FollowOption max_follow_policy;
    };

    interface LinkAttributes {
        readonly attribute FollowOption max_link_follow_policy;
    };

    interface Lookup : TraderComponents, SupportAttributes, ImportAttributes {

        typedef Istring Preference;

        enum HowManyProps { none, some, all };

        union SpecifiedProps switch ( HowManyProps ) {
            case some: PropertyNameSeq prop_names;
        };

        exception IllegalPreference {
            Preference pref;
        };

        exception IllegalPolicyName {
            PolicyName name;
        };
```

```
    exception PolicyTypeMismatch {
        Policy the_policy;
    };

    exception InvalidPolicyValue {
        Policy the_policy;
    };

    void query (
        in ServiceTypeName type,
        in Constraint constr,
        in Preference pref,
        in PolicySeq policies,

        in SpecifiedProps desired_props,
        in unsigned long how_many,
        out OfferSeq offers,
        out OfferIterator offer_itr,
        out PolicyNameSeq limits_applied
    ) raises (
        IllegalServiceType,
        UnknownServiceType,
        IllegalConstraint,
        IllegalPreference,
        IllegalPolicyName,

        PolicyTypeMismatch,
        InvalidPolicyValue,
        IllegalPropertyName,
        DuplicatePropertyName,
        DuplicatePolicyName
    );
};

interface Register : TraderComponents, SupportAttributes {

    struct OfferInfo {
        Object reference;
        ServiceTypeName type;
        PropertySeq properties;
    };

    exception InvalidObjectRef {
        Object ref;
    };

    exception UnknownPropertyName {
        PropertyName name;
    };
```

```
exception InterfaceTypeMismatch {
    ServiceTypeName type;
    Object reference;
};

exception ProxyOfferId {
    OfferId id;
};

exception MandatoryProperty {
    ServiceTypeName type;
    PropertyName name;
};

exception ReadonlyProperty {
    ServiceTypeName type;
    PropertyName name;
};

exception NoMatchingOffers {
    Constraint constr;
};

exception IllegalTraderName {
    TraderName name
};

exception UnknownTraderName {
    TraderName name;
};

exception RegisterNotSupported {
    TraderName name;
};

OfferId export (
    in Object reference,
    in ServiceTypeName type,
    in PropertySeq properties
) raises (
    InvalidObjectRef,
    IllegalServiceType,
    UnknownServiceType,
    InterfaceTypeMismatch,
    IllegalPropertyName, // e.g. prop_name = "<foo-bar"
    PropertyTypeMismatch,
    ReadonlyDynamicProperty,
    MissingMandatoryProperty,
    DuplicatePropertyName
);
```

```
    void withdraw (
    in OfferId id
) raises (
    IllegalOfferId,
    UnknownOfferId,
    ProxyOfferId
);

    OfferInfo describe (
    in OfferId id
) raises (
    IllegalOfferId,
    UnknownOfferId,
    ProxyOfferId
);

void modify (
    in OfferId id,
    in PropertyNameSeq del_list,
    in PropertySeq modify_list
) raises (
    NotImplemented,
    IllegalOfferId,
    UnknownOfferId,
    ProxyOfferId,
    IllegalPropertyName,
    UnknownPropertyName,
    PropertyTypeMismatch,
    ReadonlyDynamicProperty,
    MandatoryProperty,
    ReadonlyProperty,
    DuplicatePropertyName
);

void withdraw_using_constraint (
    in ServiceTypeName type,
    in Constraint constr
) raises (
    IllegalServiceType,
    UnknownServiceType,
    IllegalConstraint,
    NoMatchingOffers
);

Register resolve (
    in TraderName name
) raises (
    IllegalTraderName,
    UnknownTraderName,
    RegisterNotSupported
);
};
```

```
interface Link : TraderComponents, SupportAttributes, LinkAttributes {

    struct LinkInfo {
        Lookup target;
        Register target_reg;
        FollowOption def_pass_on_follow_rule;
        FollowOption limiting_follow_rule;
    };

    exception IllegalLinkName {
        LinkName name;
    };

    exception UnknownLinkName {
        LinkName name;
    };

    exception DuplicateLinkName {
        LinkName name;
    };

    exception DefaultFollowTooPermissive {
        FollowOption def_pass_on_follow_rule;
        FollowOption limiting_follow_rule;
    };

    exception LimitingFollowTooPermissive {
        FollowOption limiting_follow_rule;
        FollowOption max_link_follow_policy;
    };

    void add_link (
        in LinkName name,
        in Lookup target,
        in FollowOption def_pass_on_follow_rule,
        in FollowOption limiting_follow_rule
    ) raises (
        IllegalLinkName,
        DuplicateLinkName,
        InvalidLookupRef, // e.g. nil
        DefaultFollowTooPermissive,
        LimitingFollowTooPermissive
    );

    void remove_link (
        in LinkName name
    ) raises (
        IllegalLinkName,
        UnknownLinkName
    );
```

```
        LinkInfo describe_link (
            in LinkName name
        ) raises (
            IllegalLinkName,
            UnknownLinkName
        );

        LinkNameSeq list_links();

        void modify_link (
            in LinkName name,
            in FollowOption def_pass_on_follow_rule,
            in FollowOption limiting_follow_rule
        ) raises (
            IllegalLinkName,
            UnknownLinkName,
            DefaultFollowTooPermissive,
            LimitingFollowTooPermissive
        );
    };

    interface Proxy : TraderComponents, SupportAttributes {

        typedef Istring ConstraintRecipe;

        struct ProxyInfo {
            ServiceTypeName type;
            Lookup target;
            PropertySeq properties;
            boolean if_match_all;
            ConstraintRecipe recipe;
            PolicySeq policies_to_pass_on;
        };

        exception IllegalRecipe {
            ConstraintRecipe recipe;
        };

        exception NotProxyOfferId {
            OfferId id;
        };

        OfferId export_proxy (
            in Lookup target,
            in ServiceTypeName type,
            in PropertySeq properties,
            in boolean if_match_all,
            in ConstraintRecipe recipe,
            in PolicySeq policies_to_pass_on
        ) raises (
            IllegalServiceType,
```

```
            UnknownServiceType,
            InvalidLookupRef, // e.g. nil
            IllegalPropertyName,
            PropertyTypeMismatch,
            ReadonlyDynamicProperty,
            MissingMandatoryProperty,
            IllegalRecipe,
            DuplicatePropertyName,
            DuplicatePolicyName
        );

        void withdraw_proxy (
            in OfferId id
        ) raises (
            IllegalOfferId,
            UnknownOfferId,
            NotProxyOfferId
        );

        ProxyInfo describe_proxy (
            in OfferId id
        ) raises (
            IllegalOfferId,
            UnknownOfferId,
            NotProxyOfferId
        );
};

    interface Admin : TraderComponents, SupportAttributes, ImportAttributes,
                      LinkAttributes {

        typedef sequence<octet> OctetSeq;

        readonly attribute OctetSeq request_id_stem;

        unsigned long set_def_search_card (in unsigned long value);
        unsigned long set_max_search_card (in unsigned long value);

        unsigned long set_def_match_card (in unsigned long value);
        unsigned long set_max_match_card (in unsigned long value);

        unsigned long set_def_return_card (in unsigned long value);
        unsigned long set_max_return_card (in unsigned long value);

        unsigned long set_max_list (in unsigned long value);

        boolean set_supports_modifiable_properties (in boolean value);
        boolean set_supports_dynamic_properties (in boolean value);
        boolean set_supports_proxy_offers (in boolean value);

        unsigned long set_def_hop_count (in unsigned long value);
        unsigned long set_max_hop_count (in unsigned long value);
```

```
FollowOption set_def_follow_policy (in FollowOption policy);
FollowOption set_max_follow_policy (in FollowOption policy);
FollowOption set_max_link_follow_policy (in FollowOption policy);

TypeRepository set_type_repos (in TypeRepository repository);

OctetSeq set_request_id_stem (in OctetSeq stem);

void list_offers (
    in unsigned long how_many,
    out OfferIdSeq ids,
    out OfferIdIterator id_itr
) raises (
    NotImplemented
);

void list_proxies (
    in unsigned long how_many,
    out OfferIdSeq ids,
    out OfferIdIterator id_itr
) raises (
    NotImplemented
);
};

interface OfferIterator {

    unsigned long max_left (
    ) raises (
        UnknownMaxLeft
    );

    boolean next_n (
        in unsigned long n,
        out OfferSeq offers
    );

    void destroy ();
};

interface OfferIdIterator {

    unsigned long max_left (
    ) raises (
        UnknownMaxLeft
    );

    boolean next_n (
        in unsigned long n,
        out OfferIdSeq ids
    );
```

```
            void destroy ();
        };

    }; /* end module CosTrading */
    module CosTradingDynamic {

        exception DPEvalFailure {
            CosTrading::PropertyName name;
            // CORBA::TypeCode returned_type;
            TypeCode returned_type;
            any extra_info;
        };

        interface DynamicPropEval {

            any evalDP (
                in CosTrading::PropertyName name,
                // in CORBA::TypeCode returned_type,
                in TypeCode returned_type,
                in any extra_info
            ) raises (
                DPEvalFailure
            );
        };

        struct DynamicProp {
            DynamicPropEval eval_if;
            // CORBA::TypeCode returned_type;
            TypeCode returned_type;
            any extra_info;
        };
    }; /* end module CosTradingDynamic */

    module CosTradingRepos {

        interface ServiceTypeRepository {

        // local types
            typedef sequence<CosTrading::ServiceTypeName> ServiceTypeNameSeq;
            enum PropertyMode {
                PROP_NORMAL, PROP_READONLY,
                PROP_MANDATORY, PROP_MANDATORY_READONLY
            };
            struct PropStruct {
                CosTrading::PropertyName name;
                // CORBA::TypeCode value_type;
                TypeCode value_type;
                PropertyMode mode;
            };
            typedef sequence<PropStruct> PropStructSeq;
```

```
typedef CosTrading::Istring Identifier; // IR::Identifier
struct IncarnationNumber {
    unsigned long high;
    unsigned long low;
};

struct TypeStruct {
    Identifier if_name;
    PropStructSeq props;
    ServiceTypeNameSeq super_types;
    boolean masked;
    IncarnationNumber incarnation;
};

enum ListOption { all, since };
union SpecifiedServiceTypes switch ( ListOption ) {
    case since: IncarnationNumber incarnation;
};

// local exceptions
exception ServiceTypeExists {
    CosTrading::ServiceTypeName name;
};
exception InterfaceTypeMismatch {
    CosTrading::ServiceTypeName base_service;
    Identifier base_if;
    CosTrading::ServiceTypeName derived_service;
    Identifier derived_if;
};

exception HasSubTypes {
    CosTrading::ServiceTypeName the_type;
    CosTrading::ServiceTypeName sub_type;
};
exception AlreadyMasked {
    CosTrading::ServiceTypeName name;
};
exception NotMasked {
    CosTrading::ServiceTypeName name;
};
exception ValueTypeRedefinition {
    CosTrading::ServiceTypeName type_1;
    PropStruct definition_1;
    CosTrading::ServiceTypeName type_2;
    PropStruct definition_2;
};
exception DuplicateServiceTypeName {
    CosTrading::ServiceTypeName name;
};
```

```
// attributes
    readonly attribute IncarnationNumber incarnation;

// operation signatures
    IncarnationNumber add_type (
        in CosTrading::ServiceTypeName name,
        in Identifier if_name,
        in PropStructSeq props,
        in ServiceTypeNameSeq super_types
    ) raises (
        CosTrading::IllegalServiceType,
        ServiceTypeExists,
        InterfaceTypeMismatch,
        CosTrading::IllegalPropertyName,
        CosTrading::DuplicatePropertyName,
        ValueTypeRedefinition,
        CosTrading::UnknownServiceType,
        DuplicateServiceTypeName
    );

    void remove_type (
        in CosTrading::ServiceTypeName name
    ) raises (
        CosTrading::IllegalServiceType,
        CosTrading::UnknownServiceType,
        HasSubTypes
    );

    ServiceTypeNameSeq list_types (
        in SpecifiedServiceTypes which_types
    );

    TypeStruct describe_type (
        in CosTrading::ServiceTypeName name
    ) raises (
        CosTrading::IllegalServiceType,
        CosTrading::UnknownServiceType
    );

    TypeStruct fully_describe_type (
        in CosTrading::ServiceTypeName name
    ) raises (
        CosTrading::IllegalServiceType,
        CosTrading::UnknownServiceType
    );

    void mask_type (
        in CosTrading::ServiceTypeName name
    ) raises (
        CosTrading::IllegalServiceType,
        CosTrading::UnknownServiceType,
```

```
          AlreadyMasked
     );

     void unmask_type (
          in CosTrading::ServiceTypeName name
     ) raises (
          CosTrading::IllegalServiceType,
          CosTrading::UnknownServiceType,
          NotMasked
     );

   };
}; /* end module CosTradingRepos */s
```

3.2.2   OrbixWeb
PrintClient.java

```java
import IE.Iona.Orbix2._CORBA;
import IE.Iona.Orbix2.CORBA.*;
import IE.Iona.Orbix2.CORBA.UserException;
import IE.Iona.Orbix2.CORBA.SystemException;
import IE.Iona.Orbix2.CORBA.Any;
import IE.Iona.Orbix2.CORBA.Object.*;

import java.lang.String;

public class PrintClient {

  private static final boolean IIOP = true;

  public static void main(String args[]) {

   if( args.length < 2 || args.length > 4 ) {
        System.out.println(
 "usage: PrintClient trader_ior_file printfile [constraint [preference]]");
        System.exit( 1 );
    }

    // some general purpose variables
    Any policy_any;
    if(IIOP)
        policy_any = new Any(_CORBA.IT_INTEROPERABLE_OR_KIND);
    else
        policy_any = new IE.Iona.Orbix2.CORBA.Any();
    IE.Iona.Orbix2.CORBA.Object.Ref obj;

    // get reference to trader lookup interface
    CosTrading.Lookup.Ref my_lookup = null;
    try {
        IORFile ior_file = new IORFile( args[0] );
        obj = _CORBA.Orbix.string_to_object(
```

```
                ior_file.get_ior_string() );
        my_lookup = CosTrading.Lookup._narrow( obj );
}
catch(IE.Iona.Orbix2.CORBA.SystemException se) {
        System.err.println("CORBA System Exception: " + se);
        System.exit(1);
}

// determine the constraint
String constr;
if( args.length > 2 )
        constr = args[2];
else
        constr = "";

// determine the prefs
String prefs;

if (args.length > 3 )
        prefs = args[3];
else
        // if no preference, compare the offers for shortest queue
        prefs = "min queue_len";

// set some basic policies
CosTrading.PolicySeq query_pols = new CosTrading.PolicySeq(2);

//declare variables needed in the query()
short num_offers = 3;
String service_type = "PrinterST";
CosTrading.PolicyValue policy_value;
CosTrading.PropertyNameSeq desired_prop_names;
CosTrading.Lookup.SpecifiedProps desired_props = null;
CosTrading.OfferSeq return_offers = new CosTrading.OfferSeq();
CosTrading.OfferIterator.Holder iter =
        new CosTrading.OfferIterator.Holder();
CosTrading.PolicyNameSeq limits =
        new CosTrading.PolicyNameSeq();

 try {
        // we want at most 3 offers back
        policy_any.insertShort( num_offers );
        policy_value = new CosTrading.PolicyValue(policy_any);
        query_pols.buffer[0] =
                new CosTrading.Policy("return_card", policy_value);

        // we want to use dynamic props to find printer queue length
        policy_any.insertBoolean(true);
        policy_value = new CosTrading.PolicyValue(policy_any);
        query_pols.buffer[1] =
                new CosTrading.Policy("use_dynamic_properties", policy_value);
```

```
            // we want back only the name property
            desired_prop_names = new CosTrading.PropertyNameSeq(1);
            desired_prop_names.buffer[0] = "name";
            desired_props = new CosTrading.Lookup.SpecifiedProps();
            // the value of CosTrading.Lookup.HowManyProps.some is 1
            desired_props.prop_names(desired_prop_names, (int) 1);
        }
    catch (IE.Iona.Orbix2.CORBA.SystemException se) {
            System.err.println("Query failed: " + se);
            System.exit(1);
        }

        // make a query
        try {
            my_lookup.query( service_type,
                             constr,
                             prefs,
                             query_pols,
                             desired_props,
                             num_offers,
                             return_offers,
                             iter,
                             limits);
        }
        // catch some important exceptions
        catch (IE.Iona.Orbix2.CORBA.UserException ue) {
            System.err.println("Query failed - User Exception: " + ue);
            System.exit(1);
        }
        catch (IE.Iona.Orbix2.CORBA.SystemException se) {
            System.err.println("Query failed: " + se);
            System.exit(1);
        }

        // send job to printer
        int i = 0;
        boolean printed = false;
        String pname = "";

        Any return_any;
        if(IIOP)
            return_any = new Any(_CORBA.IT_INTEROPERABLE_OR_KIND);
        else
            return_any = new IE.Iona.Orbix2.CORBA.Any();
        // we'll try all the returned printers until one works

    while (i < return_offers.length - 1 && !printed) {
            try {
                return_any =
                    return_offers.buffer[i].properties.buffer[0].value;
                pname = return_any.extractString();
                Printer.Ref printer =
                    Printer._narrow(return_offers.buffer[i].reference);
```

```
            printer.print_file( args[1] );
            printed = true;
            System.out.println("File " + args[1] +
                " sent to printer " + pname);
        }
        catch (Printer.PrinterOffLine pol) {
            System.out.println("Printer " + pname + " offline!");
        }
        catch (IE.Iona.Orbix2.CORBA.SystemException se) {
            System.out.println("Printer " + pname +
                                " raised: " + se);
        }
        i++;
    }

}
```

4   *Building Applications*

4.1   Interface Specification

4.1.1   RoomBooking.idl

module RoomBooking {

interface Meeting {

   // A meeting has two read-only attributes which describes
   // the purpose and the participants of that meeting.

   readonly attribute string purpose;
   readonly attribute string participants;
};

interface MeetingFactory {

// A meeting factory creates meeting objects.

   Meeting CreateMeeting(in string purpose, in string participants);
};

interface Room {

   // A Room provides operations to view, make and cancel bookings.
   // Making a booking means associating a meeting with a time slot
   // (for this particular room).

   // Meetings can be held between the usual business hours.
   // For the sake of simplicity there are 8 slots at which meetings
   // can take place.

   enum Slot {am9, am10, am11, pm12, pm1, pm2, pm3, pm4};

```
// since IDL does not provide means to determine the cardinality
// of an enum, a corresponding constant MaxSlots is defined.

const short MaxSlots = 8;

// Meetings associates all meetings (of a day) with time slots
// for a room.

typedef Meeting Meetings( MaxSlots );

exception NoMeetingInThisSlot {};
exception SlotAlreadyTaken {};

// The attribute name names a room.

readonly attribute string name;

// View returns the bookings of a room.
// For simplicity, the implementation handles only bookings
// for one day.

Meetings View();

void Book( in Slot a_slot, in Meeting a_meeting )
        raises(SlotAlreadyTaken);

void Cancel( in Slot a_slot )
        raises(NoMeetingInThisSlot);
   };
};
```

4.2   Visibroker

4.2.1   *MeetingFactoryImpl.java*

```
// MeetingFactoryImpl.java

class MeetingFactoryImpl extends RoomBooking._sk_MeetingFactory {

    private CORBA.ORB orb;
    private CORBA.BOA boa;

    // constructor
    MeetingFactoryImpl() {

        try {
            // initialize ORB
            orb = CORBA.ORB.init();

            // initialize BOA
            boa = orb.BOA_init();
        }
        catch(CORBA.SystemException e) {
            System.out.println(e); }
    }
```

```
// method
public RoomBooking.Meeting CreateMeeting(
    String purpose, String participants )
    throws CORBA.SystemException {

    MeetingImpl new_meeting = new MeetingImpl(purpose, participants);

    try {
        boa.obj_is_ready( new_meeting );
    }
    catch(CORBA.SystemException e) {
        System.out.println(e); }
    return new_meeting;
    }
}
```

4.2.2   *MeetingFactoryServer.java*

```
// MeetingFactoryServer.java

import java.io.*;

public class MeetingFactoryServer {

    public static void main(String[] args) {

        String str_name;

        if( args.length != 0 ) {
        System.out.println("Usage: java MeetingFactoryServer");
        System.exit( 1 );
        }

        str_name = new String(
            "/BuildingApplications/MeetingFactories/MeetingFactory");

        try {
            //initialize ORB
            CORBA.ORB orb = CORBA.ORB.init();

            // initialize BOA
            CORBA.BOA boa = orb.BOA_init();

            // create the MeetingFactory object
            MeetingFactoryImpl meeting_factory = new MeetingFactoryImpl();

            // export the object reference
            boa.obj_is_ready(meeting_factory);

            // register with naming service
            // get IOR for naming service from file
            IORFile ior_file = new IORFile("CosNaming.ior");
```

```
        EasyNaming easy_naming =
            new EasyNaming( orb, ior_file.get_ior_string() );

        // rebind the new meeting factory
        easy_naming.rebind_from_string( str_name, meeting_factory );

        // wait for requests
        boa.impl_is_ready();
    }
    catch(CORBA.UserException ue) {
        System.err.println(ue);
    }
    catch(CORBA.SystemException se) {
        System.err.println(se);
    }
  }
}
```

4.2.3 MeetingImpl.java

```
// MeetingImpl.java

class MeetingImpl extĪends RoomBooking._sk_Meeting{

    private String purpose;
    private String participants;

    // constructor
    MeetingImpl( String _purpose, String _participants) {

        // initialise private variables
        purpose = new String( _purpose );
        participants = new String( _participants );
    }

    // attributes
    public String purpose() throws CORBA.SystemException {
        return purpose;
    }

    public String participants() throws CORBA.SystemException {
        return participants;
    }
}
```

4.2.4 RemoteIORFileImpl.java

```
import java.io.RandomAccessFile;
import IORFile.*;

public class RemoteIORFileImpl extends _sk_RemoteIORFile {
```

```
        private String ior_string;

        // constructor
        public RemoteIORFileImpl( String file_name ) {

            super( file_name );

            try {
                RandomAccessFile file = new RandomAccessFile( file_name, "r");
                ior_string = new String( file.readLine() );
            }
            catch ( java.io.IOException io_exception )
                    { System.out.println( io_exception ); }
        }


        // methods

        public String get_ior_string() {
            return ior_string;
        }
    }
```

4.2.5   *RemoteIORFileServer.java*

```
// RemoteIORFileServer.java

import java.io.*;

public class RemoteIORFileServer {

    public static void main(String[] args) {

        String str_name;

        if( args.length != 1 ) {
        System.out.println("Usage: java RemoteIORFileServer file-name");
        System.exit( 1 );
        }

        try {
            //initialize ORB
            CORBA.ORB orb = CORBA.ORB.init();

            // initialize BOA
            CORBA.BOA boa = orb.BOA_init();

            // create the RemoteIORFileImpl object
            RemoteIORFileImpl remote_ior_file =
                new RemoteIORFileImpl( args[0] );

            // export the object reference
            boa.obj_is_ready(remote_ior_file);
```

```
                // wait for requests
                boa.impl_is_ready();
            }
            catch(CORBA.SystemException se) {
                System.err.println(se);
            }
        }
    }
```

4.2.6   *RoomBookingClient.java*

```
import java.awt.*;
import IORFile.*;

public class RoomBookingClient {

    public Button view_button;
    public Button book_button;
    public Button cancel_button;
    public Button[][] slot_button;

    private TextField participants_tf;
    private TextField purpose_tf;

    private Panel main_panel;
    private Panel title_panel;

    private boolean[][] booked;

    private int selected_room;
    private int selected_slot;

    private CORBA.ORB orb;
    private CosNaming.NamingContext room_context;
    private EasyNaming easy_naming;

    private RoomBooking.MeetingFactory meeting_factory;
    private RoomBooking.Room[] rooms;
    private RoomBooking.Meeting meetings[];

    private String ior;

    Color green = new Color( 0, 94, 86 );
    Color red = new Color( 255, 61, 61 );

    // constructor for applets
    // using bind mechanism to get a root context via remote IOR server
    RoomBookingClient( java.applet.Applet applet ) {

        try {
            // initialize the ORB
            orb = CORBA.ORB.init( applet );
```

```
            // proprietary bind to a remote IOR file server
            RemoteIORFile remote_ior_file =
                RemoteIORFile_var.bind("CosNaming.ior");

            easy_naming = new EasyNaming( orb,
                remote_ior_file.get_ior_string() );
        }
        catch(CORBA.SystemException system_exception ) {
            System.err.println( "constructor RoomBookingClient: " +
                system_exception );
        }
    }

    // constructor for applications
    // using a stringified IOR to get a root context
    RoomBookingClient() {

        try {
            // initialize the ORB
            orb = CORBA.ORB.init();

            IORFile ior_file = new IORFile("CosNaming.ior");
            easy_naming = new EasyNaming( orb, ior_file.get_ior_string() );
        }
        catch(CORBA.SystemException system_exception ) {
            System.err.println( "constructor RoomBookingClient: " +
                system_exception );
        }
    }

    public int no_of_rooms() {
        return rooms.length;
    }

    public void init_GUI( java.awt.Container gui ) {

        // initialize widgets

        gui.setBackground( Color.white );

        view_button = new Button("Back");
        view_button.setFont(new Font("Helvetica", Font.BOLD, 14));
        view_button.setBackground( red );

        book_button = new Button("Book");
        book_button.setFont(new Font("Helvetica", Font.BOLD, 14));
        book_button.setBackground( red );

        cancel_button = new Button("Cancel");
        cancel_button.setFont(new Font("Helvetica", Font.BOLD, 14));
        cancel_button.setBackground( red );
```

```
    main_panel = new Panel();
    title_panel = new Panel();

    title_panel.setLayout( new GridLayout(3, 1));
    title_panel.setFont(new Font("Helvetica", Font.BOLD, 20));
    title_panel.setBackground( red );
    title_panel.add( new Label("", Label.CENTER) );
    title_panel.add( new Label("Room Booking System", Label.CENTER) );
    title_panel.add( new Label("", Label.CENTER) );

    gui.setLayout(new BorderLayout() );
    gui.add( "North", title_panel );
    gui.add( "Center", main_panel );
    gui.resize( 500, 300 );
    gui.show();
}


public void init_from_ns() {

    // initialize from Naming Service
    try {
        // get room context
        room_context = CosNaming.NamingContext_var.narrow(
            easy_naming.resolve_from_string(
            "/BuildingApplications/Rooms" ) );
        if( room_context == null ) {
            System.err.println( "Room context is null," );
            System.err.println( "exiting ..." );
            System.exit( 1 );
        }

        // get MeetingFactory from Naming Service
        meeting_factory = RoomBooking.MeetingFactory_var.narrow(
            easy_naming.resolve_from_string(
            "/BuildingApplications/MeetingFactories/MeetingFactory") );
        if( meeting_factory == null ) {
            System.err.println(
                "No Meeting Factory registred at Naming Service" );
            System.err.println( "exiting ..." );
            System.exit( 1 );
        }
    }

    catch(CORBA.SystemException system_exception ) {
        System.err.println( "Initialize ORB: " + system_exception );
    }
    catch(CORBA.UserException naming_exception) {
        System.err.println( "Initialize ORB: " + naming_exception );
    }
}
```

```
public boolean view() {

    try {
        // list rooms
        // initialize binding list and binding iterator
        // _var objects for out parameter
        CosNaming.BindingList_var bl_var =
               new CosNaming.BindingList_var();
        CosNaming.BindingIterator_var bi_var =
               new CosNaming.BindingIterator_var();

        // we are lazy and consider only 20 rooms
        // although there could be more in the binding iterator
        room_context.list( 20, bl_var, bi_var );

        // create an array of Room and initialize it by resolving
        // the entries in the Room context of the Naming Service
        rooms = new RoomBooking.Room[ bl_var.value.length ];
        for( int i = 0; i < bl_var.value.length; i++ ) {
            System.out.println( "Room " + i + " : " +
            bl_var.value[i].binding_name[0].id );
            rooms[i] = RoomBooking.Room_var.narrow(
                room_context.resolve( bl_var.value[i].binding_name ));
        }
        // be fiendly with system resources
        if( bi_var.value != null )
            bi_var.value.destroy();

        // create labels and slots according to the number of rooms
        Label[] r_label = new Label[rooms.length];
        slot_button =
            new Button[rooms.length] [RoomBooking._Room.MaxSlots.value];
        booked =
            new boolean[rooms.length] [RoomBooking._Room.MaxSlots.value];
        main_panel.removeAll();

        // define layout for the table
        GridBagLayout gridbag = new GridBagLayout();
        GridBagConstraints c = new GridBagConstraints();
        main_panel.setLayout(gridbag);

        c.fill = GridBagConstraints.BOTH;

        c.gridwidth = 2;
        c.gridheight = 1;
        Label room_label = new Label("Rooms", Label.CENTER );
        room_label.setFont(new Font("Helvetica", Font.BOLD, 14));
        gridbag.setConstraints( room_label, c);
        main_panel.add( room_label );
```

```
c.gridwidth = 4;
c.gridheight = 1;
Label am_label = new Label("AM", Label.CENTER );
am_label.setFont(new Font("Helvetica", Font.BOLD, 14));
gridbag.setConstraints( am_label, c);
main_panel.add( am_label );

c.gridheight = 1;
c.gridwidth = GridBagConstraints.REMAINDER;
Label pm_label = new Label("PM", Label.CENTER );
pm_label.setFont(new Font("Helvetica", Font.BOLD, 14));
gridbag.setConstraints( pm_label, c);
main_panel.add( pm_label );

c.gridwidth = 2;
c.gridheight = 1;
Label e_label = new Label("");
gridbag.setConstraints( e_label, c);
main_panel.add( e_label );

c.gridwidth = 1;
c.gridheight = 1;
Label label9 = new Label(" 9", Label.CENTER );
label9.setFont(new Font("Helvetica", Font.BOLD, 14));
gridbag.setConstraints( label9, c);
main_panel.add( label9 );

c.gridwidth = 1;
c.gridheight = 1;
Label label10 = new Label("10", Label.CENTER );
label10.setFont(new Font("Helvetica", Font.BOLD, 14));
gridbag.setConstraints( label10, c);
main_panel.add( label10 );

c.gridwidth = 1;
c.gridheight = 1;
Label label11 = new Label("11", Label.CENTER );
label11.setFont(new Font("Helvetica", Font.BOLD, 14));
gridbag.setConstraints( label11, c);
main_panel.add( label11 );

c.gridwidth = 1;
c.gridheight = 1;
Label label12 = new Label("12", Label.CENTER );
label12.setFont(new Font("Helvetica", Font.BOLD, 14));
gridbag.setConstraints( label12, c);
main_panel.add( label12 );

c.gridwidth = 1;
c.gridheight = 1;
```

```
Label label1 = new Label(" 1", Label.CENTER );
label1.setFont(new Font("Helvetica", Font.BOLD, 14));
gridbag.setConstraints( label1, c);
main_panel.add( label1 );

c.gridwidth = 1;
c.gridheight = 1;
Label label2 = new Label(" 2", Label.CENTER );
label2.setFont(new Font("Helvetica", Font.BOLD, 14));
gridbag.setConstraints( label2, c);
main_panel.add( label2 );

c.gridwidth = 1;
c.gridheight = 1;
Label label3 = new Label(" 3", Label.CENTER );
label3.setFont(new Font("Helvetica", Font.BOLD, 14));
gridbag.setConstraints( label3, c);
main_panel.add( label3 );

c.gridwidth = GridBagConstraints.REMAINDER;
c.gridheight = 1;
Label label4 = new Label(" 4", Label.CENTER );
label4.setFont(new Font("Helvetica", Font.BOLD, 14));
gridbag.setConstraints( label4, c);
main_panel.add( label4 );

// show the label with the room name
for( int i = 0; i < rooms.length; i++ ) {
    c.gridwidth = 2;
    c.gridheight = 1;
    r_label[i] = new Label( rooms[i].name() );
    r_label[i].setFont(new Font("Helvetica", Font.BOLD, 14));
    gridbag.setConstraints( r_label[i], c);
    main_panel.add( r_label[i] );

    // call view operation on the i-th room object and
    // create book or free button
    System.out.println(orb.object_to_string(rooms[i]));
    meetings = rooms[i].View();
    c.gridheight = 1;
    for( int j = 0; j < meetings.length; j++ ) {
        if( j == meetings.length - 1 )
            c.gridwidth = GridBagConstraints.REMAINDER;
        else
            c.gridwidth = 1;
        if( meetings[j] == null ) {
            // slot is free
            slot_button[i] [j] = new Button("Book");
            slot_button[i] [j].setBackground( green );
            slot_button[i] [j].setForeground( Color.white );
            slot_button[i] [j].setFont(new Font("Helvetica",
                Font.BOLD, 14));
```

```
                    booked[i] [j] = false;
                }

                else {
                    // slot is booked - view or cancel
                    slot_button[i] [j] = new Button("View");
                    slot_button[i] [j].setBackground( red );
                    slot_button[i] [j].setFont(new Font("Helvetica",
                        Font.BOLD, 14));
                    booked[i] [j] = true;
                }
                gridbag.setConstraints( slot_button[i] [j], c);
                main_panel.add( slot_button[i] [j] );
            }
        }

        c.gridwidth = 4;
        c.gridheight = 1;
        Label e1_label = new Label("");
        gridbag.setConstraints( e1_label, c);
        main_panel.add( e1_label );

        c.gridheight = 1;
        c.gridwidth = GridBagConstraints.REMAINDER;
        Label e2_label = new Label("");
        gridbag.setConstraints( e2_label, c);
        main_panel.add( e2_label );

        c.gridheight = 1;
        c.gridwidth = GridBagConstraints.REMAINDER;
        Label e3_label = new Label("");
        gridbag.setConstraints( e3_label, c);
        main_panel.add( e3_label );

        main_panel.layout();
    }

    catch(CORBA.SystemException system_exception) {
        System.err.println("View: " + system_exception);
    }
    catch(CORBA.UserException naming_exception) {
        System.err.println("View: " + naming_exception);
    }
    return true;
}

public boolean cancel() {
    try {
        rooms[selected_room].Cancel( selected_slot );
    }
    catch(RoomBooking._Room.NoMeetingInThisSlot no_meeting ) {
        System.err.println("Cancel :" + no_meeting );
    }
```

```
        catch(CORBA.SystemException system_exception) {
            System.err.println("Cancel :" + system_exception);
        }

        // show bookings of all rooms
        return view();
    }

    public boolean process_slot( int _selected_room, int _selected_slot ) {

        selected_room = _selected_room;
        selected_slot = _selected_slot;

        if( booked[selected_room] [selected_slot] ) {
            // view the meeting details, potentially cancel
            meeting_details();
        }
        else {
            // get meeting details and book
            booking_form();
        }
        return true;
    }

    public boolean meeting_details() {

        // clean main panel
        main_panel.removeAll();

        // call view operation on the selected room
        try {
            meetings = rooms[selected_room].View();
        }
        catch(CORBA.SystemException system_exception ) {
            System.out.println("meeting_details: " + system_exception );
        }

        // create new form for displaying meeting details
        GridBagLayout gridbag = new GridBagLayout();
        GridBagConstraints c = new GridBagConstraints();
        main_panel.setLayout(gridbag);

        c.gridwidth = GridBagConstraints.REMAINDER;
        Label header_label = new Label("Meeting details");
        gridbag.setConstraints( header_label, c);
        main_panel.add( header_label );

        c.gridwidth = 1;
        c.gridheight = 1;
        c.fill = GridBagConstraints.BOTH;
```

```
Label purpose_label = new Label("Purpose: ");
gridbag.setConstraints( purpose_label, c);
main_panel.add( purpose_label );

c.gridheight = 1;
c.gridwidth = 2;
c.gridwidth = GridBagConstraints.REMAINDER;
purpose_tf = new TextField();
purpose_tf.setEditable(false);

try {
    purpose_tf.setText( meetings[selected_slot].purpose() );
}
catch(CORBA.SystemException system_exception) {
    System.out.println(system_exception);
}
gridbag.setConstraints( purpose_tf, c);
main_panel.add( purpose_tf );

c.gridwidth = 1;
c.gridheight = 1;
c.fill = GridBagConstraints.BOTH;
Label participants_label = new Label("Participants: ");
gridbag.setConstraints( participants_label, c);
main_panel.add( participants_label );

c.gridheight = 1;
c.gridwidth = 2;
c.gridwidth = GridBagConstraints.REMAINDER;
participants_tf = new TextField();
participants_tf = new TextField();
participants_tf.setEditable(false);

try {
    participants_tf.setText(
        meetings[selected_slot].participants() );
}
catch(CORBA.SystemException system_exception) {
    System.out.println(system_exception);
}
gridbag.setConstraints( participants_tf, c);
main_panel.add( participants_tf );

c.gridheight = 1;
c.gridwidth = 3;
c.gridwidth = GridBagConstraints.REMAINDER;
gridbag.setConstraints( view_button, c);
main_panel.add( view_button );

gridbag.setConstraints( cancel_button, c);
main_panel.add( cancel_button );
```

```
        main_panel.layout();
        main_panel.repaint();
        return true;
    }

    public void booking_form() {

        // clean main panel
        main_panel.removeAll();

        GridBagLayout gridbag = new GridBagLayout();
        GridBagConstraints c = new GridBagConstraints();
        main_panel.setLayout(gridbag);

        c.gridwidth = GridBagConstraints.REMAINDER;
        Label header_label = new Label(
            "Please, enter details of the meeting.");
        gridbag.setConstraints( header_label, c);
        main_panel.add( header_label );

        c.gridwidth = 1;
        c.gridheight = 1;
        c.fill = GridBagConstraints.BOTH;
        Label purpose_label = new Label("Purpose: ");
        gridbag.setConstraints( purpose_label, c);
        main_panel.add( purpose_label );

        c.gridheight = 1;
        c.gridwidth = 2;
        c.gridwidth = GridBagConstraints.REMAINDER;
        purpose_tf = new TextField();
        gridbag.setConstraints( purpose_tf, c);
        main_panel.add( purpose_tf );

        c.gridwidth = 1;
        c.gridheight = 1;
        c.fill = GridBagConstraints.BOTH;
        Label participants_label = new Label("Participants: ");
        gridbag.setConstraints( participants_label, c);
        main_panel.add( participants_label );

        c.gridheight = 1;
        c.gridwidth = 2;
        c.gridwidth = GridBagConstraints.REMAINDER;
        participants_tf = new TextField();
        gridbag.setConstraints( participants_tf, c);
        main_panel.add( participants_tf );

        c.gridwidth = GridBagConstraints.REMAINDER;
        gridbag.setConstraints( book_button, c);
        main_panel.add( book_button );
        main_panel.layout();
```

```java
        main_panel.repaint();
    }


    public boolean book() {
        try {
            RoomBooking.Meeting meeting =
                meeting_factory.CreateMeeting(
                    purpose_tf.getText(),
                    participants_tf.getText() );
            System.out.println( "meeting created" );
            String p = meeting.purpose();
            System.out.println("Purpose: "+p);
            rooms[selected_room].Book( selected_slot, meeting );
            System.out.println( "room is booked" );
        }
        catch(RoomBooking._Room.SlotAlreadyTaken already_taken ) {
            System.out.println( "book :" + already_taken );
        }
        catch(CORBA.SystemException system_exception ) {
            System.out.println( "book :" + system_exception );
        }

        // show bookings of all rooms
        return view();
    }
}
```

4.2.7 *RoomBookingClientApplet.java*

```java
import java.awt.*;

public class RoomBookingClientApplet extends java.applet.Applet {

private RoomBookingClient client;

    // override init method of Class Applet
    public void init() {

        // create a RoomBookingClient client -
        // using the applet constructor
        client = new RoomBookingClient( this );

        // initialize the GUI
        client.init_GUI( this );

        // initialize the Naming Service
        client.init_from_ns();

        // view existing bookings
        client.view();
    }
```

```
        // catch and process events
        public boolean action(Event ev, java.lang.Object arg) {

            if(ev.target == client.view_button)
                return client.view();
            if(ev.target == client.book_button)
                return client.book();
            if(ev.target == client.cancel_button)
                return client.cancel();

            // look for free/book button pressed
            for( int i = 0; i < client.no_of_rooms(); i++ ) {
                for( int j = 0; j < RoomBooking.Room_.MaxSlots.value; j++ ) {
                    if( ev.target == client.slot_button[i] [j] ) {
                        return client.process_slot( i, j );
                    }
                }
            }
            return false;
        }

    }
```

4.2.8   *RoomBookingClientApplication.java*

```
import java.awt.*;

public class RoomBookingClientApplication extends Frame implements Runnable

    private static RoomBookingClient client;

    // constructor
    RoomBookingClientApplication() {
        super( "Room Booking System" );
    }

    // implement method run() of interface Runnable
    public void run() {
        while( true ) { ; }
    }

    public static void main( String args[]) {

        // create an object of its own class
        RoomBookingClientApplication gui =
            new RoomBookingClientApplication();

        // create a RoomBookingClient object -
        // using the application constructor
        client = new RoomBookingClient();
```

```
        // initialize the GUI
        client.init_GUI( gui );

        // initialize the Naming Service
        client.init_from_ns();

        // view existing bookings
        client.view();
    }

    // catch and process events
    public boolean action(Event ev, java.lang.Object arg) {

        if(ev.target == client.view_button)
            return client.view();
        if(ev.target == client.book_button)
            return client.book();
        if(ev.target == client.cancel_button)
            return client.cancel();

        // look for free/book button pressed
        for( int i = 0; i < client.no_of_rooms(); i++ )
            for( int j = 0; j < RoomBooking._Room.MaxSlots.value; j++ )
                if( ev.target == client.slot_button[i] [j] ) {
                    return client.process_slot( i, j );
                }
        return false;
    }
}
```

4.2.9 *RoomImpl.java*

```
// RoomImpl.java

class RoomImpl extends RoomBooking._sk_Room {

    private String name;
    private RoomBooking.Meeting[] meetings;

    // constructor
    RoomImpl( String _name ) {
        name = new String( _name );
        meetings =
            new RoomBooking.Meeting[ RoomBooking._Room.MaxSlots.value ];
    }

    // attributes
    public String name() throws CORBA.SystemException {
        return name;
    }
```

```java
    // methods
    public RoomBooking.Meeting[] View() throws CORBA.SystemException {
        return meetings;
    }

    public void Book( int slot, RoomBooking.Meeting meeting )
        throws CORBA.SystemException, RoomBooking._Room.SlotAlreadyTaken {

        if( meetings[slot] == null ) {
                meetings[slot] = meeting;
        }
        else {
            throw new RoomBooking._Room.SlotAlreadyTaken();
        }
        return;
    }

    public void Cancel( int slot )
        throws CORBA.SystemException, RoomBooking._Room.NoMeetingInThisSlot

        if( meetings[slot] != null ) {
            meetings[slot] = null;
        }
        else {
            throw new RoomBooking._Room.NoMeetingInThisSlot();
        }
    }
}
```

4.2.10 RoomServer.java

```java
//RoomServer.java

import java.io.*;

public class RoomServer {

    public static void main(String[] args) {

        String context_name, str_name;

        if( args.length != 1 ) {
            System.out.println("Usage: java RoomServer room-name");
            System.exit( 1 );
        }

        // context_name = new String("/BuildingApplications/Rooms/");
        context_name = new String("/X/Rooms/");

        try {
            //init
```

```
        CORBA.ORB orb = CORBA.ORB.init();
        CORBA.BOA boa = orb.BOA_init();

        // create the Room object
        RoomImpl room = new RoomImpl( args[0] );

        // export the object reference
        boa.obj_is_ready(room);

        // register with naming service
        // get IOR for Naming Service from file
        IORFile ior_file = new IORFile("CosNaming.ior");

        EasyNaming easy_naming =
            new EasyNaming( orb, ior_file.get_ior_string() );

        str_name = context_name + args[0];

        easy_naming.bind_from_string( str_name, room );

        // wait for requests
        boa.impl_is_ready();
    }

    catch( CosNaming._NamingContext.AlreadyBound already_bound ) {
        System.err.println("Room " + context_name + args[0] +
            " already bound.");
        System.err.println("exiting ...");
    }
    catch(CORBA.UserException ue) {
        System.err.println(ue);
        System.err.println("Room " + context_name + args[0] +
            " already bound. ");
    }
    catch(CORBA.SystemException se) {
        System.err.println(se);
    }
  }
}
```

4.2.11   RoomBookingClientApplet.html

```
<html>
<header>
<title>
Room Booking Applet
</title>
<BODY BGCOLOR=15085A TEXT=FFD700 LINK==FFFFFF VLINK=FFFFFF ALINK=FFFFFF>
<center>
<pre>
```

```
</pre>
<h1>
Room Booking Applet
</h1>
</center>
<pre>

</pre>
<center>
<applet code=RoomBookingClientApplet.class width=600 height=300>
</applet>
</center>
</body>
</html>
```

5 Advanced Features

5.1 Talk

Interface Specification
Talk.idl

```
module Talk {
   interface Listener {
     void message( in string msg );
   };
};
```

5.1.2 Visibroker
TalkAppletServer.java

```
import CORBA.*;
import IORFile.*;
import java.awt.*;

class ListenerImpl extends Talk._sk_Listener {

    private TalkAppletServer talk_applet;

    // constructor
    ListenerImpl( TalkAppletServer _applet ) {
        talk_applet = _applet;
    }

    // method
    public void message( String msg ) throws CORBA.SystemException {

        talk_applet.display( msg );
        return;
```

```
        }
    }

public class TalkAppletServer extends java.applet.Applet {

    private CORBA.ORB orb;
    private EasyNaming easy_naming;
    private RemoteIORFile remote_ior_file;
    private Talk.Listener listener;
    private ListenerImpl listener_impl;
    private Panel button_panel;
    private Panel text_panel;
    private Button register_button;
    private Button resolve_button;
    private Button send_button;
    private Button quit_button;
    private TextField in_field;
    private TextField out_field;
    private String my_name;

    public void init() {
        register_button = new Button("register");
        register_button.setFont(new Font("Helvetica", Font.BOLD, 20));
        resolve_button = new Button("resolve");
        resolve_button.setFont(new Font("Helvetica", Font.BOLD, 20));
        send_button = new Button("send");
        send_button.setFont(new Font("Helvetica", Font.BOLD, 20));
        quit_button = new Button("quit");
        quit_button.setFont(new Font("Helvetica", Font.BOLD, 20));
        in_field = new TextField();
        in_field.setFont(new Font("Helvetica", Font.BOLD, 14));
        out_field = new TextField();
        out_field.setEditable(false);
        out_field.setFont(new Font("Helvetica", Font.BOLD, 14));

        button_panel = new Panel();
        text_panel = new Panel();

        button_panel.setLayout( new GridLayout(1,4));
        button_panel.add( register_button );
        button_panel.add( resolve_button );
        button_panel.add( send_button );
        button_panel.add( quit_button );

        text_panel.setLayout( new GridLayout(2,1));
        text_panel.add( in_field );
        text_panel.add( out_field );

        setLayout( new BorderLayout());
        add( "Center", text_panel );
        add( "South", button_panel );
```

```
        try {
            //init ORB
            orb = CORBA.ORB.init( this );

            //init Basic Object Adapter
            CORBA.BOA boa = orb.BOA_init();

            // create a Listener object
            listener_impl = new ListenerImpl( this );

            // proprietary bind to a remote IOR file server
            remote_ior_file =
                RemoteIORFile_var.bind("CosNaming.ior");

            easy_naming = new EasyNaming( orb,
                remote_ior_file.get_ior_string() );

            // export the object reference
            boa.obj_is_ready( listener_impl );

        }

        catch(CORBA.SystemException e) {
            System.err.println(e);
            System.exit( 0 );
        }
    }

    public void register() {

        try {
            my_name = new String( in_field.getText() );
            easy_naming.bind_from_string( my_name, listener_impl );
        }
        catch(CORBA.UserException ue) {
            out_field.setText( "register " + my_name + " failed: " + ue );
        }
        catch(CORBA.SystemException se) {
            out_field.setText( "CORBA System Exception: " + se );
        }
    }

    public void quit() {

        try {
            easy_naming.unbind_from_string( my_name );
        }
        catch(CORBA.UserException ue) {
            System.err.println(ue);
        }
        catch(CORBA.SystemException se) {
```

```
            System.err.println(se);
        }
    }

    public void connect() {

        // invoke the operation
        try {

            //resolve name
            // and narrowed it to Talk.Listener
            listener = Talk.Listener_var.narrow(
                easy_naming.resolve_from_string( in_field.getText() ) );

            // send initial message
            listener.message( "Connected to " + my_name );
        }

        // catch CORBA system exceptions
        catch(CORBA.UserException ue) {
            out_field.setText( "resolve failed: " + ue );
        }
        catch(CORBA.SystemException se) {
            out_field.setText( "CORBA System Exception: " + se );
        }
        return;
    }

    public void display( String msg ) {

        out_field.setText( msg );
        return;
    }

    public boolean action(Event ev, java.lang.Object arg) {

        // catch and process events
        if(ev.target == resolve_button ) {

            // resolve to name and connect
            connect();
            return true;
        }

        if(ev.target == register_button ) {

            // register yourself
            register();
            return true;
        }
```

```
                 if(ev.target == quit_button ) {

                     // quit
                     quit();
                     return true;
                 }

                 if(ev.target == send_button ) {

                     // invoke the operation
                     try {
                         listener.message( in_field.getText() );
                     }

                     // catch CORBA system exceptions
                     catch(CORBA.SystemException ex) {
                         out_field.setText( "CORBA System Exception: " + ex );
                     }
                     return true;
                 }
                 return false;
         }
}
```

TalkClient.java

```
import CORBA.*;
import java.awt.*;

public class TalkClient {

    public static void main(String args[]) {

        try {

            CORBA.ORB orb = CORBA.ORB.init();

            // get object reference from command-line argument
            CORBA.Object obj = orb.string_to_object( args[0] );

            // and narrowed it to SimpleHelloWorld.GoodDay
            Talk.Interact interact = Talk.Interact_var.narrow( obj );

            System.err.println( "interact connected" );

            interact.send( "Hello World" );
        }

        // catch CORBA system exceptions
        catch(CORBA.SystemException ex) {
            System.err.println(ex);
        }
```

```
        }

}
```

5.1.3   Talk.html

```html
<html>
<header>
<! -- TalkAppletServer.html -->
<title>
Talk Example
</title>
<BODY BGCOLOR=15085A TEXT=FFD700 LINK==FFFFFF VLINK=FFFFFF ALINK=FFFFFF>
<center>
<pre>

</pre>
<h1>
Talk to Me
</h1>
</center>
<pre>

</pre>
<center>
<applet code=TalkAppletServer.class width=500 height=150>

</applet>
</center>

<pre>

</pre>

</body>
</html>
```

5.2   Tie

5.2.1   Interface Specification
HelloWorld.idl

```
module HelloWorld {
    interface GoodDay {
        string hello(
            out short hour,
            out short minute );
    };
};
```

5.2.2 *Visibroker*
GoodDayImpl.java

```java
import java.util.Date;

class GoodDayImpl implements HelloWorld.GoodDayOperations {

    private String locality;

    // constructor
    GoodDayImpl( String m_locality ) {
        locality = new String( m_locality );
    }

    // method
    public String hello(
            CORBA.short_var hour,
            CORBA.short_var minute
        ) throws CORBA.SystemException {

        // get local time of the server
        Date date = new Date();
        hour.value = (short) date.getHours();
        minute.value = (short) date.getMinutes();

        return locality;
    }
}
```

HelloWorldApplet.java

```java
import java.awt.*;
import HelloWorld.*;
import CORBA.*;

public class HelloWorldApplet extends java.applet.Applet {

    private CORBA.short_var minute;
    private CORBA.short_var hour;

    private HelloWorld.GoodDay good_day;
    private String text;
    private String locality;
    private Button hello_world_button;
    private TextField text_field;

    public void init() {

        minute = new CORBA.short_var();
        hour = new CORBA.short_var();

        hello_world_button = new Button("Invoke remote method");
        hello_world_button.setFont(new Font("Helvetica",
```

```
            Font.BOLD, 20));
        text_field = new TextField();
        text_field.setEditable(false);
        text_field.setFont(new Font("Helvetica", Font.BOLD, 14));

        setLayout( new GridLayout(2,1));
        add( hello_world_button );
        add( text_field );

        try {
            // initilize the ORB (using this applet)
            CORBA.ORB orb = CORBA.ORB.init( this );

            // bind to "HelloWorld.GoodDay"
            good_day = HelloWorld.GoodDay_var.bind();
        }

        // catch CORBA system exceptions
        catch(CORBA.SystemException ex) {
            System.err.println(ex);
        }
    }

    public boolean action(Event ev, java.lang.Object arg) {
        // catch and process events
        if(ev.target == hello_world_button ) {
            // invoke the operation
            try {
                locality = new String( good_day.hello( hour, minute ) );
            }
            // catch CORBA system exceptions
            catch(CORBA.SystemException ex) {
                System.err.println(ex);
            }
            if( minute.value < 10 )
                text = new String("The local time in " + locality +
                    " is " + hour.value + ":0" + minute.value + "." );
            else
                text = new String("The local time in " + locality +
                    " is " + hour.value + ":" + minute.value + "." );
            text_field.setText( text );
            return true;
        }
        return false;
    }
}
```

HelloWorldClient.java

```
import java.io.*;

public class HelloWorldClient {
```

```java
    public static void main(String args[]) {

        // create _var objects for out parameters
            CORBA.short_var minute = new CORBA.short_var();
            CORBA.short_var hour = new CORBA.short_var();

            try {
            // initilize the ORB
            CORBA.ORB orb = CORBA.ORB.init();

            // get object reference from command-line argument
            CORBA.Object obj = orb.string_to_object( args[0] );

            // and narrowed it to HelloWorld.GoodDay
            HelloWorld.GoodDay good_day =
                HelloWorld.GoodDay_var.narrow( obj );

            // invoke the operation
            String locality = new String(
                good_day.hello( hour, minute ) );

            // print results to stdout
            System.out.println("Hello World!");
            if( minute.value < 10 )
                System.out.println("The local time in " + locality +
                    " is " + hour.value + ":0" + minute.value + "." );
            else
                System.out.println("The local time in " + locality +
                    " is " + hour.value + ":" + minute.value + "." );
        }

        // catch CORBA system exceptions
        catch(CORBA.SystemException ex) {
            System.err.println(ex);
        }
    }
}
```

HelloWorldTieServer.java

```java
public class HelloWorldTieServer {

    public static void main(String[] args) {
        try {
            //init orb
            CORBA.ORB orb = CORBA.ORB.init();

            //init basic object adapter
            CORBA.BOA boa = orb.BOA_init();

            // create an implementation object
            GoodDayImpl good_day_impl = new GoodDayImpl( args[0] );
```

```
            // create a Tie object
            HelloWorld._tie_GoodDay good_day_pseudo_impl =
                new HelloWorld._tie_GoodDay( good_day_impl );

            // export the object reference
            boa.obj_is_ready( good_day_pseudo_impl );
            System.out.println(
                orb.object_to_string( good_day_pseudo_impl ) );

            // wait for requests
            boa.impl_is_ready();
        }

        catch(CORBA.SystemException e) {
            System.err.println(e);
        }
    }
}
```

5.3   DII

5.3.1   *Interface Specification*
HelloWorld.idl

```
module HelloWorld {
  interface GoodDay {
    string hello(
        out short hour,
        out short minute );
  };
};
```

5.3.2   *Visibroker*
DiiAnySupport.java

```
import CORBA.*;

public class DiiAnySupport {

    DiiAnySupport() { ; }

    // creates an Any and initializes it with a dummy
    // value of the type specified by the type code

    Any TC2Any( TypeCode tc, int mode )
        throws NotYetImplemented, CORBA.SystemException {

    switch ( tc.kind() ) {
```

```
        case CORBA.TCKind.tk_short:
          return new CORBA.Any().from_short((short)0);

        case CORBA.TCKind.tk_long:
          return new CORBA.Any().from_long(0);

        case CORBA.TCKind.tk_ushort:
          return new CORBA.Any().from_ushort((short)0);

        case CORBA.TCKind.tk_ulong:
          return new CORBA.Any().from_ulong(0);

        case CORBA.TCKind.tk_float:
          return new CORBA.Any().from_float((float)0.0);

        case CORBA.TCKind.tk_double:
          return new CORBA.Any().from_double(0.0);

        case CORBA.TCKind.tk_boolean:
          return new CORBA.Any().from_boolean(true);

        case CORBA.TCKind.tk_char:
          return new CORBA.Any().from_char(' ');

        case CORBA.TCKind.tk_octet:
          return new CORBA.Any().from_octet((byte)' ');

        case CORBA.TCKind.tk_string:
          return new CORBA.Any().from_string("");

        case CORBA.TCKind.tk_any:
          Any empty_any = new Any();
          return new CORBA.Any().from_any( empty_any );

        default:
          // for more complex data types, see Universal CORBA Client
          // by Gerald Vogt
          throw new NotYetImplemented( tc );
        }
      }
    }
}
```

DiiClient.java

```
import java.io.*;
import CORBA.*;

public class DiiClient {

    public static void main(String args[]) {

        // get stringified IOR from command line
        String ior = new String( args[0] );
```

```
try {
    // initilize the ORB
    CORBA.ORB orb = CORBA.ORB.init();

    // get object reference
    CORBA.Object obj = orb.string_to_object( ior );

    // browsing the Interface Repository

    // get interface definition from Interface Repository
    CORBA.InterfaceDef if_def = obj._get_interface();

    // get full interface dscription
    CORBA.InterfaceDef_.FullInterfaceDescription full_if_desc =
        if_def.describe_interface();

    int no_of_parameters;

    // print various information
    System.out.println("Quering the Interface Repository\n");
    System.out.println("interface " + full_if_desc.name + " {\n" );

    for( int i = 0; i < full_if_desc.operations.length; i++ ) {

        no_of_parameters =
            full_if_desc.operations[i].parameters.length;

            System.out.println("   " +

            // print the type code of the operation's result
            full_if_desc.operations[i].result + " " +

            // print the name of the operation
            full_if_desc.operations[i].name + " ("
        );

        // define and initialize text representations
        // for parameter modes
        String mode, in, inout, out;
        in = new String("in");
        inout = new String("inout");
        out = new String("out");

        char last_char = ',';

        // print parameters of the operations
        for( int j = 0; j < no_of_parameters; j++ ) {

            // set the right text for the parameter mode
            switch (full_if_desc.operations[i].parameters[j].mode) {
                case CORBA.ParameterMode.PARAM_IN:
                    mode = in; break;
                case CORBA.ParameterMode.PARAM_INOUT:
                    mode = inout; break;
                case CORBA.ParameterMode.PARAM_OUT:
```

```
                    mode = out; break;
                default:
                    mode = new String("unknown mode");
            }

            // deal with separating commas
            if( j == no_of_parameters - 1 )
                last_char = ' ';

            // print mode, type and name of the parameter
            System.out.println("        " +
                mode + " " +
                full_if_desc.operations[i].parameters[j].type +
                " " +
                full_if_desc.operations[i].parameters[j].name +
                last_char
            );
        }
        System.out.println("    );\n};\n");
    }

    // using the DII to make an invocation
    System.out.println("Make a DII call\n");

    // create a support object
    DiiAnySupport dii_any_support = new DiiAnySupport();

    // create and initialize result
    NVList result_list = orb.create_list( 0 );

    result_list.add_value( "",
        dii_any_support.TC2Any(
            full_if_desc.operations[0].result,
            CORBA.ParameterMode.PARAM_OUT ),
        0 );

    // create and initialize arg_list
    NVList arg_list = orb.create_list( 0 );

    no_of_parameters = full_if_desc.operations[0].parameters.length;
    for( int i = 0; i < no_of_parameters; i++ ) {

        arg_list.add_value(
            full_if_desc.operations[0].parameters[i].name,
            dii_any_support.TC2Any(
                full_if_desc.operations[0].parameters[i].type,
                full_if_desc.operations[0].parameters[i].mode ),
            full_if_desc.operations[0].parameters[i].mode + 1 );
    }

    // create request
    CORBA.Request request = obj._create_request(
```

```
                null,                             // context - not used
                full_if_desc.operations[0].name, // operation name
                arg_list,                         // NVList with arguments
                result_list.item(0)               // NamedValue for result
            );

            // invoke request
            request.invoke();

            // get result
            System.out.println("result:\n    " + request.result().value() );

            // get out parameters
            CORBA.NVList nv_list = request.arguments();
            for( int i = 0; i < no_of_parameters; i++ )
                System.out.println( nv_list.item( i ).name() +
                    ":\n    " + nv_list.item( i ).value() );
        }

    // catch CORBA system exceptions
    catch(NotYetImplemented nyi) {
        System.err.println(nyi);
    }
    // catch CORBA system exceptions
    catch(CORBA.SystemException ex) {
        System.err.println(ex);
    }
    }
}
```

NotYetImplemented.java

```
import CORBA.*;

public class NotYetImplemented extends java.lang.Exception {
    public TypeCode tc;

    NotYetImplemented( TypeCode _tc ) {
        tc = _tc;
    }
}
```

5.4 Any

5.4.1 Interface Specification
HelloWorldAny.idl

```
module HelloWorldAny {

    struct Time {
        short hour;
```

```
        short minute;
    };

    interface GoodDay {
        any hello( out any any_time );
    };
};
```

5.4.2   *Visibroker*
GoodDayImpl.java

```java
import CORBA.*;
import java.util.Date;

class GoodDayImpl extends HelloWorldAny._sk_GoodDay {

    private String m_locality;

    // constructor
    GoodDayImpl( String locality ) {
        m_locality = new String( locality );
    }

    // method
    public CORBA.Any hello(
            CORBA.Any_var any_time
        ) throws CORBA.SystemException {

        // get local time of the server
        Date date = new Date();

        // create time-structure assign hour and minute to it
        HelloWorldAny.Time struct_time = new HelloWorldAny.Time(
            (short) date.getHours(), (short) date.getMinutes() );

        // shuffle structure into any
        any_time.value = struct_time.any();

        // create any and shuffle locality into it
        CORBA.Any any_locality = new Any();
        any_locality.from_string( m_locality );

        return any_locality;
    }
}
```

HelloWorldAnyClient.java

```java
import java.util.*;
import java.io.*;
import HelloWorldAny.*;
```

```
public class HelloWorldAnyClient {

    public static void main(String args[]) {

        CORBA.Any_var any_time = new CORBA.Any_var();
        CORBA.Any any_locality;

        // get stringified IOR from command line
        String ior = new String( args[0] );

        try {
            // initialize the ORB.
            CORBA.ORB orb = CORBA.ORB.init();

            // get object reference . .
            CORBA.Object obj = orb.string_to_object( ior );
            // and narrowed it to "HelloWorld.GoodDay"
            HelloWorldAny.GoodDay good_day =
                HelloWorldAny.GoodDay_var.narrow( obj );

            // invoke the operation
            any_locality = good_day.hello( any_time );

            // create a type code object
            CORBA.TypeCode tc;

            // get type of any_time.value and print type information
            tc = any_time.value.type();
            try {
                System.out.println("IfRepId of any_time: " + tc.id() );
                System.out.println("Type code of any_time: " + tc.name() );
                for( int i = 0; i < tc.member_count(); i++ )
                    System.out.println("\tname: " + tc.member_name(i) );
            }
            catch(CORBA._TypeCode.BadKind ex_bk) {
                System.err.println("any_time: " + ex_bk);
            }
            catch(CORBA._TypeCode.Bounds ex_b) {
                System.err.println("any_time: " + ex_b);
            }

            // get length any_locality.value
            tc = any_locality.type();
            try {
                if( tc.kind() == CORBA.TCKind.tk_string )
                    System.out.println( "length of any_locality: "
                        + tc.length() );
                else
                    System.out.println(
                        "any_locality does NOT contain a string.");
            }
            catch(CORBA._TypeCode.BadKind ex_bt) {
```

```
                        System.err.println("any_locality: " + ex_bt);
                }

                // get String from any_locality
                // try
                String locality = any_locality.to_string();
                // String locality = new
                    // String( any_locality.to_string() );

                // get struct from any_time
                HelloWorldAny.Time time = new
                    HelloWorldAny.Time( any_time.value );

                // print results to stdout
                System.out.println("Print Anys:");
                System.out.println("any_locality: ");
                System.out.println( any_locality );
                System.out.println("time:");
                System.out.println( any_time.value );

                // print results to stdout
                System.out.println("Hello World!");
                if( time.minute < 10 )
                    System.out.println("The local time in " +
                        locality +
                        " is " + time.hour + ":0" +
                        time.minute + "." );
                else
                    System.out.println("The local time in " +
                        locality +
                        " is " + time.hour + ":" +
                        time.minute + "." );
            }
            // catch CORBA system exceptions
            catch(CORBA.SystemException ex) {
                System.err.println(ex);
            }
        }
    }
}
```

HelloWorldAnyServer.java

```
import CORBA.*;

public class HelloWorldAnyServer {

    public static void main(String[] args) {
        try {
            //init orb
            CORBA.ORB orb = CORBA.ORB.init();
```

```
            //init basic object adapter
            CORBA.BOA boa = orb.BOA_init();

            // create a GoodDay object
            GoodDayImpl good_day_impl = new GoodDayImpl( args[0] );

            // export the object reference
            boa.obj_is_ready(good_day_impl);
            System.out.println(good_day_impl + " is ready.");
            System.out.println( orb.object_to_string(good_day_impl) );

            // wait for requests
            boa.impl_is_ready();
        }
        catch(CORBA.SystemException e) {
            System.err.println(e);
        }
    }
}
```

Further Reading

This is a short list of books we recommend for the study of related subjects. There are two categories, literature on Java and literature on CORBA.

Books on Java

Ed Anuff, *The Java Source Book*. New York: John Wiley & Sons, 1996.

Ken Arnold and James Gosling, *The Java Programming Language*. Reading, PA: Addison-Wesley Publishing Company, 1996.

James Gosling, Frank Yellin, and The Java Team, *The Java Application Programming Interface*, Volume 1, *Core Packages*. Reading, PA: Addison-Wesley Publishing Company, 1996.

James Gosling, Frank Yellin, and The Java Team, *The Java Application Programming Interface*, Volume 2, *Window Toolkit and Applets*. Reading, PA: Addison-Wesley Publishing Company, 1996.

Books on CORBA

Thomas J. Mobray and Ron Zahavi, *The Essential CORBA—Systems Integration Using Distributed Objects*. New York: John Wiley & Sons, 1995.

Jon Siegel, *CORBA—Fundamentals and Programming*. New York: John Wiley & Sons, 1996.

Object Management Group, *CORBA Specification*. New York: John Wiley & Sons, 1995.

Object Management Group, *CORBAfacilities: Common Object Facilities Specification*. New York: John Wiley & Sons, 1995.

Object Management Group, *CORBAservices: Common Object Services Specification*. New York: John Wiley & Sons, 1995.

Glossary

1 Acronyms

AB: Architecture Board.

API: Application Programming Interface.

BOA: Basic Object Adapter.

CGI: Common Gateway Interface.

CORBA: Common Object Request Broker Architecture.

DCE: Distributed Computing Environment.

DCE-CIOP: DCE Common Inter-ORB Protocol.

DII: Dynamic Invocation Interface.

DIS: Draft International Standard.

DSI: Dynamic Skeleton Interface.

DTC: Domain Technology Committee.

ESIOP: Environment-Specific Inter-ORB Protocols.

EUSIG: End User Special Interest Group.

FDTF: Financial Domain Task Force.

GIOP: General Inter-ORB Protocol.

IDL: Interface Definition Language.

IIOP: Internet Inter-ORB Protocol.

IMCDTF: Interactive Multimedia and Electronic Commerce Domain Task Force.

IOR: Interoperable Object Reference.

IR: Interface Repository.

ISIG: Internet Special Interest Group.

ISO: International Standards Organization.

JSIG: Japan Special Interest Group.

MDTF: Manufacturing Domain Task Force.

ODP: Open Distributed Processing.

OMA: Object Management Architecture.

OMG: Object Management Group.

ORB: Object Request Broker.

PIDL: Pseudo-IDL.

PTC: Platform Technology Committee.

RFI: Request For Information.

RFP: Request For Proposal.

RMI: Remote Method Invocation.

RTSIG: Real Time Special Interest Group.

SIG: Special Interest Group.

TSIG: Transportation Special Interest Group.

UUID: Universal Unique Identifier.

2   Terms

Any: Pre-defined data type in OMG IDL which can contain self-describing values of *any* type.

Architecture Board: An OMG board which reviews proposals and technology for conformance to the OMA.

Basic Object Adapter: The ORB component which launches servers and accepts notifications about when objects come into existence, and when servers are ready to accept incoming requests.

Byte-code: Intermediate representation of programming language code. The Java byte-code is very popular and virtual machines which can execute Java byte-code are available for most hardware platforms and operating systems.

Common Facilities: See CORBAfacilities.

Common Gateway Interface: Interface at HTTP servers which allows access to resources, e.g. databases or programs outside the server.

Common Object Request Broker Architecture: Architecture for distributed object systems defined by the OMG.

Common Object Services: See CORBAservices.

CORBAfacilities: A set of published specifications for application-level object services that are applicable across industry domains, e.g. Printing Facility, Systems Management Facility.

CORBAnet: Permanent showcase to demonstrate IIOP-based ORB interoperability sponsored by the OMG and most ORB vendors. CORBAnet is hosted by the Distributed Systems Technology Centre in Brisbane, Australia. CORBAnet can be accessed at http://www.corba.net.

CORBAservices: Set of published specifications for fundamental services assisting all object implementations, e.g. Naming Service, Event Service, Object Trading Service.

Core Object Model: The fundamental object-oriented model in the OMA which defines the basic concepts on which CORBA is based.

DCE Common Inter-ORB Protocol. Environment Specific Interoperability Protocol based on DCE. The first ESIOP adopted by the OMG.

Distributed Computing Environment. Distributed middleware developed under the control of the Open Group, formerly Open Software Foundation (OSF).

Domain Task Force: Group in the OMG responsible for specifying technologies relevant to a particular industry sector. They report to the Domain Technical Committee.

Domain Technology Committee: OMG Committee which supervises several Domain Task Forces concerned with technology specification for particular domains.

Draft International Standard: ISO defines phases through which a potential International Standard must pass. Draft International Standard is the penultimate phase.

Dynamic Invocation Interface: Interface defined in CORBA which allows the invocation of operations on object references without compile-time knowledge of the objects' interface types.

Dynamic Skeleton Interface: Interface defined in CORBA which allows servers to dynamically interpret incoming invocation requests of arbitrary operations.

Environment-Specific Inter-ORB Protocols: CORBA interoperability protocols which use data formats other than the ones specified in the GIOP. See also DCE ESIOP.

General Inter-ORB Protocol: Protocol which belongs to the mandatory CORBA Interoperability protocol specifications. It defines the format of the protocol data units which can be sent via any transport. Currently there is only one transport protocol defined, namely, IIOP.

Interface Definition Language: Language to specify interfaces of objects independent of particular programming language representations. OMG has defined OMG IDL.

Interface Repository. Component of CORBA which stores type information and makes it available through standard interfaces at run time. Typically, an Interface Repository is populated by an IDL compiler when processing IDL specifications.

Interoperable Object Reference: Object reference which identifies objects independent of the ORB environment in which they have been created.

Marshal: Conversion of data into a programming-language and architecture-independent format.

Object Management Architecture: This is the overall architecture and roadmap of the OMG, of which CORBA forms a part.

Object Management Group: An international industry consortium with over 600 members which specifies an object-oriented framework for distributed computing, including CORBA.

Object Reference: Opaque data structure which identifies a single CORBA object, and enables clients to invoke operations on it, regardless of the object's location. Objects can have multiple object references.

Object Request Broker: The central component of the OMA which transmits operation invocation requests to distributed objects and returns the results to the requester.

Object Services: See CORBAservices.

OMA Reference Model: The structural model defining roles for the various components taking part in the OMA. It identifies five groups of objects to be specified: Object Request Broker, Object Services, Common Facilities, Domain Objects and Application Objects.

Open Distributed Processing: Group within ISO which is concerned with the standardization of open distributed systems.

Platform Technology Committee: OMG Committee which supervises several Task Forces concerned with specifying the ORB platform infrastructure.

Pseudo-IDL: Interface definitions for components of ORB infrastructure that will not be implemented as CORBA objects.

Request For Information: A formal request from an OMG body for submissions of information relating to a specific technology area.

Request For Proposal: A formal request from an OMG body for a submission of a technology specification in IDL with English semantics.

Special Interest Group: Member group in the OMG that has a topic of interest in common. These groups report findings to Committees within the OMG, or the Architecture Board.

TypeCode: A run-time representation of an IDL type.

Universal Unique Identifier.   Used in DCE to identify an entity.

Unmarshal: The inverse of marshaling.

Index

Compiler(s):
  calling the, 70
  IDL, 5, 53, 61, 266
  standard Java, 2
Compiling:
  applet, 75
  IDL, 63–65
  Room booking example, 182–183
  server, 79
Components, Core Model, 251
Concrete interface, 295
Concurrency Control, 256
connect(), 235, 240
Connection, ORB network, 8
ConstantDef, 305
Constants, 275
  IDL, 266
  IDL mapping, 102
Constraint string, 169
Constructor(s), 76, 88
  copy, 96
  independent client code, 203–204
  OrbixWeb sequence, 94
  Visibroker example, 174
Constructs, IDL, 266
Contained, 297–299
  interfaces derived from, 305–307
Container, 299–300
  IR, 295
  object type, 204
Container classes, 105
  predefined IDL types, 317–322
Container objects, 80
contents(), 299
content_type(), 128
Context(s), 139–142, 262
  adding names to, 146
  browsing, 150
  creating, 139
  creating new, 149
  destruction of, 149–150
  dynamic interface, 294–295
  IDL, 277
  manipulating, 139–141
  removing names from, 147
  Request object, 227
Context clause, 23–24
Context Object Tree, 141–142
Copy constructor, 96
CORBA:
  definition of, 1
  OSTF responsible for, 246
  overview, 258–259
  unique features of, 3–6

CORBAfacilities, 5
  CFTFs, 246
  Common Facilities, 257
CORBAfinancials (Financial Domain Task Force), 247
CORBAmanufacturing (Manufacturing Domain Task Force), 247
CORBAmed Task Force (Healthcare), 247
CORBAnet, 55
CORBAservices, 5, 256–257
  distributed applications, 10
  resolve_initial_references, 285
CORBAtel (Telecommunications Task Force), 247
Core Object Model, 14, 249, 250–253
  concepts defined by, 251
CosNaming, 178
CosNaming::Naming, 285
CosTrading::Lookup, 285
Costs, reduced Java, 2
C++:
  BOA language mapping, 290
  IDL syntax from, 266
  Java compared to, 3
create(), 289
create_alias_tc(), 129
create_array_tc(), 130
create_enum_tc(), 129
create_exception_tc(), 129
create_interface_tc(), 129
create_list, 131–132
create_recursive_sequence_tc(), 130
create_request(), 121, 134, 227
create_sequence_tc(), 129
create_string_tc(), 129
create_struct_tc(), 128
create_union_tc(), 128
Creating, supporting objects, 225–227
ctx(), 138

Daemon process, 18
Database Special Interest Group, 248
Data type(s), 21–23, 252–253
  basic, 85–87
  enums, 87–88
  IDL interface for, 297
  string, 87
  struct, 88–89
Data type declarations, 266
DCE-CIOP (DCE Common Inter-ORB Protocol), 29, 292–293
DCE Common Inter-ORB Protocol (DCE-CIOP), 29, 292–293